SIMUL 2020

The Twelfth International Conference on Advances in System Simulation

October 18 -22, 2020

SIMUL 2020 Editors

Frank Herrmann, OTH Regensburg, Germany

Lorena Parra, Universitat Politecnica de Valencia, Spain

Manuela Popescu, IARA, USA/EU

Printed from e-media with permission by:

Curran Associates, Inc.
57 Morehouse Lane
Red Hook, NY 12571

CURRAN ASSOCIATES INC. proceedings.com

Some format issues inherent in the e-media version may also appear in this print version.

International Academy, Research, and Industry Association (IARIA)
412 Derby Way
Wilmington, DE 19810

Phone: (408) 893-6407
Fax: (408) 527-6351

petre@iaria.org

Additional copies of this publication are available from:

Curran Associates, Inc.
57 Morehouse Lane
Red Hook, NY 12571 USA
Phone: 845-758-0400
Fax: 845-758-2633
Email: curran@proceedings.com
Web: www.proceedings.com

Table of Contents

SIMUL 2020

Forward

The Twelfth International Conference on Advances in System Simulation (SIMUL 2020), held on October 18 - 22, 2020, continued a series of events focusing on advances in simulation techniques and systems providing new simulation capabilities.

While different simulation events are already scheduled for years, SIMUL 2020 identified specific needs for ontology of models, mechanisms, and methodologies in order to make easy an appropriate tool selection. With the advent of Web Services and WEB 3.0 social simulation and human-in simulations bring new challenging situations along with more classical process simulations and distributed and parallel simulations. An update on the simulation tool considering these new simulation flavors was aimed at, too.

The conference provided a forum where researchers were able to present recent research results and new research problems and directions related to them. The conference sought contributions to stress-out large challenges in scale system simulation and advanced mechanisms and methodologies to deal with them. The accepted papers covered topics on social simulation, transport simulation, simulation tools and platforms, simulation methodologies and models, and distributed simulation.

We welcomed technical papers presenting research and practical results, position papers addressing the pros and cons of specific proposals, such as those being discussed in the standard forums or in industry consortiums, survey papers addressing the key problems and solutions on any of the above topics, short papers on work in progress, and panel proposals.

We take here the opportunity to warmly thank all the members of the SIMUL 2020 technical program committee as well as the numerous reviewers. The creation of such a broad and high quality conference program would not have been possible without their involvement. We also kindly thank all the authors that dedicated much of their time and efforts to contribute to the SIMUL 2020. We truly believe that thanks to all these efforts, the final conference program consists of top quality contributions.

This event could also not have been a reality without the support of many individuals, organizations and sponsors. We also gratefully thank the members of the SIMUL 2020 organizing committee for their help in handling the logistics and for their work that is making this professional meeting a success. We gratefully appreciate to the technical program committee co-chairs that contributed to identify the appropriate groups to submit contributions.

We hope the SIMUL 2020 was a successful international forum for the exchange of ideas and results between academia and industry and to promote further progress in simulation research.

SIMUL 2020 Publicity Chair

Lorena Parra, Universitat Politecnica de Valencia, Spain

SIMUL 2020

Committee

SIMUL 2020 Publicity Chair

Lorena Parra, Universitat Politecnica de Valencia, Spain

SIMUL 2020 Technical Program Committee

Ahmed M. Abdulkhaleq, SARAS Technology/ University of Bradford, UK
Petra Ahrweiler, Johannes Gutenberg University Mainz, Germany
Chrissanthi Angeli, University of West Attica, Greece
Alfonso Ariza Quintana, University of Malaga, Spain
Ana Paula Barbosa Póvoa, Universidade de Lisboa, Portugal
Marek Bauer, Politechnika Krakowska, Poland
John Betts, Monash University, Australia
Patrick Biemelt, University of Paderborn, Germany
Paolo Bocciarelli, University of Rome Tor Vergata, Italy
Jalil Boudjadar, Aarhus University, Denmark
Christos Bouras, University of Patras, Greece
Lelio Campanile, Università degli Studi della Campania "L. Vanvitelli", Italy
Enrique Chirivella, University of the West of Scotland, UK
Franco Cicirelli, ICAR-CNR, Italy
Fábio Coelho, CEG-IST Instituto Superior Técnico | University of Lisbon, Portugal
Duilio Curcio, University of Calabria, Italy
Andrea D'Ambrogio, University of Roma TorVergata, Italy
Gabriele D'Angelo, University of Bologna, Italy
Luis Antonio de Santa-Eulalia, Business School | Université de Sherbrooke, Canada
Alexander Ditter, Friedrich-Alexander University Erlangen-Nürnberg (FAU), Germany
Anatoli Djanatliev, University of Erlangen-Nuremberg, Germany
Julie Dugdale, University Grenoble Alps, France
Mahmoud Elbattah, Université de Picardie Jules Verne, France
Amr Eltawil, School of Innovative Design Engineering / Japan University of Science and Technology, Egypt
Diego Encinas, Informatics Research Institute LIDI - CIC - UNLP, Argentina
Fouad Erchiqui, Université du Québec en Abitibi-Témiscamingue, Canada
Zuhal Erden, Atilim University, Turkey
Sibylle Fröschle, University of Oldenburg, Germany
José Manuel Galán, Universidad de Burgos, Spain
Simon Genser, Virtual Vehicle Research GmbH, Graz, Austria
Katja Gilly de la Sierra-Llamazares, Universidad Miguel Hernández, Spain
Denis Gracanin, Virginia Tech, USA
Antoni Grau, Technical University of Catalonia, Barcelona, Spain
Andrew Greasley, Aston University, Birmingham, UK

Magdalena Hańderek, Cracow University of Technology, Poland
Thomas Hanne, University of Applied Sciences and Arts Northwestern Switzerland / Institute for Information Systems, Switzerland
Eduardo Hargreaves, Petrobras, Brazil
Frank Herrmann, University of Applied Sciences Regensburg, Germany
Tsan-sheng Hsu, Institute of Information Science | Academia Sinica, Taiwan
Xiaolin Hu, Georgia State University, Atlanta, USA
Marc-Philippe Huget, Polytech Annecy-Chambery-LISTIC | University of Savoie, France
Mauro Iacono, Università degli Studi della Campania "Luigi Vanvitelli", Italy
Lisa Jackson, Loughborough University, UK
Matthieu Jonckheere, Universidad de Buenos Aires, Argentina
Maria Julia Blas, Instituto de Desarrollo y Diseño (INGAR) | UTN-CONICET, Argentina
Youngjae Kim, Sogang University, Seoul, Korea
Dmitry G. Korzun, Petrozavodsk State University | Institute of Mathematics and Information Technology, Russia
Anatoly Kurkovsky, Georgia Gwinnett College - Greater Atlanta University System of Georgia, USA
Massimo La Scala, Politecnico di Bari, Italy
Fedor Lehocki, Slovak University of Technology in Bratislava, Slovakia
Fabian Lorig, Malmö University | IoTaP, Sweden
Emilio Luque, University Autonoma of Barcelona (UAB), Spain
Johannes Lüthi, University of Applied Sciences - Fachhochschule Kufstein Tirol, Austria
Imran Mahmood, Brunel University London, UK
Fahad Maqbool, University of Sargodha, Pakistan
Eda Marchetti, ISTI-CNR, Pisa, Italy
Romolo Marotta, University of Rome "Sapienza", Italy
Niels Martin, Research Foundation Flanders (FWO) - Hasselt University, Belgium
Omar Masmali, The University of Texas, El Paso, USA
Michele Mastroianni, Università degli Studi della Campania "Luigi Vanvitelli", Italy
Andrea Matta, Politecnico di Milano, Italy
Nuno Melão, Polytechnic Institute of Viseu, Portugal
Owen Molloy, National University of Ireland, Galway, Ireland
Sébastien Monnet, LISTIC / Savoie Mont Blanc University, France
Federico Montori, University of Bologna, Italy
Jérôme Morio, ONERA (the French Aerospace Lab), France
Paulo Moura Oliveira, Universidade de Trás-os-Montes e Alto Douro (UTAD) / INESC-TEC Porto, Portugal
Nazmun Nahar, University of Jyvaskyla, Finland
Alessandro Pellegrini, Sapienza University of Rome, Italy
Tomas Potuzak, University of West Bohemia, Czech Republic
Dipak Pudasaini, Tribhuvan University, Nepal / Ryerson University, Canada
Francesco Quaglia, University of Rome Tor Vergata, Italy
Marco Remondino, University of Genova, Italy
Dupas Rémy, University of Bordeaux, France
Oscar Rodríguez Polo, University of Alcala, Spain
Julio Sahuquillo, Universitat Politecnica de Valencia, Spain
Ignacio Sanchez-Navarro, University of the West of Scotland, UK
Nandakishore Santhi, Los Alamos National Laboratory, USA
Victorino Sanz, ETSI Informática | UNED, Spain
Paulo Jorge Sequeira Goncalves, Instituto Politecnico de Castelo Branco, Portugal

Li Shi, Snap Inc., USA
Alireza Shojaei, Mississippi State University, USA
Patrick Siarry, Université Paris-Est Créteil (UPEC), France
Carlo Simon, Hochschule Worms - University of Applied Sciences, Germany
Leszek Siwik, AGH-UST University of Science and Technology, Krakow, Poland
Yuri N. Skiba, Universidad Nacional Autónoma de México, Mexico
Azeddien M. Sllame, University of Tripoli, Libya
Fabian Speicher, RWTH Aachen University, Germany
Giandomenico Spezzano, CNR-ICAR, Italy
Renata Spolon Lobato, UNESP - São Paulo State University, Brazil
Mu-Chun Su, National Central University, Taiwan
Grażyna Suchacka, University of Opole, Poland
János Száz, Corvinus University, Hungary
Ingo J. Timm, Trier University, Germany
Klaus G. Troitzsch, Universität Koblenz-Landau, Germany
Hasan Turan, University of New South Wales, Australia
Alfonso Urquía, UNED, Spain
Vahab Vahdatzad, Harvard Medical School, Boston, USA
Durk-Jouke van der Zee, University of Groningen, Netherlands
Maria João Viamonte, Institute of Engineering (ISEP) - Polytechnic Institute of Porto (IPP), Portugal
Manuel Villen-Altamirano, Universidad de Málaga, Spain
Antonio Virdis, University of Pisa, Italy
Haoliang Wang, Adobe Research, USA
Frank Werner, Otto-von-Guericke University Magdeburg, Germany
Kuan Yew Wong, Universiti Teknologi Malaysia (UTM), Malaysia

Copyright Information

Scheduling of a Real World Filter Production with Lot-Size 1

Frank Herrmann
Ostbayerische Technische Hochschule Regensburg - University of Applied Sciences Regensburg
Innovation and Competence Centre for Production Logistics and Factory Planning (IPF)
PO box 120327, 93025 Regensburg, Germany
E-Mail: Frank.Herrmann@OTH-Regensburg.de

Abstract—**In industrial practice, a travelling crane on the ceiling of a factory hall transports products in process from one station to the next one in a production line. Due to space restrictions, there is no buffer between the stations. The production line at Fiedler Andritz, Regensburg in Germany, can be seen as an example of such a problem class. Such restrictions reduce the set of feasible schedules even more than the no-buffer restrictions discussed in the literature in the case of limited storage. Since this scheduling problem is integrated in the usual hierarchical planning, the tardiness is minimised. Due to the high number of jobs as well as the goal of a simple algorithm, scheduling is always done by priority rules at the company site. The standard approach of using the net processing time causes poor results. A simulation of the processing time is suggested. In addition, several very relevant priority rules from the literature are modified by this simulated processing and significantly better results are obtained.**

Keywords-Simulation of processing time; scheduling, flow-shop; no-buffer (blocking); no-wait; priority rules; real world application; filter production

I. Introduction

Specific products are produced by special machines, which are often grouped in a flow shop. They have to produce small batches with short response times, so scheduling algorithms are needed to ensure that under the constraint of a high average load of the flow shop, the due dates of the production orders are met. Nowadays, such special designed flow shops often have technological restrictions, which complicate the scheduling. For example, in cell manufacturing, buffer could be non-existent due to limited space and storage facilities. So, in recent years, a considerable amount of interest has arisen in no-buffer (blocking) scheduling problems and in no-wait scheduling problems, with makespan as objective criterion. Often, these production systems deliver products for other systems as well. Due to the hierarchical planning, which is implemented in enterprise resource planning systems (ERP system) (see e.g., [7]), the local completion times in one production system in many cases determine the earliest possible starting times in another production system. Thus, the delay of the operations in a production system has an impact on the effectivity of this coordination process. Therefore, tardiness is considered as objective criterion.

The paper is structured as follows. The real world application is described, followed by a literature review. Next, the algorithms are explained, then, the computational results are given and analysed and the papers ends with a conclusion.

II. A Real World Application

The problem is a modification of a partly automated production line at Fiedler Andritz in Regensburg, Germany, to produce filter (baskets) with a lot size of 1. All filters have unified constructions. They differ in varying heights of the baskets and there exist different designs.

The production line consists of 4 stations which are shown in Figure 1. Station 1 assembles 6 single batons (called consoles) on an assembly ground plate to a skeleton of a filter basket. Baton profiles are assembled into the provided slots of the filter basket skeletons. At the plunge station a wire coil is contrived in the device of a lining machine. The lining machine straightens the wire and inserts batons into the slots. To ensure stability, the span station installs span kernels in the case of outflow filter baskets and span belts in the case of inflow filter baskets. Then, the filter basket is lifted from the assembly ground plate and is transported to the welding station, at which the baton profiles are welded on the filter basket skeletons. The accomplished filter basket leaves the production line. Prior to this, the span medium is removed. An overhead travelling crane lifts a filter basket out of a station, transports it to the next station and inserts it directly in this station. This is just possible if this station is free. So, there is no buffer in the production line and each feasible schedule of jobs is a permutation of these jobs. Due to other operational issues, the crane can just be moved if all stations are inactive. Since an operation cannot be interrupted, the transport has to be performed after the completion of all operations on the stations in the flow shop. Due to further operational issues, this restriction has to be applied also to the first and the last station; note, that the crane loads S1 and unloads S4 as well. In summary, all stations are loaded and unloaded with filters during a common process and this process starts with the last station S4, followed by station S3, S2, until station S1 is reached. It is allowed that a station is empty; then this station is skipped (may be partially) in this process. In total, there are 10 part types whose processing times are listed in Table I.

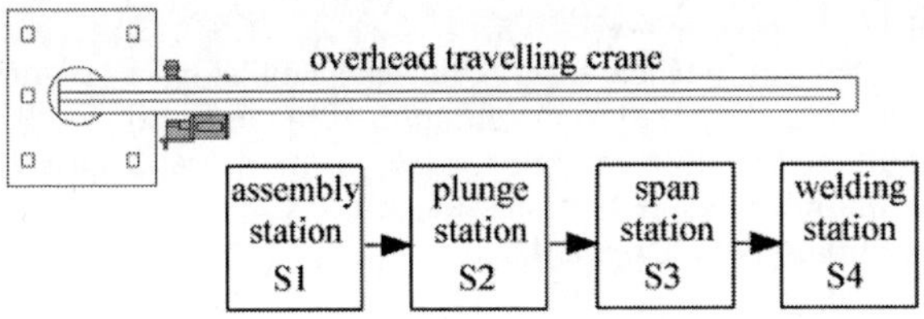

Figure 1. Structure of the production line.

At the company's production site, the jobs for filters are generated by an SAP system and produced filters are stored before they are assembled into other products or sold directly to customers. Therefore, all jobs with a release date after the beginning of a period are released at the beginning of this period. One period consists of one day with three 8 hour shifts. For this investigation, sequences of jobs of filter types with lot size 1 are randomly generated for each period t by an generating algorithm which has been designed in accordance with the proceeding in [22] and in [2]: An additional filter type F, released in period t, consumes capacity on each station during the time between t and its due date; the calculation for the capacity just uses the net processing time and does not regard the dependencies between the jobs (released so far). F is accepted as long as this consumed capacity on each station is below a maximal load level, otherwise it will be skipped to the next period. A maximal load level is an (intended) average load $(L_0(S))$ plus 0, –30% and +30% of $L_0(S)$. Over the first 5, 10, 15 etc. consecutive periods, the load level variations average to zero.

TABLE I. PROCESSING TIMES FOR ALL PART TYPES IN MINUTES.

Part type	Station				Sum of times
	S1	S2	S3	S4	
P1	100.5	50	53.5	9	213
P2	256.5	50	53.5	9	369
P3	122	135	90	75	422
P4	256.5	50	267	9	582.5
P5	182	200	135.5	140	657.5
P6	100.5	300	53.5	300	754
P7	223	250	196	220	889
P8	223	250	206.5	220	899.5
P9	100.5	300	267	300	967.5
P10	256.5	300	267	300	1123.5

In reality at the company, there are large numbers of periods with a low number of late jobs and large numbers of periods with a high (or even very high) number of late jobs. To achieve a comparable situation for this investigations, due dates are determined in a way so that scheduling with the FIFO rule (first-in-first-out) causes a specific percentage of late jobs. The company confirmed that job sequences with 30%, 50%, 70% and 85% of late jobs by scheduling with the FIFO rule (called time pressure) are comparable to the ones which occurred in the real operation. As a result of the generating algorithm's calculations the mean difference between the due dates and the release dates are between 2 and 3.5 days with a standard deviation of 0,5 days. Andritz Fiedler has confirmed that such timeframes for processing jobs are representative.

The time needed for loading and unloading a station is negligible compared to the duration of the operation itself. In addition, this task is independent from the allocation (or loading) of other stations and the required time is included in the duration of the operation.

The general scheduling problem consists of M stations and a pool of N jobs, which may change at any time, with known earliest possible starting times for release dates a_i $(1 \leq i \leq N)$ and due dates f_i $(1 \leq i \leq N)$ respectively. Also, there is the duration $t_{i,j}$ of operation $(o_{i,j})$ j $(1 \leq j \leq M)$ of job i $(1 \leq i \leq N)$, which is being worked on station j. As performance criteria average tardiness (T_{Mean}) and standard deviation of the tardiness (T_σ) are primarily analysed.

The time between two consecutive executions of the load process is determined by the maximum of the duration of the operations on the stations in the flow shop. This is called cycle time. This "load"-restriction, the no-buffer condition and the capacity of the stations are the main restrictions. Setup times are relatively small compared to operation times and are included in those.

The no-buffer condition means a relaxation of the scheduling problem with the (above) "load"-restriction. Scheduling problems with the no-buffer are proven to be NP-hard in the strong sense for more than two stations; see e.g., [5], which contains a good survey of such problems.

III. LITERATURE REVIEW

As mentioned earlier, the real application is close to the class of no-buffer (blocking) scheduling problems. Solutions for the no-buffer (blocking) scheduling problems are published in various papers. In [10], a schedule is extended by a (unscheduled) job that leads to the minimum sum of blocking times on machines which is called Profile Fitting (PF). Often, the starting point of an algorithm is the algorithm of Nawaz, Enscore and Ham, in short NEH algorithm, presented in [11], as it is the best constructive heuristic to minimize the makespan in the flow shop with blocking according to many papers, e.g., [3]. Therefore, [19] substituted the initial solution for the enumeration procedure of the NEH algorithm by a heuristic based on a makespan property proven in [18] as well as by the PF of [10]. [20] used an elaborated lower bound to realise a branch-and-bound algorithm which becomes a heuristic since the CPU time of a run is limited. Also, for minimising makespan, [4] realised and analysed a tabu search algorithm. As an alternative approach, [27] have developed a discrete particle swarm optimisation algorithm. In order to diversify the population, a random velocity perturbation for each particle is integrated according to a probability controlled by the diversity of the current population. Again, based on the NEH algorithm, [28] described a harmony search algorithm. First, the jobs (i.e., a harmony vector) are ordered by their non-increasing position value in the harmony vector, called largest position value, to obtain a job permutation. A new NEH heuristic is developed on the reasonable premise that the jobs with less total processing times should be given higher priorities for the blocking flow shop scheduling with makespan criterion. This leads to an initial solution with higher quality. With special settings as a result of the mechanism of a harmony search algorithm, better results are achieved. Also [17] presented an improved NEH-based heuristic and uses this as the initial solution procedure for their iterated greedy algorithm. A modified simulated annealing algorithm with a local search procedure is proposed by [28]. For this, an approximate solution is generated using a priority rule specific to the nature of the blocking and a variant of the NEH-insert procedure. Buffering strategies are proposed by [30] to handle random machine breakdowns for minimizing makespan in a job shop. Again, based on the PF approach of [10][12] addressed two simple constructive heuristics. Then, both heuristics and the PF are combined with the NEH heuristic to three improved constructive heuristics. Their solutions are further improved by an insertion-based local search method. The resulting three composite heuristics are tested on the well-known flow shop benchmark of [24], which is widely used as benchmark in the literature. [9] achieve for flow shop scheduling with jobs arriving at different times with a simple and constructive heuristic method very good results for the average completion time.

To the best of my knowledge, only a few studies investigate algorithms for the total tardiness objective (for flow shops with blocking). [18] have developed a lower bound which reduces the number of nodes in a branch-and-bound algorithm significantly. [21] described several versions of a local search. First, with the NEH algorithm, they explore specific characteristics of the problem. A more comprehensive local search is developed by a GRASP based (greedy randomized adaptive search procedure) search heuristic.

Priority rules are still a first choice in the case of complex scheduling problems. Thus, in [23], for a complex scheduling problem the performance of priority rules are analysed. Another example is the application of priority rules for the dispatching of AGVs in flexible job shops in [6]. It might be that in the near future several such problems will be solved by more sophisticated heuristics as genetic algorithms for example.

IV. HEURISTIC SOLUTION BY PRIORITY RULES

The real application operates in dynamic environments where real time events like station failure, tool breakage, arrival of new jobs with high priority, changes of due dates etc. may turn a feasible schedule into an infeasible one. A feasible assignment of a job is achieved by a priority rule like earliest due date (EDD), because a priority rule orders a queue in front of a station quasi immediately. So, priority rules are still analysed in many studies on scheduling; one example of a recent one is [1].

Due to the "load"-restriction, the processing time of a job A on the flow shop depends on the other jobs processed on the flow shop at the same time. Therefore, its processing time can be significantly larger than the sum of the processing times of its single operations (t_A), called net processing time of job A. A realistic processing time for a job A is achieved, if the processing on the flow shop is simulated with respect to the jobs processed on this flow shop at the same time. After four cycles $(\tau_1,\ldots,\tau_4)$, job A leaves the flow shop. So, these cycle times depend on the three jobs (X1, X2, and X3) on the flow shop as A is assigned to station 1, and the three jobs (B1, B2, and B3) following A in the sequence; this is illustrated in Figure 2.

So, $\tau_1+\tau_2+\tau_3+\tau_4$ is the (total) processing time of A (tt_A). This processing time of job A is only correct, if the tail is (structurally) identical with the three jobs which follow job A in the final permutation. Since these are not known a deviation normally occurs between this calculated processing time and the processing time which will really occur if job A is chosen.

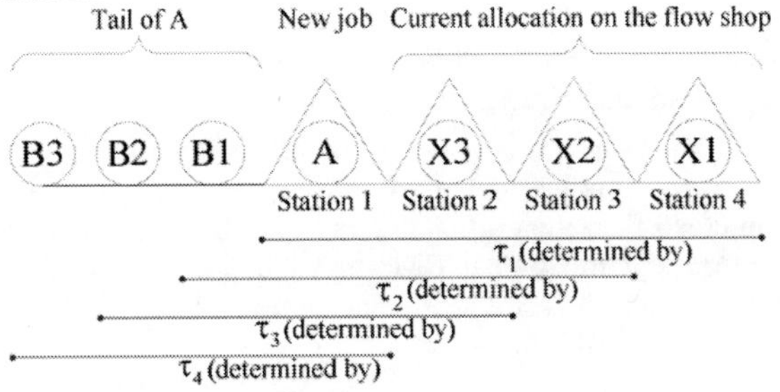

Figure 2. Calculation the processing time of a job A.

As known, tardiness is improved by assigning jobs with a small slack; the slack for job i is defined by $f_i - t - tt_i$, where t is the current time and f_i is the due date of job i. Investigations by the author (see also [2]) show, that for many job shop problems the rules

$$\text{CR+SPT} = \begin{cases} \frac{f_i - t}{tt_i}, & f_i - t - tt_i > 0 \\ tt_i, & f_i - t - tt_i \le 0 \end{cases}$$

(tt_i is the shortest processing time – the SPT rule; $\frac{f_i - t}{tt_i}$ is the critical ratio (CR)), ODD (EDD-rule – here) and $SL/OPN = \frac{f_i - t - tt_i}{M}$ (slack rule (SL) – here) are Pareto optimal to the average, the standard deviation and the maximum tardiness.

In addition, two more rules are applied, after adaption to this production line. One is the rule RR, proposed by [15], which seeks to minimize both mean flow time and mean tardiness of jobs. The priority index is $(f_i - t - tt_i)\cdot e^{-\eta} + e^{\eta}\cdot tt_i$, with utilisation level η of the entire flow shop defined by $\eta = \frac{b}{b+j}$ with b being the busy time and j being the idle time of the entire flow shop; the job with the lowest priority index will be processed next.

The other one is based on an optimal solution for the single-station weighted tardiness scheduling problem and was proposed by [14] as the weighted slack-based scheduling rule RM. The priority index is: $\frac{1}{\pi_i}\cdot e^{-\frac{k}{\bar{t}}\cdot\max\{f_i - t - tt_i, 0\}}$. As local processing time costing $\pi_i^l = tt_i$ is used, called RM local, and as global processing time costing $\pi_i^g = \sum_{i \in U_t} tt_i$, where U_t is the set of unfinished jobs in the pool of orders, excluding job i, is used, called RM global; [8] considered additional resource costs which do not fit to our problem or have already been integrated (in other parameters); e.g., a (static) bottleneck resource cost is not applicable because it is assumed that each station is temporary a bottleneck.

V. COMPUTATIONAL RESULTS

The real world application is realised in the simulation tool "Plant Simulation" together with an implementation of the above mentioned hierarchical planning as realised in ERP systems, used in industrial practice. Average tardiness (T_{Mean}) and standard deviation of the tardiness (T_{σ}) reach a steady state by a simulation horizon of 5000 periods.

A large number of preliminary studies show that the parameter k has a significant impact on the performance of the local and the global RM rule and the best results are achieved with $k = 1$. In [26], k has a negligible influence, but they regard an RCPSP.

The impact of the simulated processing time is analysed first. Due to its implementation, its concrete values depend from the (3) jobs on the flow shop and the (3) jobs following. So, the values should be independent from the priority rules and the time pressure. But, it could be that individual rules prefer permutations of jobs in a cycle. This is observed in experiments with the (above explained) priority rules. In these experiments the mean, the standard deviation, the minimum and the maximum of the simulated processing times are measured. The measured values for all part types and all rules are between those for the SPT rule and the SL rule which are listed in Table II. These results demonstrate a huge deviation from the net processing time

TABLE II. NET PROCESSING TIME (NET) AND SIMULATED PROCESSING TIME IN MINUTES FOR THE RULES SPT AND SL.

Part type	SPT				
	Mean	Net	Standard deviation	Mini-mum	Maxi-mum
P1	1116.5	213	151.8	885	1349.5
P2	1159.8	369	100.45	1061	1349.5
P3	1088.6	422	138.1	929	1349.5
P4	1151.7	582.5	96.4	1061	1349.5
P5	1162.9	657.5	88.5	1063.5	1349.5
P6	1233.3	754	95.3	1098.5	1376
P7	1228.1	889	60.1	1164.5	1349.5
P8	1225.5	889.5	57.8	1164.5	1349.5
P9	1237.2	967.5	93.9	1098.5	1376
P10	1322.8	1123.5	27.9	1098.5	1376
	SL				
	Mean	Net	Standard deviation	Mini-mum	Maxi-mum
P1	1179	213	126.5	885	1349.5
P2	1192.6	369	112.3	885	1349.5
P3	1179.3	422	118.1	885	1349.5
P4	1181.7	582.5	111.5	885	1349.5
P5	1184.6	657.5	106.5	885	1349.5
P6	1198.3	754	106.1	885	1376
P7	1203.8	889	101.7	885	1376
P8	1207.9	889.5	98.2	885	1376
P9	1215.9	967.5	98.1	885	1376
P10	1225.9	1123.5	97.5	885	1376

Furthermore, the experiments show a significant impact by the tail. The values in Table II are representative for many tails. Exceptions occur if each tail only consists of jobs with a small net processing time, as with part type P1, or a high one, as with part type P10. In the first case, the simulated processing times have small mean values, e.g., for part type P1 901,1 minutes and for part type P10 1067,6 minutes, and in the second case the mean values are large, e.g., 1248,5 minutes for part type P1 and 1269,2 minutes for part type P10. The standard deviations are in the first case huge, e.g., for part type P1 173,1 minutes and for part type P10 187,6 minutes, and the second case low e.g., for part type P1 77,4 minutes and part type P10 61,3 minutes.

As indicated by these results, the performance of a priority rule is influenced by the concrete tail. Instead of regarding all 1000 possible tails, the study is limited on tails whose part types have similar net processing times and those whose part types have significantly different net processing times. The experiments for each priority rule show both significant and minor deviations. These significant deviations are not exceptions and the reduction is almost one-third (or even more). Results which are close to the best possible results are achieved, if each tail consists of jobs of part type P4 only (i.e., P4, P4, P4); this tail is used in the following. Experiments show that an accidental tail (i.e., the part types for a tail are randomly selected) is a very good alternative.

Table III contains the percental changes by using simulated processing times instead of net processing times. Due to the characteristic behaviour of the SPT rule and the SL rule to T_{Mean} and T_{σ} (see above), both are analysed first. The SPT rule benefits most from a more realistic processing time. In case of the SL rule, there are just small improvements but often significant deteriorations. As long as the CR+SPT rule uses CR – which is some kind of slack – there are deteriorations for T_{Mean}. Since the net processing time is much smaller than the simulated processing time, the CR+SPT rule with simulated processing time decides earlier according to SPT as the CR+SPT rule with net processing time which explains the improvement. Both rules RR and RM are a combination of slack and shortest processing time (SPT). The RR rule benefits from a more precise processing time. A smaller (percental) improvement compared to the SPT rule is caused by already better values if net processing is used and the impact of the slack; The impact of the slack is shown most clearly by a time pressure of 85%. Much better (percental) improvements for T_{Mean} in case of a small time pressure is caused because RR rule prefers critical jobs with positive slack much better than the SPT rule (which does not take due dates into account). The RM rule prefers small jobs if there is no slack and otherwise jobs with small slack. Depending on the degree of influence of the slack on the priority, it can be expected that their changes are between those of the rules SL and CR+SPT. The values in Table III confirm this conclusion primarily for the rule RM global. The concrete values depend on the time pressure. In the case of rule RM local, the percental improvements for T_{Mean} and for T_{σ} with small time pressure are comparable to the ones of the SPT rule. In the case of T_{σ} a better processing time causes an increase of the (absolute) values for this rule on the level of the values of the SPT rule, except for a low time pressure.

TABLE III. CHANGE BY USING SIMULATED PROCESSING TIME INSTEAD OF NET PROCESSING TIME IN PERCENT, COMPARED TO THE RESULT WITH NET PROCESSING TIME.

Rule	Time pressure			
T_{Mean}	30%	50%	70%	85%
SPT	57.6	10.3	12.3	25.8
SL	-41.2	-2.3	0.23	-17
CR+SPT	-4	-10.3	-7.4	8.9
RR	75.3	4.2	3.9	11.9
RM local	48.9	10.4	11.7	21.5
RM global	3.3	-10.9	-4	-5.8
T_σ	30%	50%	70%	85%
SPT	68.65	31.3	27.2	48.11
SL	-20.1	1.2	3.4	-19
CR+SPT	51.4	34.1	37.1	48.6
RR	69.8	14.3	14.4	23.6
RM local	68.3	-21.2	-25.5	-242.8
RM global	50	-10.1	10.4	67.9

The absolute values, listed in Table IV (just the ones by using simulated processing times), differ partially from the results published in other papers. In order to judge this and the following more detailed results, it should be pointed out that the real world problem in this paper has a very special problem structure, compared to the representative problems usually regarded in the literature. The above mentioned expectation of the SPT and the SL rule – namely small T_{Mean} at the expense of large T_σ by the first rule and the opposite by the second one – is fulfilled. For many job shop and flow shop problems the CR+SPT rule outperforms the best results from the SPT and the SL rule. For this real world application CR+SPT delivers always, with one exception, results, which are much worse than the ones of all other rules. Since the rules RR and RM also combine slack and SPT, the worse results of CR+SPT are caused by a too late switch from preferring jobs with small slack to jobs with small SPT. Compared to other job shop problems this is more significant because just a misguided decision causes long cycles, which reduces the remaining slack for all other jobs much more than in the case of typical job shop problems. In addition, these long cycles could be very ineffective in terms of large times on some stations without any processing.

The performance of the RR rule for the real world application is primarily compared with the results in [16], because in [15] an open shop problem is regarded. In [16], the RR rule delivers better results than the other rules except for one case. In detail, in most of the cases, the improvements are less significant (partially much less) and the sequences of the regarded rules according to both performance criteria, are different. The results of the priority rules in [16] and in [15] are significantly impacted by the station utilisation levels, which are primarily 80% and 95%. In addition [16], uses an allowance factor and [15] uses the due date tightness, which both have a much smaller impact than the station utilisation level. In this investigation the time pressure is only increased by using tighter due dates while the load on the stations remains unchanged. Therefore, it can be expected that the time pressure here has a similar effect as the allowance factor in [16] or the due date tightness in [15]. A much larger impact is caused by a significant fluctuation of the load in the periods, so there are some periods where the load is either much higher than 95% and or much lower than 80% (as in [16] or in [15]). Thus a tighter due date has a more significant effect in periods with relative very high load than in periods with a relative very small load. In total, this seems to cause the different amount of improvement.

TABLE IV. ABSOLUTE PERFORMANCE MEASURES FOR PRIORITY RULES WITH SIMULATED PROCESSING TIME IN MINUTES.

Rule	Time pressure			
T_{Mean}	30%	50%	70%	85%
SPT	99.1	323.3	326.2	646.9
SL	161.6	321.5	344.7	1149.8
EDD	103.4	300.2	342.2	948.7
CR+SPT	581.97	575.7	574.6	1032.7
RR	40.7	279.5	313.5	823.1
RM local	55.3	267.1	278.6	626.2
RM global	134.9	346.7	359.2	1008.5
T_σ	30%	50%	70%	85%
SPT	314.5	449.2	473.4	826.7
SL	353.4	315.3	326.6	787.6
EDD	243.1	293.1	328.9	643.4
CR+SPT	2023.9	916.4	901.2	1464.1
RR	125.1	282.8	305.7	564.6
RM local	235.9	425.8	454.1	1187.4
RM global	395.5	456.2	464.6	890.04

The poor results of RM global compared with RM local (with one exception) contradicts the results in [8]. The same happens in the investigation of [26]. The local processing time costing prefers more often jobs with short processing times than the global processing time costing. This procedure explains the much better results in the case of those time pressures for which the SPT rule delivers a much better T_{Mean} than to the SL rule. In the other cases,i this procedure is beneficial if many tardy jobs are waiting in front of the flow job. Finally, in the flow shop in [26] with parallel resources and setup states the differences in the results of the rules are smaller than in this investigation and vice versa for the more general problem structure in [26].

Overall, the simulated processing times should be used in the priority rules. Then, the rules RR and RM local deliver the best mean tardiness. RR is beneficial with low and RM local with (very) high time pressure. The RR rule delivers the best standard deviation of the tardiness (for all time pressures).

VI. CONCLUSIONS

This paper presents a real world flow shop scheduling problem with more restrictive restrictions than the ones normally regarded in literature. To ensure online scheduling this investigation is restricted to those priority rules, which are considered in literature as being very effective. The substitution of the net processing time, normally used in priority rules, by a simulated one delivers often significant better results. Some tests with optimisation solutions for a small test problem indicate that priority rules do not recognise when to prefer large variances of cycle times or small ones, respectively, and that the schedules of priority rules have outliers in the cycle times, which are usually avoided by optimal solutions. With this and other characteristics of optimal solutions an efficient metaheuristic like local search or genetic algorithm shall be developed next.

Up to now, the workers for the manual tasks are not scheduled. In addition, limited resources, like the available number of coils or assembly ground plates, occur at some company sites. Such requirements are also left to future investigations.

REFERENCES

[1] A. El-Bouri, "A cooperative dispatching approach for minimizing mean tardiness in a dynamic flowshop", in Computers & Operations Research, Volume 39, Issue 7 (July), pp. 1305–1314, 2012.

[2] S. Engell, F. Herrmann, and M. Moser, "Priority rules and predictive control algorithms for on-line scheduling of FMS", in Computer Control of Flexible Manufacturing Systems, S.B. Joshi and J.S. Smith (Eds.). Chapman & Hall, London, pp. 75–107, 1994.

[3] J. M. Framinan, R. Leisten, and C. Rajendran, "Different initial sequences for the heuristic of Nawaz, Enscore and Ham to minimize makespan, idletime or flowtime in the static permutation flowshop sequencing problem", in International Journal of Production Research, 41, pp. 121–148, 2003.

[4] J. Grabowski and J. Pempera, "The permutation flow shop problem with blocking. A tabu search approach", in Omega, 35 (3), 302–311, 2007.

[5] N. G. Hall and C. Sriskandarajah, "A survey of machine scheduling problems with blocking and no-wait in process", in Operations Research 44 (3), pp. 510–525, 1996.

[6] J. Heger and T. Voß, "Dynamic priority based dispatching of AGVs in flexible job shops", in Procedia CIRP, Volume 79, pp. 445–449, 2019.

[7] F. R. Jacobs, W. Berry, D. Whybark, and T. Vollmann, "Manufacturing Planning and Control for Supply Chain Management", in McGraw-Hill/Irwin (New York), 6 edition, 2010.

[8] S. Lawrence and T. Morton, "Resource-constrained multi-project scheduling with tardy costs: Comparing myopic, bottleneck, and resource pricing heuristics.", in European Journal of Operational Research 64, pp. 168–187, 1993.

[9] G. Li, N. Li, N. Sambandam, S. P. Sethi, and F. Zhang, "Flow shop scheduling with jobs arriving at different times" in International Journal of Production Economics, Volume 206, 2018, pp. 250–260, 2018.

[10] S. T. McCormick, M. L. Pinedo, S. Shenker, and B. Wolf. "Sequencing in an assembly line with blocking to minimize cycle time". Operations Research, 37 (6), pp. 925–935, 1989.

[11] M. Nawaz, E. E. Enscore, and I. Ham, "A heuristic algorithm for the m-machine, n-job flow sequencing problem", in Omega, 11(1), pp. 91–95, 1983.

[12] Q. Pan and L. Wang, "Effective heuristics for the blocking flowshop scheduling problem with makespan minimization", in *Omega*, 40 (2), pp. 218–229, 2012

[13] R. M. V. Rachamadugu, "Technical Note –A Note on the Weighted Tardiness Problem", in Operations Research, 35, pp. 450–452, 1987.

[14] R. M. V. Rachamadugu and T.E. Morton, "Myopic heuristics for the single machine weighted tardiness problem", Working Paper No. 28-81-82, Graduate School of Industrial Administration, Carnegie-Mellon University, Pittsburgh, PA, 1982.

[15] T. S. Raghu and C. Rajendran, "An efficient dynamic dispatching rule for scheduling in a job shop" in International Journal of Production Economics 32, pp. 301–313, 1993.

[16] C. Rajendran and O. Holthaus, "A comparative study of dispatching rules in dynamic flowshops and job shops", in European Journal of Operational Research, 116 (1), pp. 156–170, 1999.

[17] I. Ribas, R. Companys, and X. Tort-Martorell, "An iterated greedy algorithm for the flowshop scheduling problem with blocking", in Omega, 39, pp. 293–301, 2011.

[18] D. P. Ronconi and V. A. Armentano, "Lower Bounding Schemes for Flowshops with Blocking In-Process", in Journal of the Operational Research Society, 52 (11), pp. 1289–1297, 2001.

[19] D. P. Ronconi "A note on constructive heuristics for the flow-shop problem with blocking". International Journal of Production Economics, pp. 39–48, 2004.

[20] D. P. Ronconi "A branch-and-bound algorithm to minimize the makespan in a flowshop with blocking", Annals of Operations Research, (138), pp. 53–65, 2005.

[21] D. P. Ronconi and L. Henrique. "Some heuristic algorithms for total tardiness minimization in a flow shop with blocking", Omega, 37 (2), pp. 272–281, 2009

[22] R. S. Russel, E. M. Dar-El, and B. W. Taylor, "A comparative analysis of the COVERT job sequencing rule using various shop performance measures", in International Journal of Production Research, 25 (10), pp. 1523–1540, 1987.

[23] K. D. Sweeney, D. C. Sweeney, and J. F. Campbell, "The performance of priority dispatching rules in a complex job shop: A study on the Upper Mississippi River", in International Journal of Production Economics, Volume 216, pp. 154–172, 2019.

[24] E. Taillard. "Benchmarks for basic scheduling problems", in European Journal of Operational Research, 64 (2), pp. 278–285, 1993.

[25] A. P. Vepsatainen and T. E. Morton, "Priority rules for job shops with weighted tardiness costs", in Management Science 33/8, pp. 95–103, 1987.

[26] S. Voß and A. Witt, "Hybrid Flow Shop Scheduling as a Multi-Mode Multi-Project Scheduling Problem with Batching Requirements: A real-world application", in International Journal of Production Economics 105, pp. 445–458, 2007.

[27] X. Wang and L. Tang, "A discrete particle swarm optimization algorithm with self-adaptive diversity control for the permutation flow shop problem with blocking", in Applied Soft Computing, (12, 2), pp. 652–662, 2012.

[28] L. Wang, Q.-K. Pan, and M.F. Tasgetiren, "A hybrid harmony search algorithm for the blocking permutation flow shop scheduling problem", in Computers & Industrial Engineering, 61 (1), pp. 76–83, 2011.

[29] C. Wang S. Song, S. J. N. D. Gupta, and C. Wu, "A three-phase algorithm for flowshop scheduling with blocking to minimize makespan", in Computers & Operations Research, 39 (11), pp. 2880–2887, 2012.

[30] Z. Wu, S. Sun, and S. Yu, "Optimizing makespan and stability risks in job shop scheduling", in Computers & Operations Research, Volume 122, 2020.

Enhancing Charging & Parking Processes of AGV Systems: Progressive Theoretical Considerations

Maximilian Selmair

BMW Group
80788 Munich, Germany
Email: maximilian.selmair@bmw.de

Tobias Maurer

Regensburg University
of Applied Sciences
93049 Regensburg, Germany
Email: tobias1.maurer
@st.oth-regensburg.de

***Abstract*—This paper presents our work in progress for the development of an efficient charging & parking strategy. Our research aim is to develop a strategy that not only provides an efficient approach to charging Automated Guided Vehicle (AGV) batteries, but also reduces traffic density in a highly utilised large-scale AGV system. Alongside the current state-of-the-art solution, three new allocation methods are introduced: *Trivial+*, *Pearl Chain* and a method based on the *Generalised Assignment Problem (GAP)*. These four methods vary in their scope, in terms of number of vehicles considered, when calculating a decision for a specific vehicle. Furthermore, two types of availability rules for vehicles are introduced and evaluated. Their combination with the allocation methods lay the foundation for future research. All allocation methods and availability rules are explained in detail and this is followed by a summary of the expected outcomes.**

***Keywords*—AGVs; Automated Guided Vehicles; Battery Charging; Charging Strategy.**

I. Introduction

Due to the increasing demand for individualised goods, and tighter production schedules, production and the related logistics have needed to become more and more flexible [1]. It follows that internal logistics have to adapt efficiently to the increasing dynamics and complexity of production processes. The visionary concept of Logistics 4.0 is proposed to offer a wide range of solutions for this [2] [3]. The use of AGVs, in particular, is gaining attention and is becoming the focal point of researchers across different industries [4]–[7].

AGVs are ready for use at any time of day, can be installed with relatively little effort and can move freely in their application environment, due to the lack of required physical guiding systems [8]. The increasing environmental flexibility means that vehicles can be used for a greater range of scenarios [5]. Taking into consideration the progressing flexibility and technological advances, Automated Guided Vehicles have the potential to play an important role in factory logistics [9]. Yet, it is proposed that the organisational complexity increases alongside with greater flexibility of application [10].

Besides the apparent problem of efficient task processing, other issues relevant to the resource efficient operation of the entire system require consideration. More specifically, this paper focuses on scheduling the charging and parking missions of the vehicles. Although this issue may seem to be trivial at first, it becomes increasingly complex for large-scaled and highly utilised systems. By choosing an optimal strategy, the vehicle fleet can be reduced to a minimum number of vehicles and thus fewer resources are necessary. The lower number of AGVs results in less traffic density, which in turn leads to fewer traffic jams and less blocked pathways [5]. As such, the charging strategy is proposed to be an important aspect and has the potential to improve the total performance of such a material flow system [11]. According to Ryck et al., this topic has not been explored in great detail so far [12].

Therefore, this paper considers and evaluates existing methods discussed in the relevant literature, and proposes concepts to address the issue of scheduling the charging and parking missions of the vehicles efficiently.

This paper is structured as follows: in Section II, we outline the environmental requirements that provide the theoretical framework of this study and Section III provides an overview of the relevant literature. The strategies that we have developed are introduced in Section IV . Finally, Section V and Section VI describe the experimental environment and the predicted outcomes of the projected simulation study. Its results are going to be presented in a subsequent publication.

II. Environmental Requirements

This section describes the parameters of our study, stipulated by the constraints of a research project undertaken by the BMW Group, to which we are contributing. For the automatisation of the the internal material flow, the BMW Group has developed the so-called Smart Transport Robot (STR) (see Figure 1), designed to substitute common tucker trains which currently play a central role in the automotive material handling processes. The industrial use-case of BMW Group specifies the following requirements:

1) Every vehicle can carry one load carrier at a time.
2) All transportation requests are issued randomly and therefore unknown prior to their receipt.
3) Vehicles without a task are required to either recharge or park.

Fig. 1. BMW's STR in its natural habitat.

A. Optimisation Objective and Key Performance Indicators

The overall goal of an automotive transport vehicle system is to complete all tasks on time. This requirement is considered to be a hard constraint, which is non-negotiable to the detriment of any other Key Performance Indicators (KPIs). That is, in order to meet this requirement, other resource intensive variables are minimised to save resources. An important resource in an automotive production environment are the pathways. These are not only utilised by AGVs, but also by forklifts, tow trains, bicycles and pedestrians. In order to maximise their availability for purposes other than AGVs, the subsequent charging and parking strategy was developed.

Additional KPIs applied to evaluate the quality of loading strategies in terms of their flexibility, efficiency and scalability will be introduced below. In this context, flexibility is defined as the availability of as many vehicles as possible at any time, allowing for an immediate reaction to short notice events, such as highly-prioritised urgent tasks.

In order to assess the efficiency of a charging strategy, it is necessary to take into account the non-linear quality of the charging process. That is, the amount of time required to recharge a battery to a predetermined level depends on the initial State of Charge (SOC). This KPI can be evaluated by accessing the utilisation records of the charging stations.

As scalability is also an important variable of such a system, the required computational power needs to be considered. Consequently, a low computing effort is more likely to ensure that a later expansion of the fleet will not cause performance issues based on a lack of computational power.

Thus, a total of five KPIs are used to compare and evaluate the strategies presented in this paper.

B. Source of Energy

The Smart Transport Robot is supplied with energy from a lithium-ion battery module of BMW's electric vehicle i3. Side fact: the i3 is built of eight such modules. Each module contains twelve battery cells and has 48 V as well as a capacity of 120 Ah. The time required to fully charge one module by means of a common method like Constant Current Constant Voltage (CCCV) is 3.2 h. However, fast-charge methods are likely to reduce this duration substantially. The charging current for this method decreases from 38 and 36 A. CCCV and also other fast-charge methods have in common that they are are able to charge faster in a relatively small SOC than in a high one [13]–[15].

Lithium-ion batteries have a number of advantageous properties relevant to the practical application of AGVs. Especially the minimal negative memory effects of short charging periods over a few minutes should be emphasised. The memory effect refers to a loss of capacity which results from frequent partial discharges. This feature allows for efficient, short charging processes and continuous use over 24 hours [16]–[18]. More advantageous properties are, e. g. the long life-cycle, low levels of self-discharge, their price and their relatively small size and weight [16].

C. Task Allocation and Prioritisation

The tasks are allocated by a central operating optimisation algorithm in this experimental setting. The algorithm ensures that all tasks are performed on time, whilst minimising the driving effort of the vehicle fleet measured in meters. For this purpose, all driving efforts are transferred to a matrix that constitutes the associated GAP (for more details see Section IV-A4). The solution to the GAP, referred to as Vogel's Approximation Method for non-quadratic Matrices (VAM-nq), was developed by Selmair et al. [3], and is an extension of the original Vogel's Approximation Method (VAM) introduced by Reinfeld et al. [19]. Unlike exact methods like the *Hungarian Method*, proposed by Kuhn [20], and *Integer Linear Programming*, VAM-nq approximates a solution for the GAP. As a result, the quality of the solution is sufficient for most cases, but the algorithm computes solutions substantially faster than exact methods. For a detailed review, we refer the reader to Selmair et al. [3].

To ensure that all tasks are performed on time, the system uses a prioritisation method to schedule all tasks. This method ensures that the system uses the temporal flexibility of each task to minimise the driving effort of the AGVs. Extensive research has been conducted about this prioritisation method by Selmair et al. [21].

III. Relevant Literature

This section presents a description of the state-of-the-art planning strategies summarised in Table I and explains their findings, identifies possible weaknesses and defines potential for consolidation. Based on a review of the relevant literature, the following key components of an allocation method are identified:

- Timing of the charging process
- Choice of a charging station
- Duration of the charging process

Table I serves as the basis for a comparison and summary of planning strategies provided by studies on battery charging. On the basis of these studies, the findings are evaluated and examples of specific research are selected.

TABLE I. OVERVIEW OF ALLOCATION METHODS

	Timing	*Selection Criteria*	*Duration*
Ebben 2001 [22]	Intermediate / Charge Range	Heuristics	Duration of Battery Exchange
Kawakami & Takata 2012 [23]	Min. Deterioration	-	Duration of Battery Exchange
Zou et al. 2018 [24]	Intermediate / Below Threshold	-	Handling Time / Fully Loaded
Kabir & Suzuki 2018a [25]	Below Threshold	Heuristics	Duration of Battery Exchange
Kabir & Suzuki 2018b [11]	Below Threshold	Nearest Station	Fully Loaded / Above Threshold
Colling et al. 2019 [26]	Scheduled	Permanent Assignment	Fully Loaded
Selmair et al. 2019 [9]	Intermediate / Below Threshold	Minimal Costs	Fully Loaded / Displaced
Zhan et al. 2019 [27]	Below Threshold	Heuristics	Fully Loaded / Above Threshold

A. *Timing of the Charging Process*

The trigger that prompts the charging process is usually a predefined low battery charge level and it coincides with a point in time when a vehicle is not performing a task [9] [11] [22] [24] [25] [27]. In an effort to determine the optimal timing, Kawakami et al., for instance, focus on minimising battery deterioration [23]. However, as previously established, this aspect is deemed to be negligible when it comes to lithium-ion batteries.

Interestingly, Colling et al. distributed vehicles equally, by using charging cycles and thus focused the attention on the overall system [26]. However, the mentioned study is carried out on a system with six AGVs, it remains uncertain whether this method can be implemented for a larger system.

Charging idle vehicles, even if their battery charge levels are above the triggering SOC, also referred to as intermediate charging, is also suggested to be a feasible tool to enhance a charging strategy [9] [22] [24]. Possibilities for intermediate charging and the consideration of the SOC in comparison with other vehicles on the field or in charging stations could lead to an increase in flexibility, efficiency and scalability of the system. These considerations should also be taken into account and tested when developing the charging strategy.

B. *Selecting a Charging Station*

Heuristics can be particularly helpful in selecting a suitable charging station. Commonly, this involves selecting charging stations based on either their distance to an agent or that can be used with the least overall delay [11] [22] [27]. The total delay consists of the travel time to a station and the waiting time required by an AGV to use the charging station. In contrast, predetermining charging stations without monitoring the distance to and availability of charging stations, as implemented by Colling et al., does not appear to be feasible for a flexible and scalable system [26].

In fact, using heuristics can increase efficiency and flexibility. Furthermore, if the parameters allowed for the displacement of vehicles currently at a charging station by vehicles with a higher need for recharging, it is assumed that efficiency and flexibility can be increased.

C. *Duration of the Charging Process*

The duration of a charging process can either be defined as the time required to physically replace a battery [11] [22] [23] or to reach its planned SOC [24] [26]. Kabir et al. and Zhan et al. suggest that batteries should only be charged to a level of 90 % or 95 % to shorten the inefficient phase of a battery charge (see Section II-B) [25] [27]. All the mentioned studies have in common that only the condition of one AGV is considered in any decision. Selmair et al. provides a first method that take into account the condition of more than a single vehicle [9]. In their paper, two vehicles are compared with each other by using an objective function that includes the distance of a vehicle to an occupied station as well as the SOC of both. The following conclusions can be drawn from Selmair et al.: the possibility to interrupt a charging process due to tasks or displacements can increase flexibility. For this purpose, accurate parameters are necessary in order to achieve robust processes to attain a high level of flexibility.

IV. Developed Strategies

This section describes potential *strategies* for charging and parking vehicles, which maintain the availability of the vehicle fleet on the one hand, and minimise the distance travelled on the other. Every *strategy* can be divided into two aspects: the first is the *allocation method* itself (Subsection A) and the second pertains to the availability of a vehicle, referred to as *availability rule*, for tasks or charging and parking processes (Subsection B).

Table II illustrates the two aspects of the strategies in the form of a morphological box. Every combination of the left and the right column represents a strategy – with one exception: for the *Trivial* allocation method, which is derived from the current state of the art, only the first *availability rule* is applied.

TABLE II. THE TWO COMPONENTS OF A CHARGING & PARKING STRATEGY

Allocation Method	*Availability Rule*
Trivial	Hard Constraint
Trivial+	Soft Constraint
Pearl Chain	
GAP	

A. Allocation Methods

The four allocation methods are presented in the order of their scope, in terms of numbers of vehicles considered by each method. Therefore, the first allocation method – namely *Trivial* – only takes into account the vehicle that requires either charging or parking. This allocation method is common in today's industrial transport vehicle applications (see Table I).

The *Trivial* allocation method is followed by three new allocation methods, which consider other factors than merely the vehicle that requires a charging or parking station. These are in namely *Trivial+*, *Parl Chain* and *GAP*. Their scope is illustrated in Figure 2.

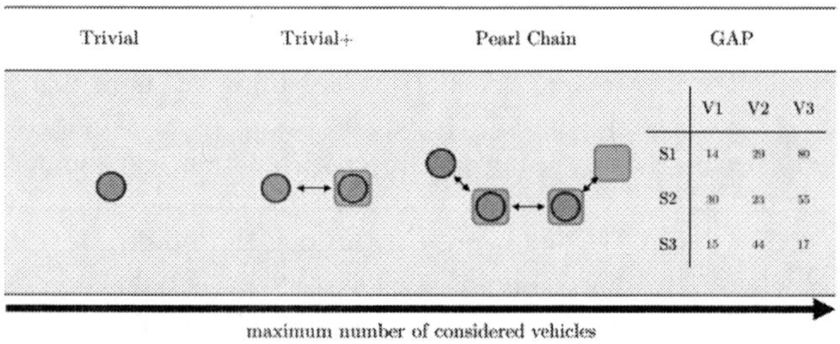

Fig. 2. The four allocation methods and their illustrated scope.

1) Trivial Allocation Method:

The *Trivial* allocation method combines the methods most frequently encountered in the literature review. They are mostly utilised in threshold-rules and nearest-agent-first allocations. Table III shows an overview structured by the defined key components, followed by their specification.

The triggering moment, in which the charging process is prompted, is predefined as the moment when the battery falls below a certain SOC (e. g., below 15 %). As soon as the current transport tasks are completed, the AGV drives to the nearest vacant charging station and the charging process continues until the battery has reached a specific SOC (e. g., above 95 %). This process can only be disrupted by the *Availability Rules of Vehicles* (see Subsection IV-B). If a vehicle is not in the process of performing a task and all charging stations are occupied, it is assigned to a parking station. Vehicles in a parking station can be pulled out by performing a task or if their charge level falls below a specific threshold (e. g., below 15 %).

TABLE III. SCHEDULING RULES FOR THE TRIVIAL CHARGING & PARKING ALLOCATION METHOD

	Timing	*Selection Criteria*	*Duration*
Charging	Below Threshold	Nearest Station	Above Threshold / Call for Task
Parking	No Task / Above Threshold / No vacant Charging Station	Nearest Station	Above Threshold / Call for Task

TABLE IV. SCHEDULING RULES FOR THE TRIVIAL+ CHARGING & PARKING ALLOCATION METHOD

	Timing	*Selection Criteria*	*Duration*
Charging	Intermediate / Below Threshold	Minimal Costs	Above Threshold / Call for Task / Displaced
Parking	No task / Above Threshold / No vacant Charging Station	Nearest Station	Above Threshold / Call for Task

2) Trivial+ Allocation Method:

The Trivial+ allocation method is designed to be more flexible, with the help of the insights gained from the literature review. The key difference to the *Trivial* allocation method is that intermediate charging are now feasible and vehicles can be displaced from their charging stations. This requires that the vehicle which has to be allocated must be compared to a vehicle within a occupied station. A description of this method is included in the Table IV and text below.

With *Trivial+*, vehicles can now be assigned to charging stations regardless of their SOC. This introduces the concept of intermediate charging. Vehicles with a very low SOC (e. g., less than 15 %) will still be allocated exclusively and therefore with priority to charging stations.

Additionally, occupied charging stations will also be considered for allocation if the occupying vehicle has a, e. g. 25 %, higher battery charge level than the vehicle seeking a charging station. This ensures that charging stations are not occupied by vehicles that have a significantly higher battery level than those seeking to recharge. Within the parameters of *Trivial+*, the driving distance to the stations remains the most important criterion for selecting a charging station. The relevant station with the lowest costs (sum of driving distance and optional additional costs) will be assigned. For occupied stations, additional costs are imposed on the vehicle that has to vacate its current station and travel to a new one. These extra costs ensure that vehicles in charging stations are not immediately displaced at will if there is a more efficient alternative for the seeking vehicle.

The charging process is carried out until the vehicle has either reached a sufficient charge level (e. g. above 95 %), gets displaced or receives a task as soon as the charge level has reached a minimum level (e. g. above 25 %).

The allocation of parking stations is unaffected by these modifications to the methods and works the same way as described for the *Trivial* allocation method.

3) Pearl Chain Allocation Method:

The *Pearl Chain* allocation method is based on the basic principle of the *Trivial+* allocation method. However, this allocation method not only compares the battery level of both vehicles, like the *Trivial+*, but also examines whether displacements are efficient considering the total distance in meters that the vehicles would have to travel. Furthermore, a distinction is made between two situations:

1) If the seeking vehicle has, for instance, a 40 % lower battery level than the occupying vehicle, displacement is permitted without further constraints.
2) If the seeking vehicle's battery level is, for example, between 20 % and 40 % lower than that of the occupying vehicle, displacement is permitted if the total distance travelled by both vehicles is shorter than the distance to other charging station options. The travelling effort of the vehicle that needs to charge for a potential displace is calculated as follows:

$$C = D_{V_S} + D_{V_D} + M_D,$$

where D_{V_S} represents the travelling effort of the seeking vehicle to the occupied charging station, whereas D_{V_D} stands for effort involved for the displaced vehicle to travel to another station as described below. Finally, M_D represents the potential effort required for the displaced vehicle to maneuver out of its station.
The displaced vehicle is permitted to choose between the stations listed below this paragraph. This principle prevents performance issues, by a reasonable restriction of the solution space. Therefore, the "pearl chain" has a maximum length of three vehicles (see Figure 2).
- Vacant charging stations
- Vacant parking stations
- Occupied charging stations which fulfill the case described in Situation 1
3) If the seeking vehicle's battery level is not at least 20 % lower than that of the occupied vehicle, a displacement is not permitted.

4) Allocation Method based on the Generalised Assignment Problem:

The GAP finds its roots in the research field of applied mathematics [28]. This problem, in its original form, consists of a number of agents and a number of tasks. Any task can be assigned to one of the agents. The total costs arising from a solution may vary, depending on each chosen agent-task assignment [29]. The optimal solution is defined as the one that maximises the total profit by minimising the associated costs.

Our idea for charging & parking vehicles by using the GAP, is to transfer the demands (in the mathematical context *costs*) of vehicles for driving to a station into a GAP. By using this method, a number of vehicles can be assigned to a number of stations by minimising the driving effort and meeting defined constraints at the same time.

These costs can be manipulated to ensure that vehicles are being assigned, on the basis of their SOC, to the closest stations according to their, even if this means bypassing some in order to allow prioritised vehicles access to these. This mechanism ensures that vehicles of a fleet with a relatively low SOC will have lower costs for charging stations than others, and will have greater priority to access charging stations. The constraints are defined as extra costs added to the driving distance to a station in meters. These extra costs are proposed as follows:

1) An occupied charging station is only accessible to vehicles whose battery charge level is 10 or more percentage points lower than that of the occupying vehicle. The theoretical allocation of a vehicle that does not fulfill this requirement is sanctioned with a penalty cost of 10,000 units and should not be accepted by a balanced system for any reason.
2) An occupied parking station is not accessible for any seeking vehicles with a battery charge level lower than the level of the vehicle currently occupying the station. The theoretical allocation of a vehicle that does not fulfill this requirement is sanctioned with a penalty cost of 10,000 units and should not be accepted by a balanced system for any reason.
3) The theoretical allocation of vehicles, with a battery level below 30 %, to a parking station will be sanctioned with a value of 1,000 units. This ensures that such vehicles will only park if no other option is available.
4) If a vehicle is occupying a charging or parking station, maneuver costs of 7 units are added.

In our opinion, the constraints formulated above will increase the likelihood of the efficient assignment of charging and parking stations. Constraint 1 allows the assignment to

Fig. 3. Exemplary two-bin principle: the full container is facing the production line. The empty container has already been collected. Replenishment will be delivered shortly.

an occupied charging station if the occupying vehicle can be assigned to any other station and the demand vehicle's battery level is at least 10 % below the battery level of the vehicle currently occupying the charging station. Due to Constraint 4, maneuver costs are also factored into every effort undertaken by a vehicle to vacate a station. Simultaneously, Constraint 2 allows vehicles in parking stations to become displaced by others if it is beneficial to the overall system in terms of distance travelled. Constraint 3 ensures that vehicles with a battery level lower than 30 % are more likely to be assigned to charging stations than to parking stations. This was determined to ensure that the vehicles' batteries are not depleted entirely – provided that enough charging stations are in the system.

B. Availability Rules of Vehicles

The defined availability rules for vehicles constitute an interface between the task allocation and the charging & parking strategy. These rules regulate the number of vehicles available for performing tasks within the system. These rules can been amended by applying two types of constraints: hard or soft constraints.

A hard constraint cannot be disregarded for any reason. By their nature, they can be easily explained and understood. Such a constraint can be formulated as follows:

- A vehicle on the field or at a parking station is available for tasks when its SOC is above, e. g. 25 %
- If a vehicle is charging, it will become available for tasks as soon as its SOC exceeds, e. g. 70 %

Soft constraints can be modelled – for example – by manipulating costs in some manner in order to change the system's behaviour to a desired behaviour. In the presented case, where the system assigns vehicles to tasks by taking into account their distance to these and their SOC, such a soft constraint can be formulated to sanction vehicles with extra costs if they are in a charging process or only have little battery left. Such a formulation can be defined as follows:

- A vehicle incurs extra costs in addition to the travelling distance in meters to a new task if it is located at a charging station. These extra costs can be calculated for example as:

$$(-1 * SOC) + 70$$

These extra costs will be negative for vehicles with a SOC above 70 %. Therefore, the system will reward these vehicles when it allocates tasks to them. They are more likely to be chosen than other vehicles on the field or parking, even if the distance to the task is the same. On the other hand, the extra costs will be positive if a charging vehicle's SOC is below 70 %. Then, this vehicle will receive penalty costs and is therefore less likely to be considered in comparison to other vehicles with the same distance. The lower a vehicle's SOC, the higher the penalty costs and the less probable their chance of receiving a new task.

V. Experimental Environment

The model layout, as shown in Figure 4, is designed to represent a typical automotive flow production system. There are three types of warehouses designed in this layout:

1) a full goods warehouse,
2) a storage for empties and
3) a mixed storage facility that serves as a full and empties warehouse.

The full goods warehouses (1 and 2 in Figure 4) are the starting points of the intracompany supply chain. The empty dollies are collected to be prepared for reuse in Warehouse 2 and 3. In the center of the layout there are three production lines that represent a flow production. Along the production lines are work stations, also called fitpoints (see Figure 3). Every work station is supplied by a predefined warehouse at certain intervals. These intervals are determined by the number of parts stored in a dolly, the frequency at which a part is required and the cycle-time of the production line. The replenishment is carried out by using a two-bin system, an example of which is shown in Figure 3. As soon as an empty container is collected, a full one is delivered by an AGV from the warehouse. There is only space for one vehicle at each station at a time. Thus, if a second vehicle was required to enter a station that is currently occupied, it has to wait in front of it and will block the pathway for other vehicles, potentially causing delays. Parking stations are established between some fitpoints along the production line (see blue house-symbols in Figure 4). The charging stations are visualised by green dots and are placed at the end of each production line.

VI. Predicted Outcomes

During the development of the previously presented allocation methods and availability rules, we endeavoured to predict

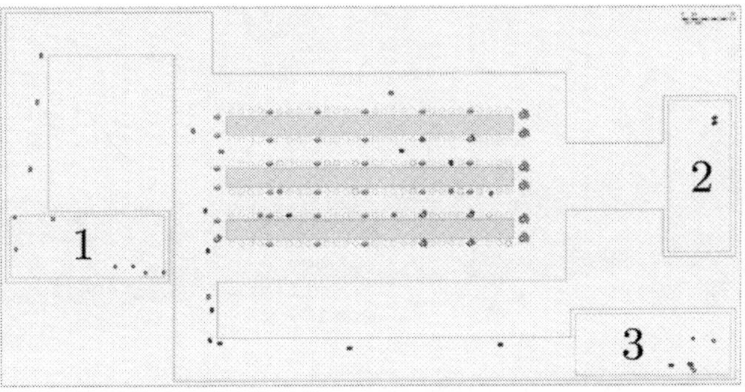

Fig. 4. Planned simulation environment consisting of three production lanes, two warehouses and one station for empty dollies.

TABLE V. PREDICTED PROPERTIES OF THE STRATEGIES

	Resource-saving	*Flexibility*	*Efficiency*	*Scalability*
Trivial	−	−−	−	++
Trivial+	0	++	++	+
Pearl Chain	+	++	+	+
GAP	++	++	+	−

the advantages and disadvantages of the resulting strategies. For this purpose, these strategies were evaluated according to the previously defined KPIs presented in Table V. It has to be highlighted that these outcomes are merely of a predictive nature. Future simulations will evaluate the strategies and their characteristics in more detail.

In summary, it is assumed that each strategy has certain strengths, but these may be disadvantageous for other characteristics like traffic density. The *Trivial* allocation method is expected to be easily scalable due to its simplicity, as this method does not require any significant computational effort. As such, any additional vehicles do not influence the individual calculation process. However, for this allocation method, the vehicles' current status, such as their position and SOC, are not compared with each other, which does not support an efficient and flexible allocation process as defined beforehand. In the *Trivial+* and *Pearl Chain* allocation method, vehicles are compared with each other in terms of their position and SOC. The resulting data are used to decide whether it is beneficial to initiate a displacement process, in which lower charged vehicles are prioritised. Furthermore, by recharging vehicles with a low SOC, the previously described loading curve, i. e. the lower the battery level, the faster the charging process, can be taken advantage of. For these reasons, positive effects in flexibility and efficiency are expected for both methods. *Pearl Chain* also compares whether certain displacements are beneficial when considering the total driving distances measured in meters. Although this requires greater computational effort of the entire system, it predicted to be more resource efficient in terms of available pathways. Due to the holistic approach of the *GAP* allocation method, a positive result is expected for the KPIs *resource-saving, flexibility, efficiency*. However, this holistic approach is expected to result in a statistically significant higher computational effort. This effort increases exponentially with the size of the system. This fact suggests that the *GAP* allocation method is unlikely to be a scalable method.

In summary, it is suggested that the combination of these *allocation methods* and *availability rules*, as illustrated in Table V, holds significant potential for any industrial setting in which AGVs are applied on a larger scale.

VII. Conclusion

In this paper, we have published our work in progress pertaining to the development of an efficient charging & parking strategy, which will reduce traffic density in a high utilised large-scale system. Alongside a state-of-the-art solution, three new methods were introduced: *Trivial+*, *Pearl Chain* and *GAP*. These methods vary in scope when calculating a decision for a specific vehicle. While *Trivial+* compares two vehicles, *Pearl Chain* is able to consider up to four vehicles for a decision and *GAP* actually takes all vehicles with a demand for a station into account. Furthermore, two types of availability rules for vehicles were proposed. Combining these *availability rules* with the various *allocation methods*, provides several strategies that could be examined in future research.

To analyse a system's behaviour and the efficiency of all strategies, a simulation study is proposed to finalise this research. Within a simulated industrial production area, each strategy will be simulated and the resulting decisions scrutinised thoroughly, and finally, the entire performance will be compared to all other strategies.

References

[1] M. t. Hompel, "Individualisierung als logistisch-technisches Prinzip (Individualisation as a logistical-technical principle)," in *Internet der Dinge in der Intralogistik*, W. Günthner and M. t. Hompel, Eds. Berlin, Heidelberg: Springer Berlin Heidelberg, 2010, pp. 3–7.

[2] K.-I. Voigt, J. M. Müller, J. W. Veile, W. Becker, and M. Stradtmann, "Industrie 4.0 – Risiken für kleine und mittlere Unternehmen (Industry 4.0 - Risks for small and middle companies)," in *Geschäftsmodelle in der digitalen Welt*, W. Becker, B. Eierle, A. Fliaster, B. Ivens, A. Leischnig, A. Pflaum, and E. Sucky, Eds. Wiesbaden: Springer, 2019, pp. 517–538.

[3] M. Selmair, A. Swinarew, K.-J. Meier, and Y. Wang, "Solving non-quadratic matrices in assignment problems with an improved version of vogel's approximation method," in *ECMS 2019 Proceedings edited 2019*, 2019a, pp. 261–266.

[4] M. t. Hompel and M. Henke, "Logistik 4.0 (Logistic 4.0)," in *Industrie 4.0 in Produktion, Automatisierung und Logistik*, T. Bauernhansl, M. t. Hompel, and B. Vogel-Heuser, Eds. Wiesbaden: Springer Fachmedien Wiesbaden, 2014, pp. 615–624.

[5] P. Pagani, D. Colling, and K. Furmans, "A neural network-based algorithm with genetic training for a combined job and energy management for AGVs," *Logistics Journal: Proceedings*, 2018.

[6] A. Leupold, F. Senger, U. Weber, and T. Kappler, "Industrial IoT," *Digitale Welt*, vol. 2, no. 3, pp. 78–84, 2018.

[7] H. Schöning, "Industry 4.0," *it - Information Technology*, vol. 60, no. 3, pp. 121–123, 2018.

[8] H. Maier, *Grundlagen der Robotik (Basics of Robotics)*, 2nd ed., ser. Lehrbuch Studium, 2019.
[9] M. Selmair, S. Hauers, and L. Gustafsson-Ende, "Scheduling charging operations of autonomous AGVs in automotive in-house logistics," *Simulation in Production and Logistics 2019*, 2019.
[10] V. Plenk and F. Ficker, "Industrie 4.0 (Industry 4.0)," in *Digitalisierung: Segen oder Fluch*, D. Wolff and R. Göbel, Eds. Berlin, Heidelberg: Springer, 2018, pp. 29–53.
[11] Q. S. Kabir and Y. Suzuki, "Comparative analysis of different routing heuristics for the battery management of automated guided vehicles," *International Journal of Production Research*, vol. 57, no. 2, pp. 624–641, 2018a.
[12] M. De Ryck, M. Versteyhe, and K. Shariatmadar, "Resource management in decentralized industrial automated guided vehicle systems," *Journal of Manufacturing Systems*, vol. 54, pp. 204–214, 2020b.
[13] D. Fasthuber, "Integration der Ladeinfrastruktur in das elektrische Energiesystem (integration of a charging infrastructure in an electric energy system)," *e & i Elektrotechnik und Informationstechnik*, vol. 6, no. 2, p. 125, 2020.
[14] P. Keil and A. Jossen, "Charging protocols for lithium-ion batteries and their impact on cycle life—an experimental study with different 18650 high-power cells," *Journal of Energy Storage*, vol. 6, pp. 125–141, 2016.
[15] W. Shen, T. T. Vo, and A. Kapoor, "Charging algorithms of lithium-ion batteries: An overview," in *2012 7th IEEE Conference on Industrial Electronics and Applications (ICIEA)*. IEEE, 2012, pp. 1567–1572.
[16] D. U. Sauer, G. Fuchs, B. Lunz, and M. Leuthold, "Technology overview on electricity storage - overview on the potential and on the deployment perspectives of electricity storage technologies."
[17] T. Sasaki, Y. Ukyo, and P. Novák, "Memory effect in a lithium-ion battery," *Nature materials*, vol. 12, no. 6, pp. 569–575, 2013.
[18] E. Rahimzei, K. Sann, and M. Vogel, *Kompendium: Li-Ionen-Batterien im BMWi Förderprogramm IKT für Elektromobilität II: Smart Car – Smart Grid – Smart Traffic, Grundlagen, Bewertungskriterien, Gesetze und Normen*. VDE Verband der Elektrotechnik: Frankfurt a. M., 2015.
[19] N. V. Reinfeld and W. R. Vogel, *Mathematical Programming*, Prentice-Hall, Englewood Cliffs, 1958.
[20] H. W. Kuhn, "The hungarian method for the assignment problem," *Naval Research Logistics Quarterly*, vol. 2, no. 1-2, pp. 83–97, 1955.
[21] M. Selmair, V. Pankratz, and K.-J. Meier, "Efficient task prioritisation for autonomous transport systems," in *ECMS 2020 Proceedings edited by Mike Steglich, Christian Mueller, Gaby Neumann, Mathias Walther*. ECMS, 2020, pp. 322–327.
[22] M. Ebben, *Logistic control in automated transportation networks*. Enschede: Twente Univ. Press, 2001.
[23] T. Kawakami and S. Takata, "Battery life cycle management for automatic guided vehicle systems," in *Design for Innovative Value Towards a Sustainable Society*, M. Matsumoto, Y. Umeda, K. Masui, and S. Fukushige, Eds. Dordrecht: Springer Netherlands, 2012, vol. 171, pp. 403–408.
[24] B. Zou, X. Xu, Y. Gong, and R. de Koster, "Evaluating battery charging and swapping strategies in a robotic mobile fulfillment system," *European Journal of Operational Research*, vol. 267, no. 2, pp. 733–753, 2018.
[25] Q. S. Kabir and Y. Suzuki, "Increasing manufacturing flexibility through battery management of automated guided vehicles," *Computers & Industrial Engineering*, pp. 225–236, 2018b.
[26] D. Colling, J. Oehler, and K. Furmans, *Battery Charging Strategies for AGV Systems*. Wissenschaftliche Gesellschaft für Technische Logistik, 2019.
[27] X. Zhan, L. Xu, J. Zhang, and A. Li, "Study on AGVs battery charging strategy for improving utilization," *Procedia CIRP*, vol. 81, pp. 558–563, 2019.
[28] H. Kellerer, U. Pferschy, and D. Pisinger, *Knapsack problems: With 33 tables*, 1st ed. Berlin: Springer Berlin, 2010.
[29] L. Özbakir, A. Baykasoğlu, and P. Tapkan, "Bees algorithm for generalized assignment problem," *Applied Mathematics and Computation*, vol. 215, no. 11, pp. 3782–3795, 2010.

Challenges of Stochastic Project Scheduling in Manual Manufacturing: A Hybrid Simulation-Based Scheduling Approach

Mathias Kühn*, Thorsten Schmidt*, René Schöne†, Dmytro Pukhkaiev†, Uwe Aßmann†
*Chair of Material Handling, †Software Technology Group
Technische Universität Dresden, Dresden, Germany
email: {first.last}@tu-dresden.de

***Abstract*—Solving Stochastic Resource-Constrained Multi-Project Scheduling Problems (SRCMPSP) is an upcoming topic. Numerous variants, smaller batch sizes and shorter product life cycles lead to more uncertainty. In Production Planning and Control (PPC), stochastic scheduling approaches are coming into focus. The schedule thus is determined during production without following a baseline schedule. In our research project Hybrid PPC, we develop robust heuristics for stochastic project scheduling. The purpose of the approach is a central, simulation-based generation of a decentralized control system. As part of the research, we investigate benchmarking of SRCMPSP, evaluation strategies, as well as heuristic and solution robustness.**

***Keywords*—stochastic processes; scheduling algorithms; benchmark testing.**

I. Introduction

Mechanical and systems engineering is increasingly becoming a project business (large number of variants, batch size one) [1]. The main driver is the increasing individualization. This is accompanied by more fuzzy data (e.g., through reduced time for work preparation). Thus, Production Planning and Control (PPC) in project manufacturing is facing new challenges. This applies in particular to complex assembly processes that are characterized by human work. Stochastically influenced process times are inherent in the process due to the fluctuating individual performance of humans and will, therefore, continue to exist in the future. There is also a low level of interaction and data availability between PPC in this domain. Representative examples of the characteristics mentioned above are the final assembly of customer-specific machine tools, printing machines or photovoltaic systems, in which several complex projects with individual objectives compete for resources. From a scientific point of view, project planning and control problems under uncertainties belong to the problem class of Stochastic Resource-Constrained Multi-Project Scheduling Problems (SRCMPSP). A solution strategy for this problem is stochastic scheduling without a baseline schedule, which is largely a novelty in the area of project scheduling. In our research project Hybrid PPC, we research heuristics for decentralized scheduling with an evolutionary simulation based optimization approach.

In this paper, we present the research background in Section II and the scope of the research project in Section III. In Section IV, we have a detailed look on the challenge heuristic and solution robustness and show our first steps regarding modelling. The paper concludes with a short summary in Section V.

II. Research Background

Current PPC developments for mastering the challenges in a dynamic production environment are promising. In particular, the comprehensive decentralization of production control can enable the compensation of stochastic influences and process uncertainties while simultaneously improving logistic objective values [2]. So-called Cyber-Physical Production Systems (CPPS) are prerequisite in many approaches (e.g., adaptive scheduling approach [3], static scheduling policy [4]). However, the permanent automatic data acquisition and availability required for such systems is currently only partially feasible and will remain subject of research and development for the next few years [5]. The technical implementation [6] and acceptance of a continuous digital recording of human work is also unclear [7].

However, in order to use the advantages of new approaches in decentralized control, strategies are required that can be implemented with low data availability and interaction.

From a conceptual point of view, there are various approaches for such a decentralized control. For process control, mainly automatically generated heuristics [8] in form of Composite Dispatching Rules (CDR) are used and applied in various PPC concepts. Simply stated, CDRs are attributes calculated according to a rule from the information on the product, process, resource and system. While automatically generated CDRs are widely used in job-shop scheduling [8], applications of automatically generated CDRs for the solution of the Resource-Constrained Project Scheduling Problem (RCPSP) [9] and especially for the solution with a decentralized control for SRCMPSP are rather rare in literature. We can only guess the reasons for this. While the job-shop environment is traditionally stochastic, the RCPSP environment is also increasingly stochastic. Classical solutions for RCPSP by generating a baseline schedule are no longer effective and the interest in scheduling without a baseline schedule increases. One possibility for efficient scheduling without a baseline schedule are those CDRs. In addition, the SRCMPSP is more complex (e.g., more complex precedence constraints, larger

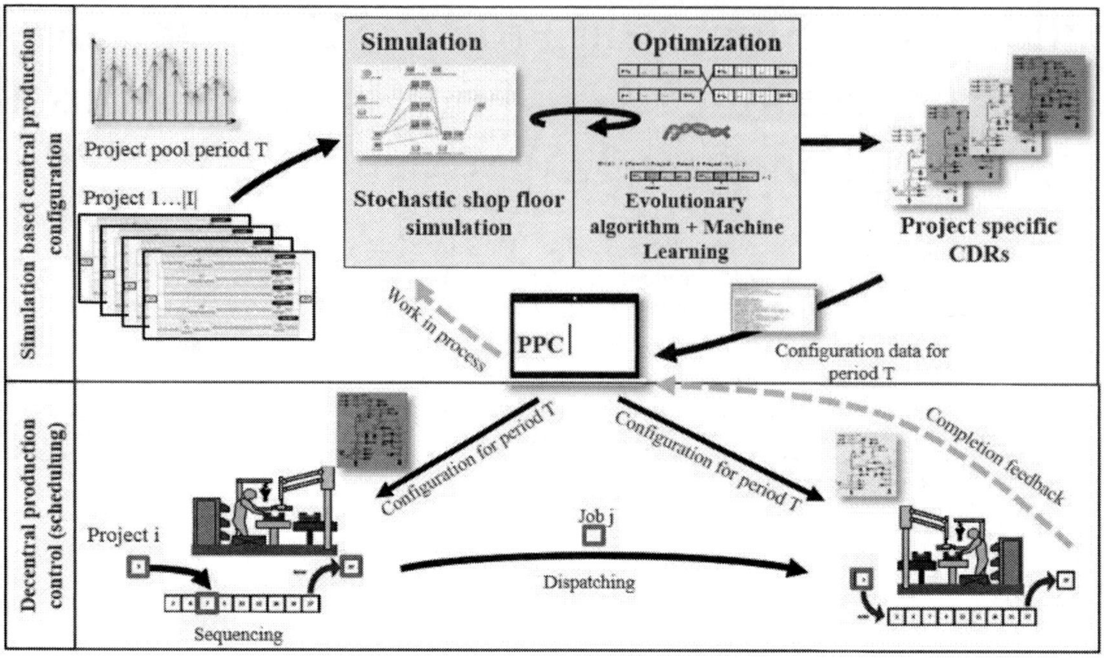

Figure 1. Proposed Hybrid PPC approach

problem size with up to 10 projects with up to 1000 jobs and up to 50 different resources) than the job-shop problem, which leads to increased requirements for PPC strategies.

III. Research Project Hybrid PPC

In order to distinguish our research from existing research in the field of decentralized control strategies due to lower data availability and interaction, we focus on the development of a method for the configuration of a CDR, which is valid for a limited period. We name this heuristic robustness. This CDR should be able to compensate process uncertainties autonomously.

In our research project *Hybrid PPC* we address different challenges and goals of the mentioned stochastic project scheduling problem (extract). We strive for the following goals:

- Best possible compensation of disturbance variables and stochastically influenced process parameters
- Multi-objective optimization: Differentiated optimization of project-specific and production system objectives
- Use of practical and easy to collect information in the production system as data basis for CDRs

To reach those goals, the following challenges arise:

- Benchmarking SRCMPSP
- Heuristic Robustness: Defining Evaluation strategies
- Investigation and applications of computational fast algorithms for generating CDRs

As mentioned, the two core components of the proposed Hybrid PPC approach is the central, simulation based configuration [10] and the decentralized control with CDRs (see Figure 1). The input for generating the CDRs is therefore a production scenario with stochastic variables, e.g., processing times, and a predefined time horizon. Based on this scenario, the central stochastic simulation starts with firstly randomly generated CDRs. Both the representation of the CDR (requirements low computation effort) and the selection of attributes (local attributes) are part of our research. In order to take advantages of different representation types, we see potential in the combination of rule-based and parameter-based representation and additional in the development of specific scheduling policies (e.g., while queue length < x, then FIFO). For improving the CDRs, evolutionary algorithms are conceivable.

Further, we want to use machine learning to generate initial solutions of CDRs (reduce computational effort) and these specific scheduling policies. Therefore, we want to derive the input parameters for the generation of the CDR based on similar model parameters. Methods of supervised learning are of particular interest here. Central configuration results in the CDR with the best statistical objective value of the different stochastic scenarios. These CDRs are transferred to the production resources and are used decentralized for scheduling. The specification of the size of the project pool / period length in correlation to heuristic robustness is also part of our research. This process is comparable to the transfer of the production schedule to production. Various options are conceivable for technical implementation. The minimum feedback quality refers to the completion of an order so that the work in process can be estimated. The success of the project is measured by whether the considered objective values are improved compared to achieved objective values of current used strategies (e.g., priority rules, list scheduling).

IV. Addressed Challenge Robustness And First Steps

A. Challenges of Robustness

In our research project, we define the robustness of heuristics to solve SRCMPSP as the capability to compensate disturbances and data uncertainty. The compensation of the disturbance correlates with the objective fulfilment. Therefore, we consider statistic values of the objective functions, so that one can also speak of solution robustness here. A low standard deviation is an indicator of high robustness.

The individual project objectives are usually in conflict with the objectives of the shop floor (see Figure 2). The first challenge is to choose the appropriate statistic for the objective functions. Usually only mean and standard deviation are considered. We also investigate other statistic parameters (e.g., range, median) if they are suitable for optimizing the objective values.

The second challenge is to find an evaluation strategy for these objectives. One concept to find a compromise could be pareto dominance [11]. However, this results in a high evaluation effort and reducing computational effort is also necessary. As an example, 10 projects with 5 objectives each means a total of 50 objective functions.

Looking on a first experiment based on previous work [12], we can underline the complexity of defining heuristic and solution robustness. For the experiment, we chose representative models of the Multi-Project Scheduling Problem Library (MPSPLIB) [13] and some industrial examples (complex printing machines). The objective function was Total Project Delay (TPD, sum of delay of all projects). Comparing mean and standard deviation of objective function values for different optimization strategies (single, pareto ranking) shows the effects in Table I. While a single optimization leads to good results for the considered objective and to bad results for the not considered objective, the pareto optimization leads to a good compromise (see Figure 3). The ratio of improvement to deterioration between the strategies is very different.

Concluding, how standard deviation and mean value correlate in the solution space cannot be determined trivially. Thus, the effects of achieving better results in one objective value on another objective value cannot be determined and are model-dependent. However, it is necessary to define additional measurements for heuristic and solution robustness according to schedule robustness [14].

B. Model description

As mentioned earlier, our problem class is a SCRMPSP. We base the description on Kolisch instances [15], which we extend by multi-objectives, setup times (based on job types), stochastically distributed job duration and resource capacity. To describe stochastics, we use examples from literature and practice. For example, the assembly time of assemblies for the interior fittings of ships is logarithmically normally distributed.

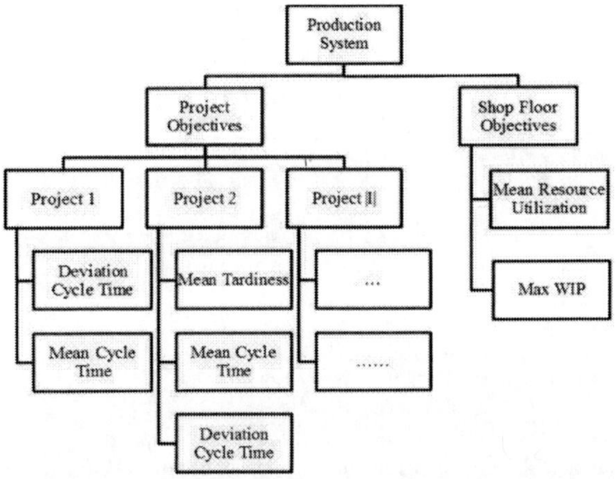

Figure 2. Shop floor objectives vs. project objectives

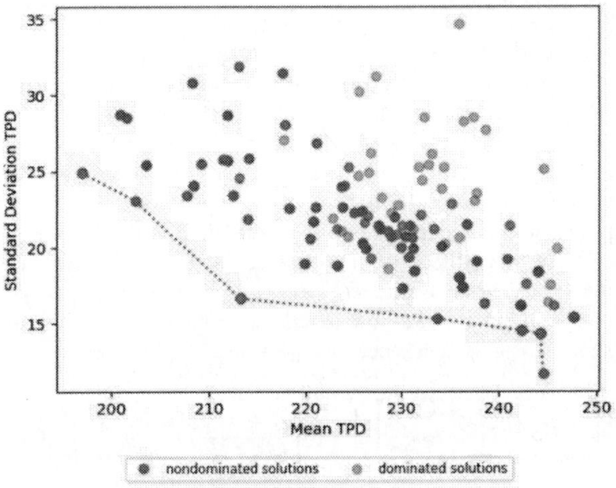

Figure 3. Result of pareto optimization (example)

The coefficient of variation is up to 0.9, which means a high uncertainty. The final problem description contains a production system with global resources and projects. Those projects comprise a list of jobs, an objective and project-local resources. Each of the jobs has a job type, a number of modes and a list of successors. A mode determines the duration and required resources of the job. A resource has a maximum capacity. Both duration of a mode and capacity of a resource can either be concrete, or stochastically distributed for some distribution.

C. Reproducible benchmark library

One of the challenges mentioned earlier is to benchmark an SRCMPSP and the comparison of different solution approaches for that problem. Our vision is to provide a benchmark architecture similar to the MPSPLIB [13]. However, the question remains: how to provide a suitable input to other participants solving a given problem instance? One can either provide stochastic distribution information, or provide

TABLE I. MEAN AND STANDARD DEVIATION OF TPD.

Model	Optimization strategy[1]					
	Mean TPD		Std TPD		Pareto TPD	
	Mean	Std	Mean	Std	Mean	Std
j30_a2_nr1	**41.3**	9.1	47.1	**6.4**	42.9	8.47
j30_a2_nr2	**54.8**	15.3	57.3	**11.6**	54.9	12.10
⋮						
PM_1	78.71	6.49	86.58	**3.68**	**74.73**	7.95
PM_2	**57.84**	4.93	69.03	**1.97**	64.95	3.93
PM_3	**65.29**	8.18	84.9	**3.11**	68.18	5.72

[1] Considering different objective strategies: mean, standard deviation (std) and pareto-optimization (mean and standard deviation) of TPD (time units), evaluation of mean and std for each strategy

"scenarios", i.e., a finite number of concrete values for all stochastically distributed values. The former is more concise, but not necessarily comparable whereas the latter is comparable, but more verbose.

D. Current status

We began to implement a process for generating problem instances of our problem class (see Figure 4). For this, an existing problem generator (ProGen) [15] is used to generate a base problem. This description is parsed into and together with the missing information like stochastic distributions, the problem is extended to be fully compliant with the problem class of SRCMPSP. The current process ends with persisting that description. Next steps are a) to find ways to compute one solution for the now extended problem, and b) to find strategies to generate heuristics, as described earlier.

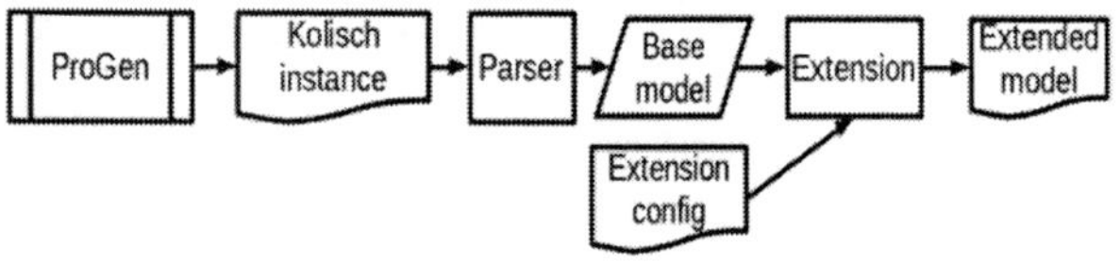

Figure 4. Extension process

V. CONCLUSION

In this paper, the research project Hybrid PPC was presented. The project takes up the PPC problem in customer-oriented project manual manufacturing and deals with fundamental questions of both scientific and practical relevance. The approach is the central configuration of a decentralized control system based on various algorithms. Therefore, we have developed a complex model of the SRCMPSP. We are currently developing an evaluation model by examining various statistical parameters of the objective function values to describe and investigate solution and heuristic robustness. Our next step is the development of a scheduler with the requirement of short computation time. In parallel, we investigate possibilities to reuse the simulation data with the aim to save computation effort. Machine Learning algorithms are promising to find correlations between models, solution approaches and objective function values based on large data sets.

ACKNOWLEDGEMENTS

This work is funded by the German Research Foundation (DFG) within the projects *Simulation-based generation of robust heuristics for self-control of manual production processes: A hybrid approach on the way to industry 4.0 (Project ID 418727532)* and *RISCOS (Project ID 280611750)*.

REFERENCES

[1] J. Bischoff *et al.*, "Tapping the Potential of Industry 4.0 in Medium-Sized Companies [Erschließen der Potenziale der Anwendung von Industrie 4.0 im Mittelstand]," Mülheim an der Ruhr, 2015, [retrieved:September, 2020]. [Online]. Available: http://publica.fraunhofer.de/documents/N-356542.html

[2] N. Vojdani and B. Erichsen, "Investigation of the impact of disruptions on processes related to production logistics using simulation," vol. 2016, 10 2016.

[3] M. Kück, J. Ehm, M. Freitag, E. M. Frazzon, and R. Pimentel, "A Data-Driven Simulation-Based Optimisation Approach for Adaptive Scheduling and Control of Dynamic Manufacturing Systems," *Advanced Materials Research*, vol. 1140, pp. 449–456, 2016.

[4] S. Grundstein, M. Freitag, and B. Scholz-Reiter, "A New Method for Autonomous Control of Complex Job Shops – Integrating Order Release, Sequencing and Capacity Control to Meet Due Dates," *Journal of Manufacturing Systems*, vol. 42, pp. 11–28, 2017.

[5] D. Spath, S. Schlund, S. Gerlach, M. Hämmerle, and T. Krause, "Outlook: Production Processes in 2030 [Ausblick: Produktionsprozesse im Jahr 2030]," in *Industry 4.0 - What will production processes look like in 2020? [Industrie 4.0 - Wie sehen Produktionsprozesse im Jahr 2020 aus?]*, A.-W. Scheer, Ed. EBOOKS, 2013.

[6] D. Spath, Ed., *Production work of the future - Industry 4.0 [Produktionsarbeit der Zukunft - Industrie 4.0]*. Stuttgart: Fraunhofer-Verl., 2013.

[7] G. Hornung, "Legal Challenges of the Industry 4.0 [Rechtliche Herausforderungen der Industrie 4.0]," in *Industry 4.0 as an Organizational Task [Industrie 4.0 als unternehmerische Gestaltungsaufgabe]*, R. Obermaier, Ed. Springer Fachmedien Wiesbaden, 2017.

[8] J. Branke, S. Nguyen, C. W. Pickardt, and M. Zhang, "Automated Design of Production Scheduling Heuristics: A Review," *IEEE Transactions on Evolutionary Computation*, vol. 20, no. 1, pp. 110–124, 2016.

[9] S. Chand, H. Singh, and T. Ray, "Evolving Heuristics for the Resource Constrained Project Scheduling Problem with Dynamic Resource Disruptions," *Swarm and Evolutionary Computation*, vol. 44, pp. 897–912, 2019.

[10] L. März, W. Krug, O. Rose, and G. Weigert, Eds., *Simulation and Optimization in Production and Logistics: Practice-Oriented Guide with Case Studies [Simulation und Optimierung in Produktion und Logistik: Praxisorientierter Leitfaden mit Fallbeispielen]*, ser. VDI-Buch. Berlin, Heidelberg: Springer Berlin Heidelberg, 2011.

[11] D. E. Goldberg, *Genetic Algorithms in Search, Optimization, and Machine Learning*, 30th ed. Boston: Addison-Wesley, 2012.

[12] M. Kühn, T. Schmidt, and M. Völker, "Simulation-Based Optimization Approach for Efficient Generation of Sequencing Heuristics for Solving the Stochastic Resource-Constrained Scheduling Problem," in *Simulation in production and logistics 2019 [Simulation in Produktion und Logistik 2019]*, M. Putz and A. Schlegel, Eds. Auerbach: Verlag Wissenschaftliche Scripten, 2019, pp. 403–412.

[13] J. Homberger, "MPSPLIB: Multi Project Scheduling Problem Library," 2008, [retrieved:September, 2020]. [Online]. Available: www.mpsplib.com

[14] Ö. Hazır, M. Haouari, and E. Erel, "Robust Scheduling and Robustness Measures for the Discrete Time/Cost Trade-Off Problem," *European Journal of Operational Research*, vol. 207, no. 2, pp. 633–643, 2010.

[15] R. Kolisch and A. Sprecher, "PSPLIB – A Project Scheduling Problem Library," *European Journal of Operational Research*, vol. 96, pp. 205–216, 1996.

A New Simulation-Based Approach to Schedule Personnel Deployment Times in Decentrally Controlled Production Systems

The Project Sim4PeP

Julia Schwemmer, Thorsten Schmidt, Michael Völker
Chair of Material Handling
TU Dresden
Dresden, Germany
e-mail: {julia.schwemmer, thorsten.schmidt, michael.voelker}@tu-dresden.de

***Abstract*—The fourth industrial revolution rises new challenges for personnel planning. On the one hand, the decentralization of production control gains a new level of flexibility. Without a fully detailed production schedule in advance, the workforce requirement will be just identified during the current processes. Therefore, it is almost impossible to deduce the concrete times of workforce requirement in advance, but this would be necessary for workforce scheduling. On the other hand, manual activities themselves will change in smart factories, resulting in a reduced deployment continuity. In order to ensure efficient resource planning, including workforce, the project Sim4PeP develops a simulation-based forecasting method to schedule workforce deployment times in a decentrally controlled production system for short- to medium-term planning horizons.**

Keywords-CPPS; simulation-based optimization; workforce requirement planning.

I. Introduction

One main topic of the fourth industrial revolution is the decentralization of production control [1]. The decentralized real-time control will gain a new level of flexibility to achieve a rapid reactivity and a demand-oriented production by handling customer-specific orders, small batches and process disturbances with minimal planning effort [1]. In this concept, orders and resources communicate autonomously and decide at lowest shop floor level (cyber-physical production system) [1]. Thereby, there is no longer a fully detailed production schedule in advance. It is not known in advance which operation of which order on which machine to what time will be processed. This "scheduling gap" also effects the workforce operations and causes a fundamental conflict: Staff schedules have to be determined some weeks in advance [2] – for individual, administrative and regulatory reasons. To enable an efficient staff schedule, that synchronizes personnel supply and demand, the times of personnel requirement times have to be known already during the scheduling of the workforce.

In addition, the changing tasks of the production workers in smart factories intensify the conflict. The scenario of a deserted factory stays still both utopian and not to be aspired [3]. Instead, the human being remains a key factor in the concept of smart factory and will take on a coordinating, controlling and directing role. Thus and due to the complexity of the system, there will be jobs with high qualification requirements and high specialization [3], which presumably arise discretely in time. At the same time, progressive automatization will increasingly eliminate simple work tasks [4], which are often accompanied by a steady deployment continuity. Accordingly, there will be more specific qualification classes and less consistent periods of working time, resulting in a further reduced deployment continuity.

Especially in countries, such as Germany or France, personnel costs are a driving force in manufacturing industry [5] that have to be optimized. Therefore, an efficient resource planning of the workforce is an essential part of Production Planning and Control (PPC) and should be a "first level resource" during the optimization process. To achieve a high workforce capacity utilisation, single tasks have to be bundled, so no (or less) idle times will occur. However, this has an effect on machine allocation and job sequence, too.

In order to solve the resulting time and planning conflict described above, the project develop a simulation-based forecasting method to schedule workforce requirements for decentrally controlled production systems.

Section 2 briefly reviews the state of the art. Section 3 introduces the concept of the new simulation-based approach and the related project. The paper concludes by a short summary and an outlook on long-term goals.

II. State of The Art

The "classic" PPC-process focuses on optimization with regard to orders or resources (in the sense of machines or unspecific form but without care of the specific attributes of workforce) [6]. The production planning creates a central production schedule from which workforce schedules are derived. Accordingly, the workforce is a "second level resource" and a subordinated optimization object in the optimization process, respectively [6]. Regarding to the changed conditions described in Section I, this approach does not work anymore at all or at least not in an efficient way.

Already at the turn of 2000, a direction of research within the PPC has emerged which especially deals with the focus of workforce scheduling and its special features (see for example [6] or [7]). These approaches take up the issues of qualification-related allocation possibilities and resource flexibility of workforce via working hours with seasonal accounts (e.g., flextime). For example in 2002, there was an AiF funded project which dealt with the integration of flexible working time models into PPC [7].

The reason to introduce flexible working hours in production is the short- to medium-term synchronization between capacity supply and demand. Consequently, the PPC is enabled to react to the volatility of the markets [6].

No literature around the millennium 2000 could deal with the later emerging idea of the future fourth industrial revolution (for example in Germany around 2012 – cf. [1][8]). Therefore, they do not deal with the essential core aspect of this research effort: The conflict between decentralized, real-time driven production control and the required lead-time of workforce resource planning.

There are also publications in the recent past developing or improving approaches to personnel planning (see for example [9] or [10]). Due to the constantly changing production requirements and influences of the rapidly changing markets, characterized by global fluctuating supply and demand relationships, more customer-specific products and shortening delivery times, personnel planning is still a current topic within PPC [9][10].

[9], for example, examined strategically as well as operationally opportunities to make personnel planning more flexible. Nevertheless, the approach does not attend to the dilemma of the time conflict of workforce scheduling in decentralized production control.

[10] developed flexibility instruments for medium- to long-term periods that is not within the scope of the presented approach.

[11] contributes an approach to allocate a highly qualified and specialized workforce under the aspects of flextime via seasonal accounts, heterogeneous deployment flexibility with regard to individual qualifications, as well as individual efficiency for the time required to fulfil the duties. However, the method is based on a deterministic production schedule with already known workforce requirement times. The same applies, for example, to [12] and [13].

[14] uses a two-stage procedure, in which the workforce is just a second level resource.

The collaborative project MyCPS [15] focuses on the integration of humans into the cyber-physical world of production. The focus is not on organizational but on technological issues, except for one project: KapaflexCy [2]. KapaflexCy enables small and medium-sized companies to implement innovative forms of working time models for more flexibility with personnel deployment schedules, individually tailored for each company. For example, they developed an app that allows employees to decide whether they want to work additional hours at requested times. In the case of short-term requirements, the employees receive requests on their smartphones. The approach thus focuses on the reactive balancing of short-term fluctuations of the capacity demand in production with the concrete and in advanced fixed allocation of workforce supply. In contrast, the core of the presented research approach involves the proactive derivation of workforce requirements based on variable production programs without a detailed production schedule known in advance. Furthermore, the focus is not only on the scheduling of additional shifts but also on the planning of the base load. The method to be developed for the research project also rejects classic shift systems.

Furthermore, some recent approaches of workforce planning and scheduling use machine-learning techniques. [16], for example, predicts the need of products and services from which it assigns work tasks to employees. In contrast to the approach presented below, [16] is an experience based approach as it mainly use history-based files. In addition, it refers to a public utility service billing company but not to the background of industrial production.

Moreover, there are scientific approaches that integrate a digital twin for employees in a self-controlling production system (see for example [17]). The twin reflects human characteristics, like behavior, skills and preferences, and strives for a better collaboration between human and automated production system, especially on intuitively interaction with technical devices [17]. However, this method does not deal with the creation of personnel deployment plans or the overall deviation of personnel requirement times sufficiently in advance. Therefore, it does not match the research focus of this contribution.

On commercial level, there are also software companies of personnel planning products that take up the changes of the fourth industrial revolution. Their products provide employee self-service portals for, e.g., wishes such as absence days or shift changes, model individual working time arrangements or the matching process of qualification requirements (see for example [18] or [19])). Nevertheless, they do not deal with the planning paradox described at the beginning.

Especially due to the thematic reference to working hours and models, legal framework conditions have to be taken into account; in Germany for example, there are [20] or [21].

To sum up the literature reviewed, the workforce should be considered as a specific resource in the PPC-process. However, none of the approaches was dealing with the dilemma of workforce requirement planning in a decentrally controlled production system.

III. Research Project Sim4PeP

A. *Simulation-Based Forecasting Method*

The research project Sim4PeP focuses on the described paradox of the lead-time for workforce scheduling and the ad-hoc decisions of the decentrally controlled production system. To solve this issue, the aim of the project is to develop a simulation-based forecasting method for the generation of workforce attendance schedules and validate the functionality of the method.

The forecasting method focuses on a short- to medium-term planning horizon (up to 6 weeks) under stochastic influences. It proceeds according to a rolling wave planning

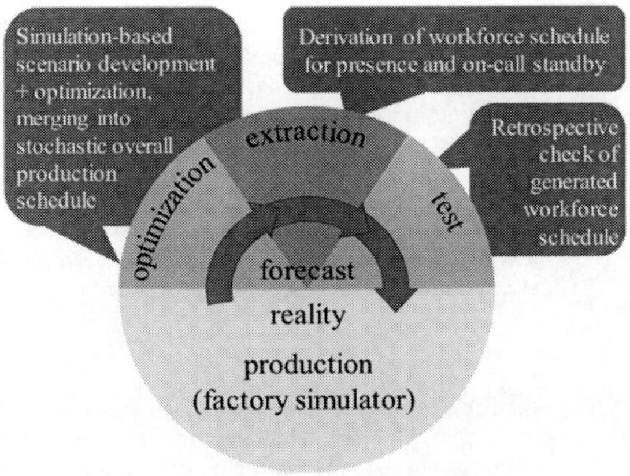

Figure 1. The three steps of the forecasting method

model and successively updates subsequent planning intervals. The method consists of three steps: optimization, extraction and test (see Figure 1).

In the first stage (optimization), a simulation-based optimization model predicts proposals of potential production schedules that consist of a timetable with resource allocations and order sequences. The objective function already includes the optimization objects "order", "machine" and "employee". Thus, the "classic" optimization objects "order" (e.g., minimizing makespan) and "machine" (e.g., maximizing capacity utilization) remain in the objective function. However, as described in the second section, the workforce working times should no longer be a subordinated optimization object, but rather a "first-level" resource due to the changed situation. Components of objective function in relation to workforce scheduling are, for example, the minimization of the total attendance time over all employees, which is for example a corporate objective. The method should not only deal with corporate objectives but also with goals of individual employees. For example, they should have the opportunity to contribute wishes of their own working hours. Thereby, the model ensures the legal or even the individually agreed working time specifications by hard model restrictions. This way, the modeling guarantees that there are, e.g., a maximum workload of 8 hours a day and adequate break times. More self-chosen and flexible working time leads to a better work-life balance and finally to a higher motivation at work [20]. Furthermore, it increases the attractiveness of the company for the workers. The forecasting method will work completely with flexible working hours and abandon from rigid shift times. So "work 4.0" is partially also available for employees in the production. In addition, the flexible working hours could enable a better synchronization of capacity supply and demand.

Due to the stochastic disturbances and uncertainty for future forecasts, as well as the autonomy in the variety of decisions of the decentral control the simulation model generates different scenarios. Weighted by the corresponding objective function value, a set of the best scenarios build a general schedule. That schedule is not exact and deterministic but rather a stochastic distribution over preferable scenarios (see Figure 2). Stochastic influences are, for example, process time deviations or machine and personnel failures.

Furthermore, this schedule already contains stochastically distributed demand times for the workforce according to qualification classes. By including the worker in the objective function of the first stage, it already meets the optimization requirement (first level resource). Stage 2 extracts the workforce attendance and when appropriate on-call standby times. However, the general schedule does not yet provide a clear, deterministic statement but the times for the staff schedules have to be deterministic. For this purpose, the method could use variable tolerance limits (see Figure 2). The derived workforce schedules have to leave as much flexibility as possible for the decentral real-time control. Therefore only the attendance times are defined, the exact allocations between work tasks (capacity demand) and the planned working times (capacity offer) are not defined, so the decentral control can still match it.

In the third stage, a retrospective test checks the generated workforce schedule by feeding the attendance times back into the simulation model. The objective function value decides whether the schedules can be released for the reality or whether it must be returned to stage 2. In the latter case, a variance of the tolerance limits can readjust the schedules.

In the research project, an extended factory simulator will replace the real production process. It incorporates further stochastic influencing variables and broader stochastic scenarios. There is not yet an adequate benchmark for the problem described in the introduction which can be applied for comparison. Using a factory simulator, the validation of

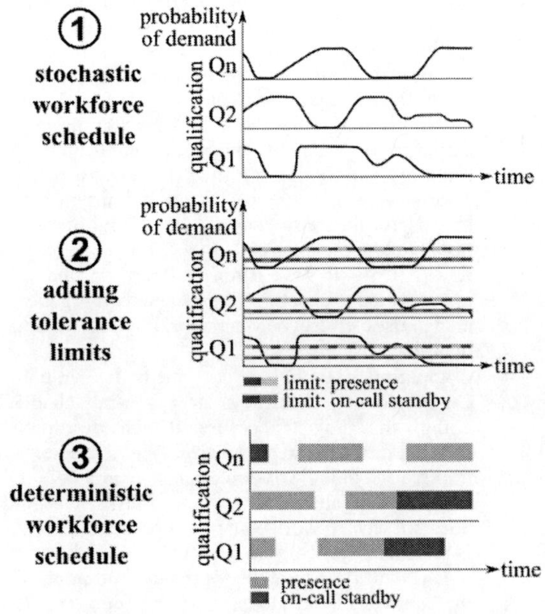

Figure 2. Derivation of the workforce schedule

the method, as well as a quality analysis of the generated plans is possible. Especially due to the stochastic problem modelling, deviations between the created personnel plans and the factory simulator are to be expected. Even in real systems application, the generated plans will not correspond one hundred percent with the actual implementation, as the forecast is still uncertain. However, it is the aim of the project to enable the method to keep these differences as small as possible by reasonable computing effort.

If the results are promising, a test on a real system can be carried out at a later project stage or in a subsequent project.

B. Research Focus

Besides the development of the forecasting method itself, it is a goal of the research project to determine feasibility, requirements and limits of this methodology. There are three main categories of research questions in the project:

- Deterministic derivation in the stochastic field: Above all, the questions arise: To what extent do the deterministic specification of the forecasted attendance requirements limit the degree of self-optimization of decentralized planning? In this context, is it feasible to achieve optimal results in terms of the overall objective? Moreover, is it feasible to achieve an optimized process for the overall system at all by determining deterministic workforce times from the stochastic forecast?
- Working time models and task bundling: What would a working time model have to look like in order to support the flexibility of decentralized control and at the same time implement a humane workforce planning? Which components of existing working time models lead to which influences within the method (e.g., flextime, overtime or division of the daily working time into parts)? How can the method match requirements from the production system (that means 24-hour operation) with the requirements regarding to the workers (e.g., 8 hours preferably during the day)? Is there a compromise? To what extent can employees contribute their preferred working hours (may possibly in different priority levels) or are core working hours necessary to ensure the basic supply of workforce? Is it possible to bundle tasks that there are no or less idle times? Does it have strong effects on the other optimization objects? Are there synergetic or antagonistic effects between working hours and task bundling?
- Computing time and method initiation: Computational efficiency is a central challenge within the project, because it can become the limiting factor of the model size. Due to the focus on the creation of the workforce schedule and not on the concrete assignment of workers to tasks, the model does not have to work on a real-time basis. Instead, it is executed cyclically (e.g. weekly). However, with regard to the later usability of the method in practice, the runtime of the models is very important. How can the models achieve a runtime improvement? May machine-learning strategies improve the metaheuristics of the simulation-based optimization? What type of triggering points will start the forecasting method (fixed time intervals vs. specific or unexpected events). How responsive are these trigger points with regard to already fixed personnel plans (e.g. drastic market changes in the occurrence of Covid19)? In which frequency do the method have to start in general? What model-internal time pattern for workforce scheduling is adequate (e.g., half-hourly)?

IV. CONCLUSIONS

The research project Sim4PeP focuses on the paradox of the creation of workforce schedules in smart factories. Therefore, the project is developing a forecasting method that contains a simulation-based optimization approach. A further goal of the research project is to determine feasibility, requirements and limits of this methodology in general.

The research approach pursues long-term goals. It brings benefits for the employees. They should have the chance to have an impact on their own individual organization of working hours. This will increase the work-life-balance, which – especially for younger employees at present time – plays a more important role than the salary [20]. The increased self-determination also leads to higher motivation and thus to higher productivity. This in turn is a corporate benefit. In addition to the companies' benefits, an efficient workforce deployment is encouraged. This results in a lean staff, which nevertheless ensures maximum flexibility and maximum production capacity. Therefore, it leads to cost advantages.

Last, the strategy "Industry 4.0" is moving forward. The research project addresses the need for novel planning and control mechanisms inside the fourth industrial revolution.

ACKNOWLEDGMENT

The Deutsche Forschungsgemeinschaft DFG is funding the project with the title "A simulation-based and flexi-time applying prediction model for scheduling personnel deployment times in the production planning process of cyber-physical systems" (project-id: 439188616).

REFERENCES

[1] German Federal Ministry of Education and Research, "Industrie 4.0. Innovationen für die Produktion von morgen (Industry 4.0. Innovations for the production of tomorrow)", Publikationsverband der Bundesregierung, Berlin, August, 2017.

[2] W. Bauer and S. Gerlach, "Selbstorganisierte Kapazitätsflexibilität in Cyber-Physical Systems: KapaflexCy. Abschlussbericht. (Self-organized flexibility of capacity in Cyber-Physical Systems: KapaflexCy. Final Report.)", Fraunhofer Verlag, Stuttgart, 2015, ISBN: 978-3-8396-0932-3.

[3] D. Spath, O. Ganschar, S. Geralch, and M. Hämmerle, "Produktionsarbeit der Zukunft (Production work of the future)", Fraunhofer Verlag, Stuttgart, 2013, ISBN: 978-3-8396-0570-7.

[4] P. Ittermann, J. Niehaus, and H. Hirsch-Kreinsen "Arbeiten in der Industrie 4.0: Trendbestimmungen und arbeitspolitische Handlungsfelder (Working in industry 4.0: Determining

trends and labour policy fields of action)", Study of Hans-Böckler-Stiftung, vol. 308, Düsseldorf, June, 2015.

[5] C. Schröder, "Industrielle Arbeitskosten im internationalen Vergleich (Industrial labour costs in international comparison)", in IW-Trends, vol. 43 (3/2016), Institut der deutschen Wirtschaft Köln, Cologne, 2016, doi: 10.2373/1864-810X.16-03-03.

[6] B. Grabot and A. Letouzey; "Short-term manpower management in manufacturing systems: new requirements and DSS prototyping", In: Computers in Industry, vol. 43, pp. 11-29, 2000.

[7] R. Schieferdecker and C. Schmidt, "Produktionsplanung und -steuerung bei flexiblen Arbeitszeiten: Arbeitszeitspezifische Planungsmodelle für eine integrierte Personalressourcen-planung (Production planning and control with flexible working hours: Working time specific planning models for integrated personnel resource planning)" AiF-founded project, project-id 12257N, 2002.

[8] German Federal Ministry of Education and Research, "Zukunftsbild „Industrie 4.0" (Vision of the future "Industry 4.0)", Publikationsverband der Bundesregierung, Bonn, July, 2015.

[9] T. Stock, "Ein Verfahren zur Personalplanung und -steuerung und Restrukturierung der Aufbauorganisation für eine bedarfsorientierte und wandlungsfähige Produktion (A method for personnel planning and control and restructuring of the organizational structure for a demand-oriented and adaptable production)", dissertation. In: Stuttgarter Beiträge zur Produktionsforschung, vol. 9, 2013, doi: 10.18419/opus-6817.

[10] M. Hämmerle, „Methoden zur strategischen Dimensionierung der Personalflexibilität in der Produktion: Wirkungsbe-wertung von Instrumenten zur Flexibilisierung der Personal-kapazität im volatilen Marktumfeld (Methods for strategic dimensioning of personnel flexibility in production: Impact assessment of instruments for making personnel capacity more flexible in a volatile market environment)", dissertation, in Schriftenreihe zu Arbeitswissenschaft und Technologie-management, vol. 26. Fraunhoferverlag, Stuttgart, 2015, ISBN 978-3-8396-0899-9.

[11] E.-A. Attia, P. Duquenne, and J. Le-Lann "Considering skills evolutions in multi-skilled workforce allocation with flexible working hours", in International Journal of Production Research, vol. 52(15), pp. 4548-4573, 2014, doi: 10.1080/00207543.2013.877613.

[12] G. Gong, R. Chiong, Q. Deng, and X. Gong, "A hybrid artificial bee colony algorithm for flexible job shop scheduling with worker flexibility", in International Journal of Production Research, 2019, doi: 10.1080/00207543.2019.1653504.

[13] X. Zheng and L. Wang "A Knowledge-Guided Fruit Fly Optimization Algorithm for Dual Resource Constrained Flexible Job-Shop Scheduling Problem". in International Journal of Production Research, vol. 54(18), pp. 5554–5566, 2016.

[14] R. Lin, G. Zhou, A. Liu, H. Lu, and T. Li, "Impact of personnel flexibility on Job Shop Scheduling". In Scientific Programming, Article ID: 3403058, Hindawi Publishing Corporation, 2016, doi: 10.1155/2016/3403058.

[15] Fraunhofer Institute for Industrial Engineering IAO, "MyCPS", available from: www.mycpstoolbox.de, [retrieved: september, 2020].

[16] N. Simeunović, I. Kamenko, V. Bugarski, M. Jovanović, and B. Lalić "Improving workforce scheduling using artificial neural networks model" in Advances in Production Engineering & Management , vol. 12 (4), pp. 337-352, APEM journal, december, 2017, doi: 10.14743/apem2017.4.262.

[17] I. Graesslera and A. Poehler "Intelligent control of an assembly station by integration of a digital twin for employees into the decentralized control system" 4th International Conference on System-Integrated Intelligence, vol. 24, pp. 185-189, Procedia Manufacturing, 2018, doi: 10.1016/j.promfg.2018.06.041.

[18] FASTEC GmbH, "Personnel Planning" available from: https://www.fastec.de/mes-fastec-4-pro/personalplanung, [retrieved: september, 2020].

[19] ATOSS Software AG, "Workforce scheduling" available from: https://www.atoss.com/en-gb/workforce-management/workforce-scheduling, [retrieved: september, 2020].

[20] German Federal Institute for Occupational Saftey and Health (baua), "Flexible Arbeitszeitmodelle: Überblick und Umsetzung (Flexible working time models: overview and implementation)", 2. edition, Dortmund, October 2019, doi: 10.21934/baua: praxis20170719.

[21] German Federal Ministry of Justice and Consumer Protection: "Arbeitszeitgesetz (law on working time)", available from: www.gesetze-im-internet.de/arbzg/BJNR117100994.html, [retrieved: september, 2020].

Provision of Model Parameters for Capacity Planning of Aircraft Maintenance Projects: A Workload Estimation Method based on Enterprise Resource Planning Data

Christian Fabig*, Michael Völker†, Thorsten Schmidt‡
Institute of Material Handling and Industrial Engineering
Technische Universität Dresden
Dresden, Germany
email: *christian.fabig@tu-dresden.de, †michael.voelker@tu-dresden.de, ‡thorsten.schmidt@tu-dresden.de

***Abstract*—Capacity planning is a major issue in aircraft Maintenance, Repair and Overhaul (MRO) companies, given that significant parts of the workload are stochastic in nature. Vast amounts of data are gathered within Enterprise Resource Planning (ERP) systems. Despite their availability, data still has to be utilized to assist the capacity planning process. Besides a quantitative characterization of the capacity planning problem in aircraft MRO, this paper proposes a method for the classification, analysis and estimation of maintenance workloads. This enables to provide model input parameters for a discrete-event simulation on a daily basis. The proposed method comprises the selection of comparable historical projects for analysis, the transformation and mapping of operation data by means of rule-based data wrangling and the characterization of maintenance workloads broken down into network activities and skills.**

***Keywords*— aircraft maintenance; workload estimation; project scheduling; simulation-based capacity planning.**

I. Introduction

Maintenance is defined as the "combination of all technical, administrative and managerial actions during the life cycle of an item intended to retain it in, or restore it to, a state in which it can perform the required function" [6]. Examples of items to be maintained include physical assets (e.g., machines, plants, buildings, ships, and aircraft). Maintenance, Repair and Overhaul (MRO) companies produce maintenance services. Thus, maintenance can be regarded as a production process that needs to be planned [16]. Far in advance to a maintenance project, an overall effort estimation is done resulting in a rough estimate of the *total project workload*. In order to carry out a capacity planning, this estimate has to be broken down into required resources and workloads of (predefined) work packages, serving as model input for specialized planning software. Performing the effort breakdown manually is cumbersome, especially when a rescheduling is needed to take production confirmations and more detailed information into account, and is prone to produce model inconsistencies. Thus, the workload estimation process ought to be supported by the Enterprise Resource Planning (ERP) system.

While *work package efforts* are estimates of the sum of working hours of (yet unknown) associated work plan activities, there usually is the possibility to compress or stretch each work package duration. From a theoretical point of view, the problem of capacity planning in aircraft MRO corresponds to a Multi-Mode Resource-Constrained Project Scheduling Problem (MRCMPSP; see [9]). In order to provide model input, ERP systems data are found to have shortcomings. For example, there may be an ambiguous classification of maintenance events, non-use of industry standards (e.g., aircraft zoning [17]) and outdated or duplicated work centers resulting from past organizational changes. These issues severely hamper data consistency and may prove them invaluable for capacity planning purposes [7]. Therefore, the objectives of this paper are as follows. Based on data from a German third-party MRO provider, (1) we quantitatively analyze the capacity planning problem in terms of routine and non-routine workloads of different types of maintenance projects and (2) propose an ERP-based method to classify maintenance operations of previously performed aircraft maintenance projects in order to estimate the workload for an integrated capacity planning process of prospective maintenance projects.

The remainder of the paper is as follows. Section II presents related work on the practical application of capacity planning models and fundamentals of aircraft maintenance. A quantitative analysis of aircraft maintenance workloads is given in Section III concerning maintenance project types, aircraft types and aircraft ages. In Section IV, we present the proposed method to classify maintenance operations based on ERP data of previously completed maintenance projects. Furthermore, we show how the evaluation can be used for estimating workloads per project network activity and skill of future projects. Section V presents an example of a maintenance workload estimation for an Airbus A380 cabin modification event that can be transferred into a simulation-based capacity planning software. Finally, in Section VI we draw conclusions on the presented method and future research opportunities.

II. Related Work

1) Practical application of capacity planning models: Significant research on allocating limited resources to competing activities has been carried out using mathematical solution techniques (see, e.g., [5][12][18]). Since large-scale problems can hardly be handled using mathematical modeling and solving techniques, simulation-based scheduling and optimization is proposed by several authors for real-life applications [11]. Concerning the field of Production Planning and Control (PPC), Carl [3] proposes a simulation model for planning and optimization of assembly lines and Pinha and Ahluwalia [15] address the short-term resource management in a ship yard using a discrete-event simulation software. In order to incorporate further aspects of real-world problems, a broad variety of model extensions of the basic Resource-Constrained Project Scheduling Problem (RCPSP) have been proposed in literature (see [9][14]). The MRCMPSP model comprises, briefly described, the following aspects (see [2][20]):

- Projects are divided into activities, which require multiple renewable (worker force, machines, tools, etc.) or non-renewable (standard parts, components, etc.) resources to be performed.
- Activities have to respect certain precedence constraints that can be modeled by means of relationships in a project network.
- Resource groups are available with limited amounts and may have certain skills and/or organizational affiliation, thus being applicable to perform a certain proportion of the activities' workload.
- Resources are not dedicated to a specific project. Thus, activities of multiple projects compete for the same set of limited resources.

However, despite considerable research effort, there exist gaps between the model capabilities and its practical application. In particular, model inputs have to be updated with ERP data (e.g., production confirmations, resource availabilities) and hand over to a planning system in order to facilitate a (daily) PPC procedure. Alfieri and Urgo [2] provide an application of project scheduling and a model formulation based on network activity workloads to one-of-a-kind production systems. Dinis and Barbosa-Póvoa [7] propose a set of generic requirements for aircraft maintenance data treatment in order to improve the MROs risk management and planning process.

One important set of parameters in MRCMPSP model formulations describes the (estimated) activity workload for a given project network. The workload of renewable *resource* k incurred by *activity* i is given as W_{ik}. Activity i can be performed in each discrete combination of processing time p_i and resource request r_{ik} that allows to reach the workload, i.e.,

$$W_{ik} \leq p_i * r_{ik}. \tag{1}$$

A mathematical formulation of the MRCMPSP is given in [20]. In Section IV, we will focus on our method for estimating W_{ik} in aircraft MRO based on ERP data.

2) Fundamentals of aircraft MRO: Concerning aircraft MRO, the following maintenance actions can be distinguished (see Figure 1):

- *Preventive maintenance* is carried out intended to assess and/or to mitigate degradation and reduce the probability of failure of an item during flight operation. Therefore, a comprehensive set of work orders is carried out at prescribed intervals of time or number of flight hours. This may require a complete or partial dismantling of the item (i.e., a 'overhaul').
- *Corrective maintenance* has to be carried out after fault recognition. It is intended to restore an item into a state in which it can perform a required function. In case of a safety-critical item corrective actions are mandatory in order to assure airworthiness before the aircraft is allowed to return to flight operation.
- *Modification & Improvement* actions are intended to change the functions of an item or to improve existing functions. This also includes available modifications that are judged by the manufacturer to be a matter of safety rather than simply product improvement.

During the planning process, actions for preventive maintenance and modification & improvement are referred to as *routine* or scheduled maintenance, defined as work orders "carried out in accordance with a specified time schedule or specified number of units of use" [6]. Corrective maintenance is referred to as *non-routine* or unscheduled maintenance, resulting from Discrepancy Reports (DR) that are detected during routine activities and thus are not completely known before inspection tasks are finished. In case of a third-party MRO provider, the customer might also inquire further services while the aircraft is already undergoing its routine maintenance. Since those Additional Service Requests (ASR) are not part of the previously assigned routine work orders, it is also regarded as non-routine. Due to the uncertainty caused by non-routine workload, proper planning is of key importance in aircraft maintenance. Multiple examples and research papers show that cost savings can be gained through a fitted, robust capacity planning and scheduling process [19]. Low and predictable costs as well as guaranteed turnaround times are the main production targets [16]. Hence, there is a need for accurate estimations of the future maintenance workloads.

III. Quantitative Analysis of Maintenance Workloads

The project samples originate from 201 maintenance projects conducted at a German third-party MRO provider between January 2013 and March 2020 on a total of 147 different aircraft from five different Airbus aircraft families. Projects are classified within that mentioned company into 'Event Types', reflecting the main objective of a maintenance project. Concerning the necessity of accurate workload estimations, so called Heavy Maintenance Checks (HMC) are of particular interest as they are complex due high intensity of workload and scope. HMC projects are labor-intensive and often subcontracted to a third-party service providers. HMC comprise the 'C-check' and the 'D-check' that have to be performed every two year and every six years, respectively [19]. We will further elaborate on the event types in Section IV.

Table I shows the comparison of event types with regard to median workloads in man-hours (MH) of work performed. As can be seen, the project workload diverges greatly from a

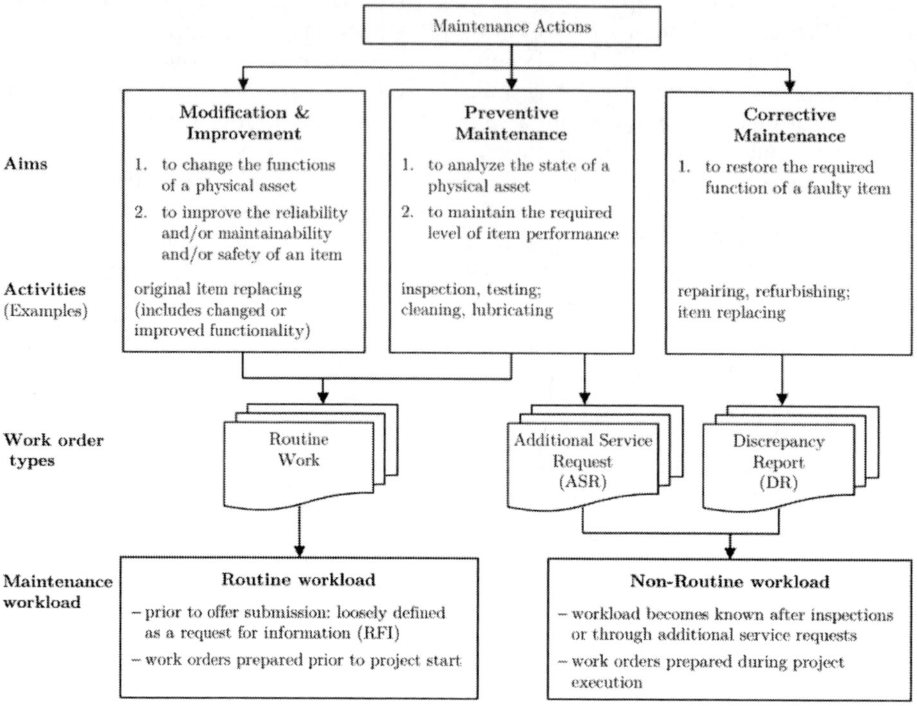

Figure 1. Maintenance actions and origin of workloads in aircraft maintenance projects

TABLE I
WORKLOAD CHARACTERISTICS OF MAINTENANCE EVENT TYPES

Event Type	# of projects [-]	Project workload [MH, median]	Routine [% of project workload]	Non-Routine [% of project workload]
COMPONENTCHANGE--ENGINES	4	464	56%	44%
COMPONENTCHANGE--GEARS	29	659	75%	25%
MODIFICATION--AVIONICS	4	718	67%	33%
CHECK--A	5	1.103	64%	36%
REPAIR--STRUCTURE	13	1.512	47%	53%
CHECK--B	23	6.659	56%	44%
CHECK--C	54	8.159	44%	56%
MODIFICATION--CABIN	28	13.010	65%	35%
CHECK--D	20	16.612	54%	46%
MODIFICATION--STRUCTURE	17	23.450	86%	14%
MODIFICATION--PTOF	4	55.210	64%	36%
Overall (median)	**201**	**6.641**	**62%**	**38%**

'component change' with less than 1,000 MH to a 'passenger-to-freighter conversion' (PtoF) with more than 55,000 MH. The share of non-routine workload for 'modification' event types is rather low (14 - 35% of total project workload) while it is comparably high for HMC (46 - 56% of total project workload). Further analyzing the non-routine workload, Figure 2 shows the median of non-routine workload by age of aircraft measured in flight hours (FH). According to the linear regression trendline, in this regard an increase occurs throughout the service life of an aircraft. However, compared to the total project workload one can see that maintenance events performed on aging aircraft

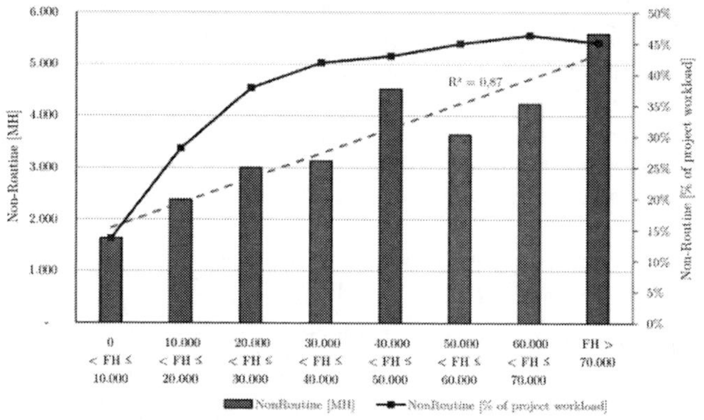

Figure 2. Median of non-routine workload by age of aircraft

(40,000 FH or more) comprise of approximately 45% non-routine workload.

IV. WORKLOAD ESTIMATION METHOD

The proposed workload estimation method consists of a set of data mining procedures based on aircraft maintenance data stored in an ERP system and of a procedure to classify and analyze the data. Two motivations have let to the development: (1) to characterize the maintenance workloads accurately despite uncertain and scare information during the offer submission process; and (2) to provide means for a simulation-based capacity planning software that allow for scheduling and

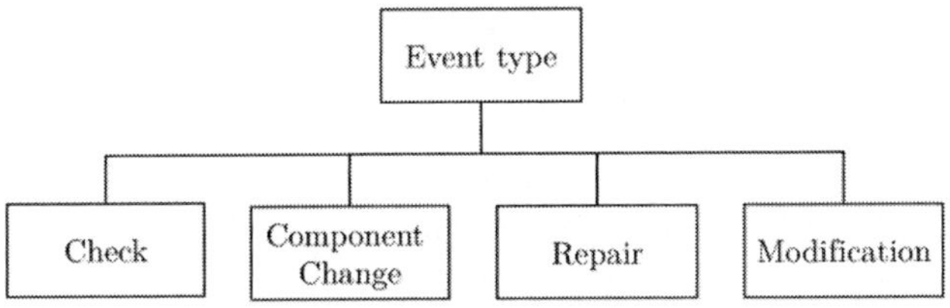

Figure 3. Event types of aircraft maintenance projects

progress control of aircraft maintenance projects. The main steps of the method are presented next.

A. Select completed projects for analysis

The starting point for estimating workloads of future maintenance projects is to select similar completed projects. In aviation, a maintenance project is called 'event'. Separately from an aircraft model, the '*Event Type*' has been established in order to gather the main purpose of an event (Figure 3). The aforementioned *checks* refer to periodic execution of scheduled inspection tasks that have to be done on all commercial and civil aircraft after a certain amount of time or usage, ranging from minor extent (A- and B-check) to major overhauls (C- and D-check). The second category is *component change* (e.g., engine change and landing gear change). Changes might occur as a separate event since the item is subject to wear and tear or, expiring lease contracts (e.g, aircraft engines and the aircraft often have separate lease contracts) and other reasons. *Repair* refers to any maintenance service with the main purpose of corrective actions. Those events include repairs such as lightning strikes, bird strikes, skin panel replacements and fuel tank resealing. The fourth category *modification* includes maintenance services with the main purpose of changing the functions of an item or to improve existing functions. Subcategories are reconfiguration of the passenger cabin, sharklet modification, avionic modification, and others. A PtoF-modification is a way to extend the economic life of an aircraft by converting it into a freighter when it reaches its useful operational service as a passenger jetliner and is one of the most extensive modifications.

An event often includes parts from two categories. E.g., a customer may want to perform a C-check including an engine change or a PtoF-modification with an accompanying A-check. In those cases the event is classified due to its main purpose, i.e., the part with the most extensive workload. When choosing similar projects out of the ERP database, the event type serves as a pre-selector. It is up to the user to either reference only one project or multiple projects of an event type for further data classification and analysis.

B. Transform and map data of completed work orders

In order to analyze the 'raw' data from the ERP system it is necessary to transform and map data into another format or into a standardized classification. Data wrangling and preparation is applied using a rule-based approach. Table II shows the rule types implemented to translate a field content or to replace it by alternatively using content from another storage location. A rule might be used for an arbitrary field of an ERP data table (e.g., work center, duration, date). Also, a combination of rules might be used whereby the order of the rules corresponds to their processing.

TABLE II
RULE TYPES FOR DATA WRANGLING

Rule type	Description
Translate Value (TV)	Translation of the field content based on the field name and content to a defined value.
Translate RegEx (TR)	Translation of the field content using a Regular Expression to a defined value.
Translate Unit (TU)	Translation of a unit field and offsetting of the associated data fields.
Replace Part (RP)	Replacement of character part of field content based on start / end position with a defined value.
Replace Content (RC)	Replacement of a field with a certain field content by the field content of an external table.
Replace Field (RF)	Replacement of a field content with field contents of an alternative field.

The Aircraft Maintenance Manual (AMM) and other manuals are available from the aircraft manufacturer Airbus SE, defining work content and workflow, required personnel skills and equipment for routine tasks. The aforementioned rules are applied to perform a data preparation and classification (1) to provide an adequate level of detail for the purpose of capacity planning and (2) to align the companies' ERP data with the AMM standards. Next, we present the classifications.

1) Aircraft locations: Among other location systems, a three-digit *'zone'* numbering system applies to every aircraft and is used within the AMM maintenance task specification [1]. Locations are refined from major zone (e.g., 200 - passenger deck), to major subzone (e.g., 210 - cockpit), to unit zone (e.g., 211 - cockpit, left hand side). However, workload estimation and capacity planning based on unit zones and even major subzones is hard to master. By grouping zones one can, obviously, characterize the workload spatially throughout the aircraft. The adequate level of detail can be controlled by the user through wrangling rules. Maintenance planning managers have defined the major zones 100 - 700 complemented with five selected major subzones (e.g., cockpit, main aviation compartment) and

TABLE III
MAJOR ZONES OF AN AIRCRAFT (EXTRACT)

Major zone	Major subzone	Description
100	-	LOWER THIRD OF FUSELAGE
	110	RADOME - NOSE CONE TO FR0
	120	MAIN AVIONICS COMPARTMENT
	130	LOWER DECK FORWARD CARGO COMP.
	140	CENTER WING BOX
	150	LOWER DECK AFT CARGO COMP.
	160	LOWER DECK BULK CARGO COMP.
	170	AFT CABIN UNDERFLOOR COMP.
	190	BELLY FAIRING, AIR CONDITION COMP.
200	-	UPPER TWO THIRDS OF FUSELAGE
300	-	REAR FUSELAGE SECTION
400	-	POWER PLANT NACELLES & PYLONS
500	-	LEFT WING
600	-	RIGHT WING
700	-	LANDING GEARS & GEAR DOORS
800	-	DOORS

four selected backshops (e.g., Non-Destructive Testing (NDT), saddler shop) as an appropriate level of detail for capacity planning purposes, resulting in a total of 16 locations.

2) Skills: Skills can be broadly defined as the ability to perform certain tasks [5]. In aircraft maintenance, a skill can be further defined as to possess a license to perform particular maintenance tasks on a specific aircraft model. A skill certificate can be held by a technician and is issued by a national aviation authority [4]. One way to model skills for tasks in an ERP system is to define a specific work center for each of them [10]. In analyzed data of the German third-party MRO provider, more than 150 work centers are currently in use and another 550 work centers are outdated or duplicated resulting from past organizational changes. Thus, in order to estimate workloads by analyzing previously performed aircraft maintenance projects the work centers have to be grouped through wrangling rules. Table IV presents the skills that maintenance planning managers have identified as an appropriate level of detail for capacity planning.

3) Network activities: Maintenance events are typically conducted in several phases. In the 'Reception' phase (I), the aircraft undergoes initial tests and preparations, e.g. docking. After that, in the 'Disassembly' phase (II), access panels, doors and aircraft components are removed in order to accomplish the maintenance actions. In the 'Inspection' phase (III) airframe, systems and components are inspected for wear and tear and other discrepancies such as dents or corrosion. Discrepancies are then corrected to ensure the items functions and airworthiness in a 'Repair & Overhaul' phase (IV). After completion of all non-routine works, the removed aircraft components, doors and panels will be reinstalled in the 'Installation' phase

TABLE IV
CONSIDERED MAINTENANCE SKILLS

Skill code	Description
A/P	Airframe & powerplant systems
AIM	Aircraft interior maintenance
E	Engineering
ERI	Electric & avionic systems
FRL	Outsourced services
KM	Painting & Composites
NDT	Non-destructive testing
QS	Quality inspection (general)
STR	Structural mechanics
TP	Work preparation

(V) before operational and functional tests of aircraft systems and components are performed in a final 'Redelivery' phase (VI). Although the above sequence of phases is technologically given, concerning the maintenance event as a whole those phase may overlap with each other since work in one location can (largely) be executed independently from that of other locations [8]. Sequence dependencies are modeled by means of a project network, as shown in Figure 4. The project network for MRO events has been defined in collaboration with maintenance managers and technicians. It includes the aforementioned MRO phases further detailed into the aircraft locations, if appropriate, and consists of a total of 56 network activities.

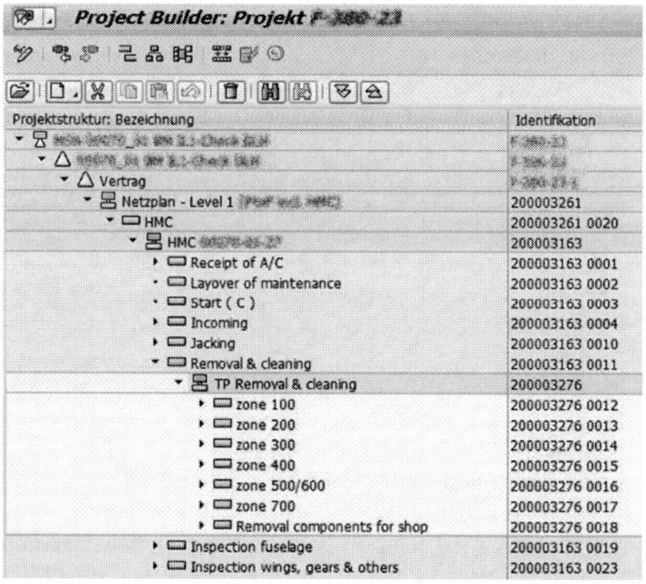

Figure 4. Network activities of a maintenance event (extract)

C. Classify and assign operations to network activities

An algorithm has been developed to assign operations listed in work orders of completed projects to the most appropriate network activities one by one. The order in which the assignment of an operations to the most appropriate network activity is checked has a decisive influence on the correct and complete classification of the operations. In general, the possible assignment of an operation to a network activity with the most specific classification (e.g., NDT inspection work in zone 140) should be checked first while its assignment to a network activity with a more general classification (e.g., inspection work in zone 100) is evaluated afterwards since the former is a subclass of the latter.

The classification and assignment process is implemented within the ERP system by extending each network activity with its classification after data wrangling in terms of aircraft location, skill, work order type, AMM reference and other attributes in an additional data table. The algorithm thus starts with checking for the matching of an operation to the network activity with the highest amount of attributes (field), i.e., the most specific classification, and subsequently those network activities with a lower amount of attributes until a matching is found. In case no matching could be found, the operation is assigned to the 'project' as the root element. Multiple values (field contents) of the same attribute are linked via a logical OR-concatenation while different attributes are linked via a logical AND-concatenation when checking the amount of attributes. A first draft version had been designed by [13]. The algorithm has been implemented in ERP system "SAP ERP 6.0", using its Advanced Business Application Programming (ABAP) language, and further improved together with maintenance planning managers.

D. Evaluate workload distribution

The analysis of the completed projects is consolidated using a *workload distribution matrix* shown in Figure 5.

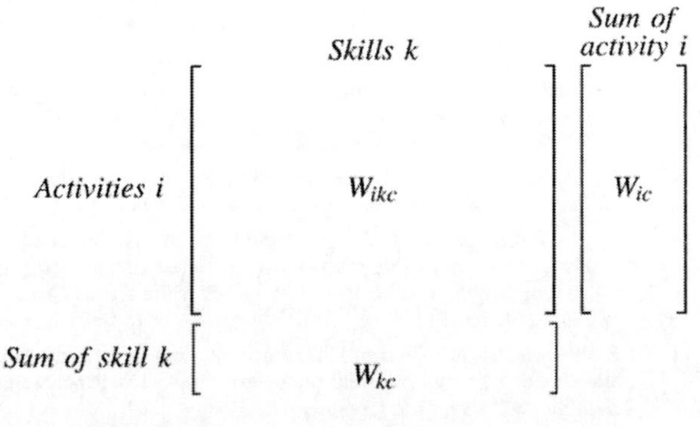

Figure 5. Structure of the workload distribution matrix

Where:

- W_{ikc} - median workload in network activity i for skill k of workload category c, in [MH],
- W_{ic} - median workload in network activity i of workload category c, in [MH],
- W_{kc} - median workload for skill k of the workload category c, in [MH].

Typically, there are several work order types that have to be mapped into a workload category c by means of the rule-based data wrangling procedure in order to differentiate '*routine*' and '*non-routine*', respectively. To quantitatively assess the workload of a prospective maintenance event for each category, the work performed through operations o from historical ERP data of completed projects p is sorted using the classifications defined in Subsection IV-B. Each matrix element is calculated as the median value of the analyzed historical projects and provides model input parameters for the left-hand side given in equation (1).

V. Case Example

Figure 6 presents an example of a maintenance workload estimation for an Airbus A380 cabin modification event. The workload distribution matrix for routine and non-routine workloads has been obtained analyzing five historical maintenance events that were classified as event type "MODIFICATION-CABIN" and assessed to be comparable to the prospective event by maintenance managers. These events contain 2,700 2,900 2,400 3,100 and 3,400 order operations, respectively. In the data wrangling procedure, the 'raw' order operation data has been transformed and mapped into the standardized classifications given in Section IV-B. Among other things, the roughly 700 work centers defined in the ERP system were mapped to the skills shown in Table IV using wrangling rules. Note that in this case example skill "NDT" is not present in the workload distribution matrix as there were no order operations having structural testing works (as could be expected for cabin modifications). On top of that, operations have been assigned to the network activities of the maintenance event (see Figure 4) and classified into workload categories. The total "routine" workload is estimated at 8,915 MH (64 %) and the total "non-routine" workload is estimated at 4,960 MH (36 %), which roughly corresponds to the workload characteristics given in Table I.

The aim is to use these results as model input for a multi-project capacity planning. An interface to a simulation-based

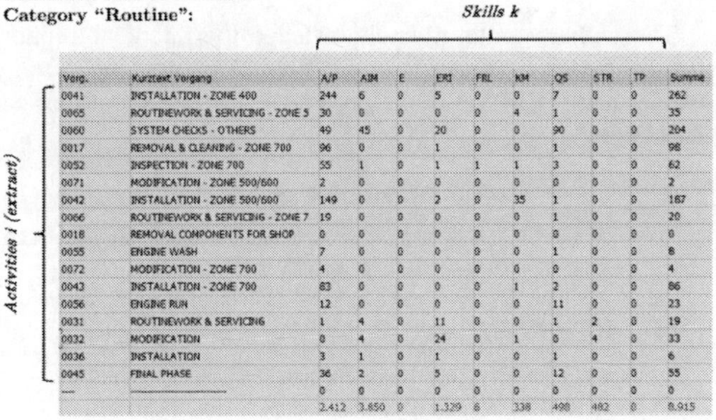

Estimated MH of Workload Category "Routine":

Skills k (columns A/P to TP); *Activities i (extract)* (rows 0041 to 0045)

Vorg.	Kurztext Vorgang	A/P	AIM	E	ERI	FRL	KM	QS	STR	TP	Summe
0041	INSTALLATION - ZONE 400	244	6	0	5	0	0	7	0	0	262
0065	ROUTINEWORK & SERVICING - ZONE 5	30	0	0	0	0	4	1	0	0	35
0060	SYSTEM CHECKS - OTHERS	49	45	0	20	0	0	90	0	0	204
0017	REMOVAL & CLEANING - ZONE 700	96	0	0	1	0	0	1	0	0	98
0052	INSPECTION - ZONE 700	55	1	0	1	1	1	3	0	0	62
0071	MODIFICATION - ZONE 500/600	2	0	0	0	0	0	0	0	0	2
0042	INSTALLATION - ZONE 500/600	149	0	0	2	0	35	1	0	0	187
0066	ROUTINEWORK & SERVICING - ZONE 7	19	0	0	0	0	0	1	0	0	20
0018	REMOVAL COMPONENTS FOR SHOP	0	0	0	0	0	0	0	0	0	0
0055	ENGINE WASH	7	0	0	0	0	0	1	0	0	8
0072	MODIFICATION - ZONE 700	4	0	0	0	0	0	0	0	0	4
0043	INSTALLATION - ZONE 700	83	0	0	0	0	1	2	0	0	86
0056	ENGINE RUN	12	0	0	0	0	0	11	0	0	23
0031	ROUTINEWORK & SERVICING	1	4	0	11	0	0	1	2	0	19
0032	MODIFICATION	0	4	0	24	0	1	0	4	0	33
0036	INSTALLATION	3	1	0	1	0	0	1	0	0	6
0045	FINAL PHASE	36	2	0	5	0	0	12	0	0	55
—	————	0	0	0	0	0	0	0	0	0	0
		2.412	3.850	0	1.329	6	338	498	482	0	8.915

Figure 6. Example of a workload estimation matrix of a cabin modification

capacity planning software has been implemented, allowing to export the workload distribution matrix as well as project networks, skills, resources, and resource availabilities (see [8]).

VI. Conclusion

The objectives of this paper were twofold: (1) to quantitatively analyze the capacity planning problem in terms of routine and non-routine workloads of different types of maintenance projects and (2) to propose an ERP-based method to classify maintenance operations of previously performed aircraft maintenance projects in order to estimate the workload for an integrated capacity planning process of prospective maintenance projects.

Regarding the first objective, results show that the workload of a maintenance project diverges greatly depending on the event type carried out. Non-routine workload has been found to be comparably high for HMC checks with 46 - 56% of total project workload. Furthermore, aging aircraft turned out to have a non-routine workload share of 45% independently from the type of maintenance event. Those amounts of uncertainty imply a serious threat to MROs capacity planning, particularly when multiple aircraft are maintained contemporaneous. As for the second objective, an ERP-integrated method for selecting comparable projects for analysis, transforming and mapping of operation data by means of rule-based data wrangling is proposed. Each operation is then assigned to one network activity of the prospective project in order to estimate routine and non-routine workloads. The workloads are further broken down into network activities and skills. This allows to characterize the maintenance workloads accurately despite uncertain and scare information as early as during the offer submission process.

Furthermore, gathered within a workload distribution matrix, the method can provide model input parameters for simulation-based capacity planning software that allow for capacity planning, scheduling and progress control of aircraft maintenance projects. This constitutes research opportunities to further enhance the multi-project planning and scheduling methods for aircraft maintenance companies, thus providing them a decisive competitive advantage.

Acknowledgment

The authors gratefully acknowledge the financial support by the Federal Ministry for Economic Affairs and Energy of Germany (BMWi) in the project MRO21 (project number 20X1714C).

References

[1] Airbus SE, *Aircraft Maintenance Manual (AMM) for Airbus A380: Electronic Document*. Blagnac Cedex, France, 2017.

[2] A. Alfieri and M. Urgo, "Project Scheduling for Aggregate Production Scheduling in Make-to-Order Environments". In: *Handbook on Project Management and Scheduling Vol.2*. Ed. by C. Schwindt and J. Zimmermann. Cham: Springer International Publishing, 2015, pp. 1249–1266.

[3] S. Carl, "Modell und Lösungsansatz zur Bestimmung kostenminimierter Ablaufpläne in Multiressourcen-Montagen (Model and solution approach for the determination of cost-minimized process schedules in multi-resource assemblies". Dissertation. Dresden: Technische Universität Dresden, 2015.

[4] G. Chen, W. He, L. C. Leung, T. Lan, and Y. Han, "Assigning licenced technicians to maintenance tasks at aircraft maintenance base: A bi-objective approach and a Chinese airline application". In: *International Journal of Production Research* 55.19, 2017, pp. 5550–5563.

[5] P. De Bruecker, J. Van den Bergh, J. Beliën, and E. Demeulemeester, "Workforce planning incorporating skills: State of the art". In: *European Journal of Operational Research* 243.1, 2015, pp. 1–16.

[6] DIN Deutsches Institut für Normung e.V., *Maintenance - Maintenance Terminology EN 13306:2017*. Berlin, 2018.

[7] D. Dinis and A. Barbosa-Póvoa, "Aircraft Maintenance Capacity Planning: A Decision Support Framework". In: *Conference Proceedings*. Ed. by T. Bousonville, T. Melo, N. Rezg, and F. Vernadat. Saarbrücken, 2017, pp. 412–417.

[8] C. Fabig and E. Winter, "A multi-level modeling approach for simulation-based capacity planning and scheduling of aircraft maintenance projects". In: *Simulation for a noble cause*. Ed. by M. Rabe. [Piscataway, NJ]: IEEE, 2018, pp. 3252–3263.

[9] S. Hartmann and D. Briskorn, "A survey of variants and extensions of the resource-constrained project scheduling problem". In: *European Journal of Operational Research* 207.1, 2010, pp. 1–14.

[10] K. Liebstückel, *Plant maintenance with SAP: Business user guide*. 4th edition. Bonn and Boston: Rheinwerk Publishing, 2017.

[11] D. Mourtzis, M. Doukas, and D. Bernidaki, "Simulation in Manufacturing: Review and Challenges". In: *Procedia CIRP* 25, 2014, pp. 213–229.

[12] A. Naber and R. Kolisch, "MIP models for resource-constrained project scheduling with flexible resource profiles". In: *European Journal of Operational Research* 239.2, 2014, pp. 335–348.

[13] J. H. Peaceman, "Conception of a Business Intelligence-based method for the causal allocation of a given effort estimation to network activities". Diploma thesis. Dresden: Technische Universität Dresden, 2018.

[14] R. Pellerin and N. Perrier, "A review of methods, techniques and tools for project planning and control". In: *International Journal of Production Research* 57.7, 2019, pp. 2160–2178.

[15] D. C. Pinha and R. S. Ahluwalia, "Flexible resource management and its effect on project cost and duration". In: *Journal of Industrial Engineering International* 15.1, 2019, pp. 119–133.

[16] C. Reményi and S. Staudacher, "Systematic simulation based approach for the identification and implementation of a scheduling rule in the aircraft engine maintenance". In: *International Journal of Production Economics* 147, 2014, pp. 94–107.

[17] T. L. Seamster and B. G. Kanki, eds., *Aviation Information Management: From Documents to Data*. Aldershot: Ashgate, 2002.

[18] E. B. Tirkolaee, A. Goli, M. Hematian, A. K. Sangaiah, and T. Han, "Multi-objective multi-mode resource constrained project scheduling problem using Pareto-based algorithms". In: *Computing* 101.6, 2019, pp. 547–570.

[19] J. Van den Bergh, J. Beliën, P. De Bruecker, and J. Peeters, "Aircraft maintenance operations: state of the art". Research Paper. Leuven: Katholieke Universiteit Leuven, 2013.

[20] T. Wauters, J. Kinable, P. Smet, W. Vancroonenburg, G. Vanden Berghe, and J. Verstichel, "The Multi-Mode Resource-Constrained Multi-Project Scheduling Problem". In: *Journal of Scheduling* 19.3, 2016, pp. 271–283.

Clock Pulse Modeling and Simulation of Push and Pull Processes in Logistics

Carlo Simon, Stefan Haag and Lara Zakfeld

Hochschule Worms
Erenburgerstr. 19, 67549 Worms, Germany
Email: {simon, haag, lara.zakfeld}@hs-worms.de

***Abstract*—This paper is about a new technique to find Petri net models for a clock pulse spotted simulation of processes in logistics and production. These models can be used to observe the raising and discharging of stocks in production in order to identify bottlenecks, to observe differences of push and pull strategies on the valued stocks, and to decide on strategic changes. For this, however, significant preliminary tasks had to be conducted first which are also the objective of this paper: a novel, Web-based Petri net modeling and simulation environment called Process-Simulation.Center (P-S.C) has been developed since existing tools are not at the least able to handle such sophisticated models. At the moment the tool worked properly, different approaches to model the described situation had to be compared. A teaching laboratory for logistics has been chosen as a sample application. The simulation now helps students to scale up their personal observations in the laboratory with respect to time, amount and value. This paper explains the situation in the laboratory, the new features of the P-S.C that enable the modeling of these processes, and the finding of the model itself. Finally, its development led to another, different approach to describe the teaching processes by a so called event triggered simulation that is shortly considered in contrast.**

Keywords–Conceptual models of timed dynamic systems; Simulation; Petri nets; Logistics; Teaching.

I. INTRODUCTION

Enterprise Resource Planning systems (ERP) can collect and integrate data using a common database, thereby representing a good basis for the overall accounting process [1]. This information can be used in all areas of a company such as sales, purchasing and finance, but also human resources or production. In many companies, they are used to plan and control manufacturing processes. These systems evaluate and name the next upcoming orders, record the progress of work by means of confirmation messages and determine production plans.

ERP systems, however, do not support their users in making decisions concerning a modified production strategy. For example, turning push processes in logistics and production into pull processes often comes along with a significant reduction of stock costs and, at the same time, an increased flexibility. Nonetheless, we observe that still many companies produce in accordance with the push principle because of over-reliance on the production strategy suggested by the ERP system, but also because of nescience of the different strategies and their effects. In order to avoid the latter, it is very important for students in the field of logistics to experience different strategies in their lectures.

However, practical experience is typically restricted concerning available time as well as amount of handled goods, machines and space. The so called *box game*, explained in Section III, for example, imparts this knowledge in a relatively simple setting. In order to extend this experience, we had the idea to develop a simulation model to overcome the mentioned limitations.

Since we work on Petri nets for decades, we decided to use Petri models to demonstrate the consequences of various processes in logistics, especially concerning the application of push and pull strategies. This, however, was a more challenging task than assumed at the beginning:

1) Especially models and simulations of pull processes rely on the possibility to distinguish between different customer orders. Hence, such processes cannot be modeled with simple Petri nets, but need Petri nets with individual tokens, so-called high-level Petri nets. Although such Petri net classes are known for many years (e.g., [2] [3]), no blueprint could be found how to develop appropriate models with them. Actually, most publications on this topic are of theoretical nature and not intended to make use of simulation results. We even assume that many of the shown models have never been tested in practice using tools. This, however, delivers new insights and new modeling techniques. Thus, one of the outcomes of this paper is a description of how the final clock pulse simulation model has been developed.
2) The above mentioned experience concerning modeling and simulation of Petri nets relies on the existence of an appropriate tool. At the present, this is a real problem. Almost all Petri net tools listed in [4] are either obsolete, do not support time aspects or Petri nets with individual tools, and none of them have modern user interfaces. They are useless for the finding of new modeling techniques for high-level Petri nets and new applications of simulation models in logistics and production. In order to overcome this limitation, we developed the Process-Simulation.Center (P-S.C), a novel, Web-based Petri net modeling and simulation environment that, among others, can be applied to the above mentioned logistics laboratory. Actually, this tool has been developed over years and its application to the box game is the last one in a series of use cases in the recent years.

In order to explain the research progress that could be achieved in the fields of the development of a tool for the conceptual modeling and simulation of processes with the aid of Petri nets, the finding of an appropriate model for the logistics problem, derived recommendations on how to find such models, and finally concerning the concrete laboratory process, this paper is organized as follows: The considered laboratory process is briefly described in Section III, while the related work is discussed in Section II. These two sections have a lot in common with the corresponding sections in [5] where a different modeling approach is considered for the same process. Section IV describes the development of the clock pulse model, explains its components, and discusses how the simulation results can be interpreted. Then, Section V shortly summarizes the specifics of the modeling approach of [5] and explains the fundamental differences between both modeling techniques. In Section VI, a conclusion both on the simulation results and the modeling approach is presented. The paper closes with an overview of planned and possible future work.

Contrary to other publications of ours, an explanation of the research agenda is omitted in this paper since this is outlined in other contemporaneous publications [5].

II. RELATED WORK

Originally, Petri nets are defined as Place/Transition (P/T) nets with anonymous tokens indicating a system's state [6]. Diverse concepts for representing high level information in Petri nets exist, with the most widely known being:

Predicate/Transition nets omit anonymous tokens for ones carrying data that can be processed and altered by use of functions encoded on transitions. When firing, these functions accept data from tokens on the preset. Functions return their results by putting appropriate tokens on the postset. The places serve as predicates according to which transitions may fire. Thus, it is possible to model interactions of tokens according to real-world influences or with each other. [2]

Colored Petri Nets integrate colors into Petri nets such that tokens, places and transitions have an assigned identity, their color. When determining if a transition is enabled, the adjacent places and their tokens are examined by color separately. This allows for more compact net representations under certain circumstances. [3] [7]

Regarding modeling, more specifically that of technical systems or business processes, time is important. Without claiming completeness, several approaches combining Petri nets and time concepts have been presented: Time Petri Nets (TPN) [8] and Timed Petri Nets (TdPN) [9] associate time with transitions, Time Place & Transition Nets (TPTN) [10] assign time with places and their marking, and Arc Timed Petri Nets (ATPN) [11] [12] associate time with the arcs of Petri nets.

The aforementioned formalisms share one concept differentiating them inherently from original Petri nets: Their state relies not only on information as given by their respective markings, but also on some kind of timer clocks. Timestamps are means to encode time information in the marking only.

Timestamp Nets introduce tokens with timestamps designating the moment the corresponding token was placed. Transitions may fire in time windows as given by two non-negative values on the transitions' incoming arcs [13]. The permeability of arcs depends on these timestamps [14].

Extended Timestamp Nets integrate the concepts of Pr/T and Timestamp nets such that tokens carry timestamps and any further information [15].

Some of the approaches may be transformed into each other quite effortlessly [16] [17]. All of the presented Petri net formalisms, however, use artificial, abstract time units. To model and simulate real-world applications, real time values should be used. To this end, date and time data types seem beneficial to be included as possible information on tokens. For reference, there are other modeling methods that were developed to combine time and process structures.

Value Stream Diagrams (VSD) establish models of flows of information and material in order to evaluate value streams. To optimize the value streams, wait times - beside other factors - need to be minimized. The value stream method exposes such wait times. This concept became widely known due to Toyotas Production System from 1930 and its advancements by Japanese engineers Taiichi Ohno and Eiji Toyoda, but dates back as far as 1914 when graphical nets were used to examine routings and other flows to help *Installing Efficiency Methods* in a manufacturing company [18] [19].
Figure 2 depicts the exemplary process as a VSD. It gives a suitable high-level overview of the whole value stream from customer to supplier, however cannot be simulated.

Business Process Model and Notation (BPMN) is a notation and representation language for modeling business processes. It is extensively used due to the relative ease of both creating and understanding models. Using BPMN, it is possible to create both high-level models of companies and low-level models of single processes in a graphical approach similar to flowcharts [20] [21].
Although there are similarities between BPMN and Petri nets, the former lack the mathematical toolset that can be used to analyze Petri nets in form of linear algebra.

If conceptual models are developed for process simulation or execution, also tools are needed in addition to the formal mathematical base. The Process-Simulation.Center (P-S.C) is a Web-based modeling and simulation environment supporting the development of P/T and Pr/T nets [22].

In P-S.C, it is possible to assign data types to places and to use these places in analogy to tables in databases. Special types for time and date are important substructures for the simulation of processes in production and logistics and enhance the mentioned approaches to timed Petri nets.

In contrast to Relational Algebra and SQL where operations like select or projection are applied to the set of all affected tuples and result in a set again, in P-S.C the tuples are processed serially. This is since, in business and production, work items are also treated one after another. A decision on the concrete sequence is made locally by the transitions of the net which also has the ability to aggregate over the tuple tokens on a place, like this is known for database systems.

Also, the P-S.C can be used to combine the process view on a system with other views. Process maps can be used to collate different processes with each other and to express the strategic value of processes as primary, supportive or managing.

The organizational structure of an institution can be combined with the Petri net view on the processes by assigning its nodes to swim lanes for the responsible organizational units. Organizational charts complete the functions of the P-S.C.

Contrary to most other conceptual modeling tools, especially those that have been developed for Petri nets, for the P-S.C a specification language has been developed with which all types of models are scripted. Due to strong algorithms for automatic layout, modelers can concentrate purely on structural aspects of the domain to be expressed.

III. A SIMULATION LABORATORY FOR PROCESSES IN LOGISTICS

The so-called *box game* has been developed at the Worms University of Applied Sciences to teach students in logistics and is used as a sample application. Despite its simplicity, very different kinds of processes that also have a high impact for practice can be observed. It is, therefore, ideal for trying out different ways of conceptual modeling and simulation.

The concrete example is a simple construction process where students assemble small and large boxes, put the smaller into the larger ones, and check the quality at the end of the process. With this process, characteristics of push and pull systems are illustrated.

Training members are present during the game. Ideally, they take part in the game in order to gain first hand experience of motivation and work situations. Being engaged in the training helps the students to recognize different types of waste, such as *overproduction*, *waiting*, and *motion*, but also the transformation of waste types. Finally, discussing the shared experiences is a major part of the learning success. A complete simulation run of the *box game* lasts approximately two to three hours.

Despite the simplicity of the used material and the low level of technical requirements, the *box game* is easily transferable to assembly work stations in a more generalized form and has a highly practical impact. Mechanical production, however, where schedules, shift patterns, changeover times or multiple machine set-ups are of particular importance, is not an objective of this training.

Figure 1 shows the spatial organization of the *box game* in the learning laboratory: five work tables are arranged in a suitable location and standard positions like interim storages are marked with adhesive tape. As can be seen, the setting can also be build up in locations such as conference rooms, training rooms, or even canteens.

The following activities have to be conducted at the five stations or (transport-wise) between them:

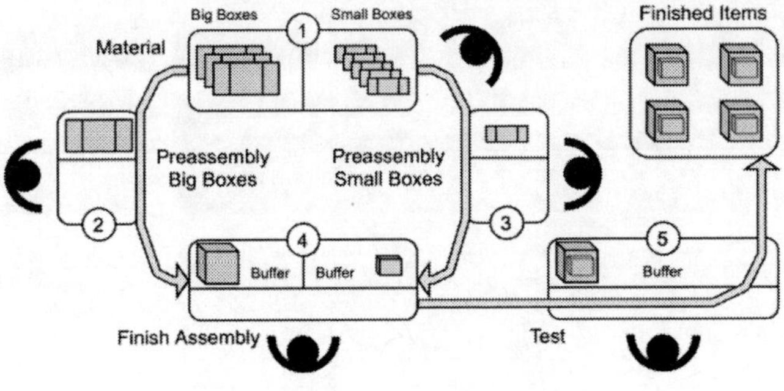

Figure 1. Layout design of the *box game*

1. **Storage (S)** Deliver boxes.
2. **Preassemble big boxes (PBB)** Fold box, close lid, and pass the box on.
3. **Preassemble small boxes (PSB)** Fold box, close lid, and pass the box on.
4. **Finish assembly (FA)** Open big box, insert small one, label small box with a post-it as "package note", close and tape big box lid up, and pass on.
5. **Test (QA)** Shake box for an acoustic quality check, apply a red dot to the upper left corner of outer box, and place the finished box in the storage area.

Beside the trainer, the following can partake in the game:

5 participants who will occupy the work stations
3 players who record the processing times
1 observer who records the inventory in the system
1 observer who records productivity levels
Possibly 2 employees who will disassemble the boxes

The initial stock of the *box game* is 75 big and 75 small boxes. However, it is not the aim to produce the entire demand in the shortest possible time, but to produce them according to the customer demand - one part every 15 seconds - without inventory and with as few employees as possible.

Figure 2 shows the value stream diagram of the *box game*. Although the processing time can be annotated in the diagram, it is hardly simulated due to a lacking mathematical foundation. Even software that replicates human intuition of value stream diagrams is missing. Nonetheless, the diagram helps to understand how the *box game* is played in detail.

Typically, the simulation is played in four rounds where each round lasts for a defined duration (e.g., 5 or 8 minutes). During the simulation, two types of principles with two batch sizes are played.

Batch size 3 - push principle: The products are passed on in batches of size 3. Each process step works functionally independent from the other and the participants are paid by the number of pieces they work on. Hence, it is the goal at each station to produce as much output as possible.

Batch size 3 - pull principle: Stations produce and pass on products in batches of size 3. Upstream stations have to hold their pieces and stop production until it is demanded by an internal or external customer. The capacity of a station and its buffer is limited to 3 items and items can only be replaced accordingly.

Batch size 1 - pull principle: The third round is played like the second one, but the batch size is reduced to one.

Improvement - pull principle: The last round is used to find improvements autonomously and to apply them as a team.

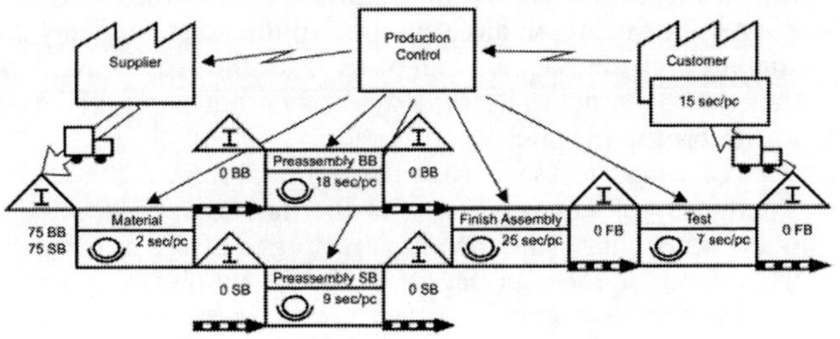

Figure 2. Value stream diagram of the *box game*

The advantage of this approach is that the participants gather personal experiences. This can hardly be replaced by a computer simulation. However, augmenting this hands-on experience by a computer simulation helps to scale up both complexity and range of the considered process.

IV. Clock Pulse Simulation Models

The aim of observing storage utilization over time necessitates a constant flow of time. To this end, the first step in modeling the *box game* is the implementation of a clock that ticks every second, as depicted in Figure 3 (upper left). A tiny Petri net consists of a time-typed place *clock*, a corresponding transition *pulse* and two arcs, one of which removes a time token from the *clock*, while the other one adds one second to the received value and puts the token back on the *clock*. Thus, each firing increments the elapsed total time by one second. At this point, it is worth mentioning that the ProcessSimulation.Center draws places such that both their labels and token quantity can be presented within the node.

The basic model of a working station - here, the folding of the big boxes, as shown in Figure 3 (lower) - consists of a place *inBB* for the attached upstream storage and a place *buildBB* for the workplace itself. An adjacent transition *deliverBB* provides the storage with feedstock coming from the *material* warehouse (and possibly information about the order volume).

The transition *startBB* gets the item with the minimal id according to the fifo principle and puts it on the workplace *buildBB*. Then, the transition *stopBB* waits for the item to be finished as indicated by the processing time (which is encoded on the item's token) and the time of the aforementioned *clock* elapsed. For this, in our models, all enabled transitions fire together in steps. This waiting is implemented as a condition on *stopBB*. Conditions and selection criteria can be displayed inside the model by clicking on the plus-symbol.

The transition *stopBB* is attached to an interim storage serving as buffer for the succeeding working station, as shown later. The place *idleBB* serves two purposes: as a semaphore that prohibits *startBB* from firing while the workplace is busy, and as a counter of the idle time of the workplace.

An observer net, as presented in Figure 3 (upper right), evaluates the costs associated with the storage. The value of place *inBBEval* is increased by the number of tokens on place *inBB* indicating the cost of the storage in that exact moment. In combination, these models allow for the observation of fluctuating storage levels, of bottlenecks, and of storage cost.

By expanding on the presented working space model and implementing the mentioned concepts, the first iteration of the *box game* - the push version as presented during a simulation run in Figure 4 - can be modeled.

As the main principle of the building net - exemplarily shown for the big boxes - can be used for the other workplaces, they can be structurally copied and then adapted with respect to the processing time.

Connected to the upstream storage places of the big and small box folding nets, there is the mentioned place for the main warehouse. The downstream storage places are linked to the interim storage serving as buffer for the finishing step.

The working station for tests is connected directly to the outgoing storage of the final assembly. As is the case for conditions, functions and data accesses on arcs can be shown or hidden, as needed.

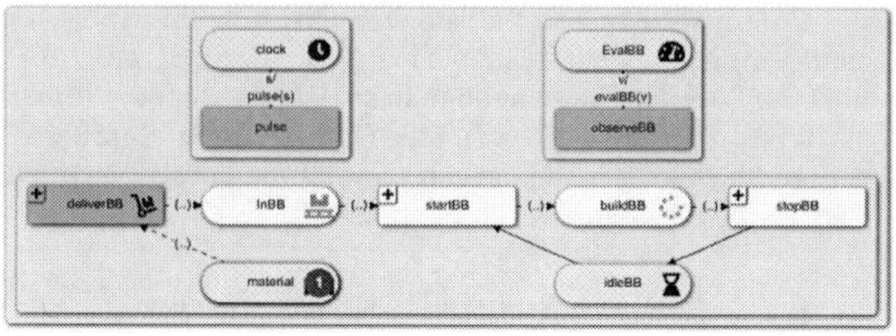

Figure 3. (upper left) Simple Petri net clock · (upper right) Observer net that evaluates the upstream storage in (lower) · (lower) Building big boxes as instance of a single working station

To further enhance the visual understanding of their respective functionality, nodes can be provided with symbols.

The pull version of the *box game* as depicted in Figure 5 is slightly more complicated, as supplementary elements are needed to implement pull requests. This is done by additional pull-transitions that keep track of the contents of upstream storage places for all three construction workplaces. As soon as these are empty, a pull request is issued, leading to a delivery.

Comparison of the two models' simulation runs show neither a change in total processing time nor one in idle times for the different workplaces, which is as expected. Differences on utilization of storage places become evident, though.

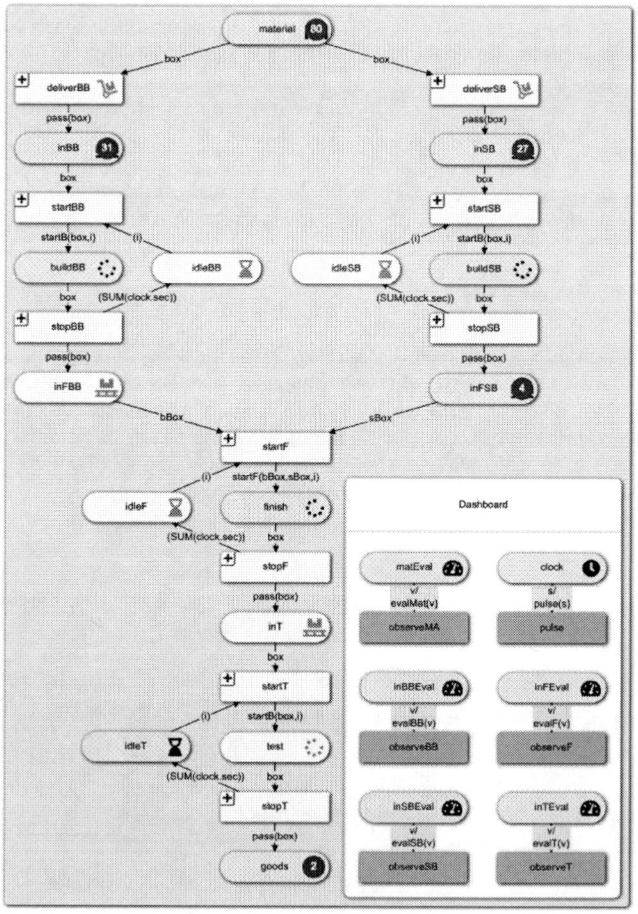

Figure 4. Pulse Clock Push Model

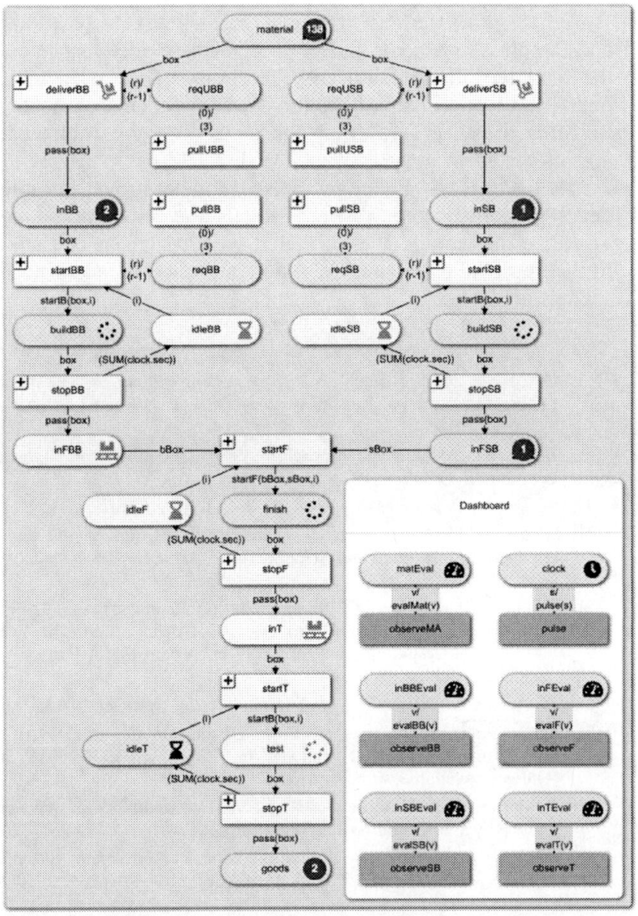

Figure 5. Pulse Clock Pull Model

The first model using push principles clearly shows the drawback of this approach: large interim storage and, as a result, high inventory costs. Figure 6 (upper) depicts the inventory on the material storage, the building buffer storages and the finished goods storage during the push simulation.

Figure 6 (lower) presents the pull simulation run's results with otherwise unaltered preconditions. The interim storage places are much less utilized as only those items are put into the assembly lines that are demanded by downstream stations.

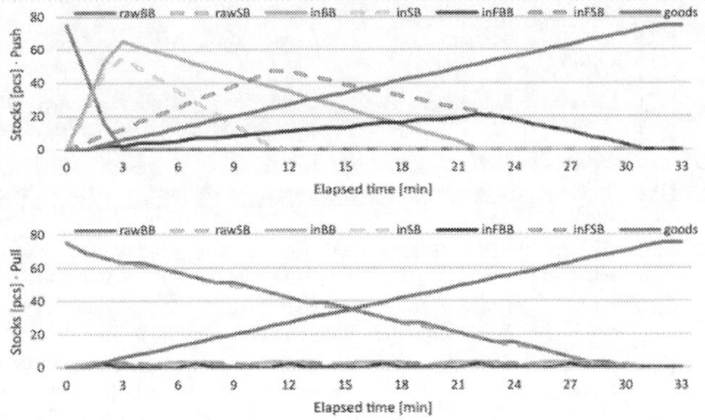

Figure 6. Stocks in the pulse clock model for Push (upper) and Pull (lower)

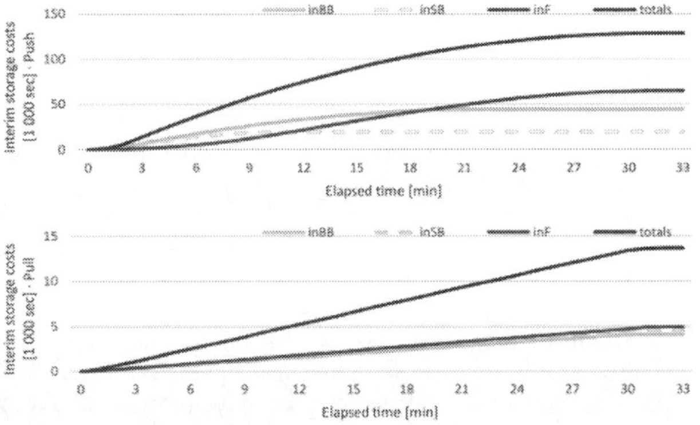

Figure 7. Inventory costs per interim storage and accumulated for Push (upper) and Pull (lower)

This is as expected, as it corresponds to the main goal behind just-in-time production schedules.

Figure 7 (upper) presents the costs of interim storage in the push model, while Figure 7 (lower) presents the same for the pull model. Also shown are the accumulated costs of all interim storage places. The finished goods storage is omitted as throughput is the same in both models, thus leading to the same costs on this storage. The material warehouse, otherwise, is put aside as the difference between the accumulated totals equals to the possible savings when externalizing the warehouse. By simply implementing pull principles, the evaluated stock cost on the interim storage places plummet. Thus, the advantages of a just-in-time production and a smaller main storage become obvious. The pull principle allows for exactly this.

What is not accounted for in these models are for example costs of transportation, as smaller batch sizes usually correspondent to higher transportation costs, leading to familiar knowledge: decreasing one muda typically increases other muda. Hence, batch size 1, which is optimal for the interim storage cost, is not necessarily the globally optimal solution.

V. An Alternative Modeling Approach

The advantage of the described way to model the box game is that the rising and discharging of the stocks can be observed throughout the simulation in a very illustrative way. The number of items in each stock is obvious for every second. Since in the P-S.C the color of and the symbol on places can change dependent on the number of tokens on the place, the advantages and disadvantages of push and pull can be demonstrated very well. As a consequence, for the students in the logistics laboratory the simulation is a demonstrative extension of their personal experience.

For the concrete example described here, 1902 steps that represent seconds (or almost 32 minutes) in the real world game are calculated for the full simulation, both for push and pull. This is a much longer period than the one that can be played by the students, because the concentration of the students decreases after about 5 minutes. But the calculation of all of these steps take time. On an iMac with 4 GHz Quad-Core Intel Core i7 processor and 16 GB RAM, the full simulation takes in a Chrome browser 8234 milliseconds. The duration for the simulation of a working day would increase linearly. This observation led to the question how to save simulation time. Actually, this can be reduced drastically if the visualization is less important compared to the concrete result.

In this case, it would be sufficient to calculate new states only in the moments of state changes. For the concrete example discussed in this paper, the simulation can be reduced from 1902 down to 79 steps for push and 228 steps for pull. On the same computer mentioned above, the simulation takes then 315 or 923 milliseconds, respectively. We call this second approach an event triggered simulation. Its benefits increase even more, if the demand interval in which changes occur vary strongly from one part of the model to the other since it takes into account local state changes.

The price that has to be paid for this is that a visualization of the simulation results must be generated in a separate working step. Also, we sensed the development of the event triggered model as more difficult compared to the clock pulse model. From this personal observation, we derive the following suggestion:

Use a clock pulse simulation if either a clock pulse visualization of the system's states is needed or if the computer is fast enough for the few simulations that must be run for the modeled system.

Use an event triggered simulation if simulation speed is necessary due the complexity of the modeled system, if fast answers are needed in production, or if a large number of variations of the production schedule or input data has to be compared. In general, the more often a specific model needs to be simulated, the more it is worth to develop an event triggered model instead of a clock pulse model.

VI. Conclusion and Future Work

The modeling exercises that had to be solved for this paper led to some new insights in the development of conceptual models for discrete timed systems. Finally, we found our personal good practice that consists of the following steps:

1. Define data types for the different stocks and other data objects, and initialize the corresponding places in accordance with the starting condition.
2. Augment the model by transitions for beginning and ending specific tasks like delivering raw materials, building or testing a box.
3. Identify the next item to be taken and the moment this will occur. This also allows for implementation of different prioritization strategies.
4. Start with modeling the simpler push principle and augment this model by pull principles.

Moreover, we now see the development of a clock pulse model as a preliminary for the development of an event triggered model. If an event triggered model is needed due to the above mentioned reasons, we suggest the following steps:

1. Develop the clock pulse model first.
2. Observe the reasons for state changes with the aid of the clock pulse model and derive the event triggered model from these observations.
3. Look for a proper visualization of the simulation results.

In order to ease the step from a clock pulse model to an event triggered model, in the future we will work on an extension of the P-S.C such that users are supported in finding the relevant moments of state changes. Probably it will be possible to automatically support the modelers in conducting this task.

What impressed us most is that what can be modeled and simulated with the aid of Petri nets is only restricted by the modelers imagination and the ability of the used tool. In opposite to other out of the box modeling environments for logistics, a user is free to lay the focus on any parameter they are interested in most.

However, two challenges exist: Modelers must be able to develop sophisticated, abstract models and must find a way to visualize the results. We hope that we have given one answer to the first challenge and see major future work concerning the second one.

References

[1] C. Caserio and S. Trucco, Enterprise Resource Planning and Business Intelligence Systems for Information Quality. Cham, Switzerland: Springer, 2018.

[2] H. J. Genrich and K. Lautenbach, "System Modelling with High-Level Petri Nets," Theoretical Computer Science, vol. 13, 1981.

[3] K. Jensen, Coloured Petri-Nets, 1st ed. Berlin: Springer, 1992.

[4] "Petri Nets Tools Database Quick Overview," https://www.informatik.uni-hamburg.de/TGI/PetriNets/tools/quick.html (last accessed 2020.09.20).

[5] S. Haag, L. Zakfeld, C. Simon, and C. Reuter, "Event Triggered Simulation of Push and Pull Processes," in SIMUL 2020: The Twelfth International Conference on Advances in System Simulation. Porto, Portugal: IARIA XPS Press.

[6] W. Reisig, Understanding Petri Nets. Berlin: Springer, 2013.

[7] M. Montali and A. Rivkin, "From DB-nets to Coloured Petri Nets with Priorities (Extended Version)," CoRR, vol. abs/1904.00058, 2019. [Online]. Available: http://arxiv.org/abs/1904.00058

[8] P. Merlin, "The Time-Petri-Net and the Recoverability of Processes," University California, Irvine, Tech. Rep., 1974.

[9] C. Ramchandani, "Analysis of Asynchronous Concurrent Systems by Timed Petri Nets," MIT, Project MAC, Technical Report 120, 1974.

[10] J. Sifakis, "Use of petri nets for performance evalutation," in Measuring, modelling and evalutating computer systems, ser. IFIP, H. Beilner and E. Gelenbe, Eds., North Holland Publ. Co., 1977, pp. 75–93.

[11] R. König and L. Quäck, Petri-Netze in der Steuerungs- und Digitaltechnik. München, Wien: Oldenbourg Verlag, 1988.

[12] H.-M. Hanisch, Petri-Netze in der Verfahrenstechnik. München: Oldenbourg, 1992.

[13] C. Ghezzi, D. Mandrioli, S. Morasca, and M. Pezzè, "A unified high-level petri net formalism for time-critical systems," IEEE Transactions On Software Engineering, vol. 17, no. 2, 1991, pp. 160–172.

[14] H.-M. Hanisch, K. Lautenbach, C. Simon, and J. Thieme, "Timestamp Nets in Technical Applications," in IEEE International Workshop on Discrete Event Systems, San Diego, CA, 1998.

[15] C. Simon, "Developing Software Controllers with Petri Nets and a Logic of Actions," in IEEE International Conference on Robotics and Automation, ICRA 2001, Seoul, Korea, 2001.

[16] K. Jensen, "High-Level Petri Nets," Informatik-Fachberichte, vol. 66, 1983, pp. 166–180.

[17] L. Popova-Zeugmann, Time and Petri Nets. Berlin: Springer, 2013.

[18] C. E. Knoeppel, Installing Efficiency Methods. The Engineering Magazine, 1915.

[19] T. Ohno, Toyota Production System. Milton Park, UK: Taylor & Francis, 1988.

[20] BPMI, "BPMN 1.0 - Business Process Model and Notation," https://www.omg.org/spec/BPMN/ (letzter Zugriff 2020.09.20), 2004.

[21] OMG, "BPMN 2.0 - Business Process Model and Notation," http://www.bpmn.org/ (last accessed 2020.09.20), 2011.

[22] C. Simon, "Web-Based Simulation Of Production Schedules With High-Level Petri Nets," in 32rd International ECMS Conference on Modelling and Simulation (ECMS 2018), L. Nolle, A. Burger, C. Tholen, J. Werner, and J. Wellhausen, Eds. Wilhelmshaven, Germany: SCS Europe, 2018, pp. 275–281.

An Agent-Based Model of Delegation Relationships With Hidden-Action: On the Effects of Heterogeneous Memory on Performance

Patrick Reinwald
Department of Management Control and Strategic Management
University of Klagenfurt
Klagenfurt, Austria
Email: patrick.reinwald@aau.at
ORCID: 0000-0002-2907-7939

Stephan Leitner
Department of Management Control and Strategic Management
University of Klagenfurt
Klagenfurt, Austria
Email: stephan.leitner@aau.at
ORCID: 0000-0001-6790-4651

Friederike Wall
Department of Management Control and Strategic Management
University of Klagenfurt
Klagenfurt, Austria
Email: friederike.wall@aau.at
ORCID: 0000-0001-8001-8558

***Abstract*—We introduce an agent-based model of delegation relationships between a principal and an agent, which is based on the standard-hidden action model introduced by Holmström and, by doing so, provide a model which can be used to further explore theoretical topics in managerial economics, such as the efficiency of incentive mechanisms. We employ the concept of agentization, i.e., we systematically transform the standard hidden-action model into an agent-based model. Our modeling approach allows for a relaxation of some of the rather "heroic" assumptions included in the standard hidden-action model, whereby we particularly focus on assumptions related to the (i) availability of information about the environment and the (ii) principal's and agent's cognitive capabilities (with a particular focus on their learning capabilities and their memory). Our analysis focuses on how close and how fast the incentive scheme, which endogenously emerges from the agent-based model, converges to the solution proposed by the standard hidden-action model. Also, we investigate whether a stable solution can emerge from the agent-based model variant. The results show that in stable environments the emergent result can nearly reach the solution proposed by the standard hidden-action model. Surprisingly, the results indicate that turbulence in the environment leads to stability in earlier time periods.**

Keywords–Agent-based modeling and simulation; Management control system; Information asymmetry; Complexity economics; Agentization.

I. Introduction

The standard hidden-action model introduced by Holmström [1] describes, in general, a delegation relation between a principal and an agent. It covers a situation in which the principal delegates a task to an agent. The agent selects an effort level in order to carry out this task, which is not observable by the principal (it is *hidden*). The agent's effort together with some environmental impact produces outcome which is to be shared between the principal and the agent. The principal's objective is to maximize her share of the outcome associated with the task while the agent strives for maximizing his share of the outcome minus his disutility from making effort to carry out the task. The standard hidden-action model proposes an incentive scheme (i.e., a rule to share the outcome) which aligns the agent's and the principal's objective so that the principal's utility finds its maximum. As only the outcome (but not the effort level) is observable for the principal, the sharing rule is based on outcome only.

In order to derive the optimal sharing rule, agency theory makes rather "heroic'" assumptions about the capabilities of both parties with respect to (i) information processing capacity, (ii) availability of information, and (iii) capability to find the optimal solution immediately. Axtell [2] argues that the most "heroic" assumptions are agent homogeneity, non-interactiveness, and the existence of equilibrium solutions and refers to them as "neoclassical sweetspot". The result of these rather "heroic" assumptions is that the explanatory and the predictive power regarding real world problems substantially decreases [3]. Critics often refer to principal-agent models as "toy problems" and argue that solutions derived from such "toy problems", where authors can "assume complicating things away", are of limited use and only merely help to solve real world problems [4]-[6].

We take up on this critique and put the "heroic" assumptions included in the standard hidden-action model [1] in the focus of this paper. In the vein of Leitner and Wall [7], we transfer the standard hidden-action model into an agent-based model following a procedure introduced by Guerrero and Axtell [8] and Leitner and Behrens [9], which allows us to relax some of the included assumptions. In particular, we relax the assumptions related to the principal's and the agent's (i) information processing capacity and (ii) the availability of information. We model situations in which the principal and the agent no longer have full information about the environment but have to learn this information over time. In consequence, they can no longer find the optimal (second-best) solution immediately, like it is the case in the standard hidden-action model. We, therefore, endow the principal and the agent with the capability to search for the best possible incentive scheme over time by employing a hillclimbing algorithm. Please notice that the optimal solution, which is derived from the standard hidden-action model for cases in which the the agent's effort is *not* observable, is referred to as *second-best solution*. The first-best solution, on the contrary, assumes that the agent's effort is observable [10], which, in consequence, means that no incentive problem in the above outlined sense arises.

The remainder of this paper is organized as follows: Section II introduces two variants of the hidden-action model. First the main features of the standard hidden-action model are presented. We, then introduce the agent-based model variant which relaxes some of the assumptions included in the standard hidden-action model. In Section III, we elaborate on the simulation setup, and introduce and discuss the results. Section IV concludes the paper and gives an outlook on future work.

II. THE HIDDEN-ACTION MODEL

This section summarizes the main features of the standard hidden-action model introduced in [1] and proposes an agent-based representation of the hidden-action problem in which the principal and the agent are endowed with limited and heterogeneous memory.

A. *The standard hidden-action model*

The standard hidden-action model, which describes a delegation relation between a principal and an agent, was first described by Holmström [1]. This model covers a situation in which a principal offers an agent a contract upon a task to be carried out and a sharing rule over the generated outcome, among other things. If the agent agrees on the condition stated in the contract, he exerts effort to complete the specified task. Together with an exogenous factor, his effort generates outcome, but this also leads to disutility for him. For the principal, however, the effort the agent had carried out is unobservable, which results in a situations where only the outcome can be used as a basis for the sharing rule. Both the principal and the agent are individual utility maximizers [10], [5]. Furthermore, it is assumed that the principal is risk neutral and characterized by her utility function

$$U_P(x, s) = x - s(x) \ , \qquad (1)$$

whereby x represents the generated outcome and $s = s(x)$ is the function for the sharing rule. As mentioned before, the outcome

$$x = f(a, \theta) \ , \qquad (2)$$

is a function of the agent's effort a and the exogenous factor θ. The agent, who is assumed to be risk averse, is characterized by the utility function

$$U_A(s, a) = V(s) - G(a) \ , \qquad (3)$$

where $V(s)$ represents the generated utility from the compensation and $G(a)$ denotes to disutulity from the exerted effort. For the contract to be effective, two additional constraints have to be fulfilled. First, the participation constraint

$$E(U_a(s, a)) \geq \bar{U} \ , \qquad (4)$$

which assures that the agent gets at least the utility he would get from the best outside option $\bar{U}$. Second, the incentive compatibility constraint

$$a \in \arg\max_{a} \ E\{U_A(s(x), a')\} \ , \qquad (5)$$

which aligns the agent's goal (maximizing his utility) with the goal of the principal. For an extensive review and the formal solution to this problem, the reader is, for example, referred to Holmström [1] and Lambert [10].

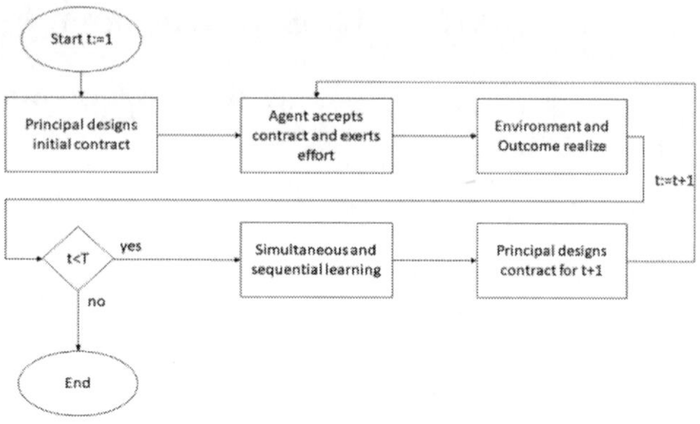

Figure 1. Flow diagram

B. *Agent-based model variant*

We transfer the standard hidden-action model [1] into an agent-based model following the agentization procedure introduced by Guerrero and Axtell [8] and Leitner and Behrens [9]. We limit the principal's and the agent's availability of information about the environment and endow them with the capability to learn about the environment over time. As a consequence of this change, the principal and the agent can no longer find the optimal (second-best) contract immediately but search for it over time. This stepwise search for the optimal contract requires us to switch from a one-periodic to a multi-periodic model in which the principal and the agent agree upon a contract in every timestep. Due to the employed learning mechanism (which is introduced below), the principal's and the agent's states of information are changing over time. We do not give the agent the possibility to allocate effort over multiple periods. A condensed overview of the sequence of the events is provided in Figure 1.

We indicate time steps by $t = 1, ..., T$. After the adjustment to a multi-periodic model, the principal's utility function introduced in (1) takes the form of

$$U_P(x_t, s(x_t)) = x_t - s(x_t) \ , \qquad (6)$$

where x_t denotes the outcome and $s(x_t)$ is the agent's compensation in time step t. The production function introduced in (2) is adapted, so that

$$x_t = a_t + \theta_t \ , \qquad (7)$$

where a_t stands for the effort-level selected by the agent from a set of all feasible actions A_t in t. A_t is a subset of A with the range from zero to the value a_t, whereby the latter refers to the effort-level which is required to achieve the second-best solution according to the standard hidden-action model. Setting the boundaries in this way is in line with [1] and assures the feasibility of the solution. We denote the effort level for which the principal designs the contract by $\tilde{a}_t$ and refer to it as incited effort. The variable θ_t denotes the realized exogenous factor in t which follows a Normal distribution. Given these adaptations, the agent's compensation function $s(x_t)$ takes the form of

$$s(x_t) = x_t * p_t \ , \qquad (8)$$

where $p_t \in [0, 1]$ is the premium parameter in t. After the adaption to a multi-periodic model, the agent's utility function takes the form of

$$U_A(s(x_t), a_t) = \overbrace{\frac{1 - e^{-\eta * s(x_t)}}{\eta}}^{V(s(x_t))} - \overbrace{\frac{a_t^2}{2}}^{G(a_t)} , \quad (9)$$

where η represents the agent's Arrow-Pratt measure of risk-aversion [11]. The agent strives for maximizing this utility function but, due to the adaptions outlined below, replaces the environmental factor θ_t by his expectation thereof. For the computation of the agent's expectation about the environmental factor see (11) and (13).

The most central change during the process of agentization is the relaxation of the availability of information about the environment for the principal and the agent. In the standard hidden-action model [1], it is assumed that both parties have knowledge about the distribution of the exogenous factor and its parameterization, so that they can compute an expected value for the environmental variable. In contrast to this, in the agent-based model variant they have to learn about the environment over time. The assumptions related to the environment are relaxed in the following way:

1) The principal and the agent no longer have full information about the environmental factor at the beginning of the simulation.
2) The principal and the agent are able to individually learn about the environment over time.
3) The principal and the agent also have the cognitive ability to store the gathered information about the environment in their memory.

These changes are implemented by a simultaneous and sequential learning model (see also [7]). Part of this learning model is not only the process of gathering and storing the information but also the application of this information to compute the estimation of the exogenous factor. Both the principal and the agent are now able to individually learn about the environment and estimate the exogenous factor in the same way: They make their conclusions about the environment on the basis of the observable outcome x_t (see (7)), which is possible because the only unknown information in the equation is the realized environmental factor. Recall, both the principal and the agent know the realized outcome x_t, the agent knows the exerted effort a_t, and the principal knows the incited effort $\tilde{a}_t$. Using this information, the principal and the agent can infer the estimations of the environmental factor from the realized outcome, according to

$$\tilde{\theta}_t = x_t - \tilde{a}_t , \quad (10)$$

and

$$\theta_t = x_t - a_t , \quad (11)$$

respectively. Furthermore, they are able to privately store the estimations in their memory until their defined cognitive capacity (m_P for the principal and m_A for the agent) is reached. Once the cognitive capacity is reached, the oldest entries are replaced by the most recent observations. Their expectation about the environmental factor is computed by averaging all privately stored and retrievable estimations of

TABLE I. NOTATION FOR THE AGENT-BASED MODEL VARIANT

Description	Parameter
Timesteps	t
Principal's utility	U_P
Agent's utility	U_A
Agent's Arrow-Pratt measure of risk-aversion	η
Agent's share of outcome in t	$s(x_t) = x_t * p_t$
Outcome	$x_t = a_t + \theta_t$
Principal's expected outcome	$\tilde{x}_{Pt}$
Premium parameter in t	p_t
Exerted effort level in t	a_t
Induced effort level by the principal in t	$\tilde{a}_t$
Set of all feasible actions in t	A_t
Exogenous (environment) variable in t	θ_t
Principal's estimation of the realized exogenous factor in t	$\tilde{\theta}_t$
Mental capability of the principal	m_P
Mental capability of the agent	m_A
Averaged expected exogenous factor of the principal	$\hat{\theta}_{Pt}$
Averaged expected exogenous factor of the agent	$\hat{\theta}_{At}$

exogenous factors, so that

$$\hat{\theta}_{Pt} = \begin{cases} \frac{1}{t-1} \sum_{n=1}^{n=t-1} \tilde{\theta}_n & \text{if } m_P = \infty, \\ \frac{1}{m_P} \sum_{\substack{\forall t \leq m_P : n=1 \\ \forall t > m_P : n=t-m_P}}^{n=t-1} \tilde{\theta}_n & \text{if } m_P < \infty , \end{cases} \quad (12)$$

for the principal and

$$\hat{\theta}_{At} = \begin{cases} \frac{1}{t-1} \sum_{n=1}^{n=t-1} \theta_n & \text{if } m_A = \infty, \\ \frac{1}{m_A} \sum_{\substack{\forall t \leq m_A : n=1 \\ \forall t > m_A : n=t-m_A}}^{n=t-1} \theta_n & \text{if } m_A < \infty , \end{cases} \quad (13)$$

for the agent.

Next, the principal randomly discovers two alternative effort levels in the search space A_t which together with $\tilde{a}_t$ serve as candidates for $\tilde{a}_{t+1}$. Using her expectation about the environment $\hat{\theta}_{Pt}$, the principal computes the expected outcome $\tilde{x}_{Pt}$ (according to (7)) and her expected utility (according to (6)) associated with all three candidates. Notice that for all effort levels the associated premium parameter is computed according to

$$p_t = \max_{p=[0,1]} U_p(\tilde{x}_{Pt}, s(\tilde{x}_{Pt})) . \quad (14)$$

Finally, the principal selects the candidate with the highest expected utility as desired effort level $\tilde{a}_{t+1}$ for period $t + 1$ and communicates the associated premium parameter p_{t+1} to the agent. In period $t + 1$, the agent starts over the procedure with selecting an effort level a_{t+1} using p_{t+1} (see Figure 1).

III. Simulations Parameters and Results

We have conducted 8 scenarios with different underlying assumptions about the cognitive capacity (memory) of the principal and the agent and two different levels of environmental turbulence.

Recall that the environmental variable is modeled to follow a Normal distribution. The variations in environmental turbulence are operationalized by altering this distribution's standard deviation which is set relative to the optimal outcome x of the standard hidden-action model (second-best solution in [1]). For the case of a rather stable environment we set $\sigma = 0.05x$ and for a rather unstable environment we set $\sigma = 0.45x$. The distribution's mean is fixed at zero.

In the 8 investigated scenarios, we have, in general, two configurations related to the cognitive capacity of the principal and the agent. The first one assumes that the principal has advantage in cognitive capacity and the second assumes the opposite situation. Each of them consist of 4 scenarios where the one in advantage always has unlimited memory and the other one has either a memory with the length of one or five. The agent's Arrow-Pratt measure is always set to $\eta = 0.5$, which characterizes a risk-averse agent.

For every scenario, we perform 700 repetitions ($R = 700$), our analysis focuses on the first 20 time steps ($t = 1, ..., 20$). In order to implement our simulation model we use MATLAB®.

We report the averaged normalized effort level carried out by the agent in every period t as performance measure. Therefore in every simulation run $r = 1, ..., R$ and for every period $t = 1, ..., T$ we track the effort level a_{tr} chosen by the agent, and normalize it by the optimal level of effort $a*$.

$$\phi_t = \frac{1}{R} \sum_{r=1}^{r=R} \frac{a_{tr}}{a*} \quad (15)$$

We report the averaged normalized effort level as a measure of performance, as provides fundamental insights into the functioning of the emergent incentive schemes without further perturbation caused by environmental turbulence.

A. Results 1: Advantage in information for the agent

First, we analyze the results in the situation with the advantage for the agent. In the two scenarios with a relatively stable environment ($\sigma = 0.05x$) we can see that performance is significantly higher (at the end of the observation period) for cases in which the principal's cognitive capacity is higher, too (in terms of an increase in memory length): As the principal's memory increases from $m_P = 1$ to $m_P = 5$, the observed final averaged normalized effort level increases from 0.9063 to 0.9474 (see the two top subplots in Figure 2). We can observe similar results for the scenarios with a rather unstable environment ($\sigma = 0.45x$). Here, the final performance measure increases from 0.8135 to 0.8785 as the principal's memory increases from $m_P = 1$ to $m_P = 5$ (see the two bottom subplots in Figure 2). Furthermore, in line with intuition, we can observe that an increase in environmental turbulence leads to a decrease in the effort exerted by the agent.

We further analyze the effect of the principal's memory on the average variance of the results (i.e., the average variance of the effort exerted by the agent throughout the entire observation period): For the scenarios in a rather unstable environment, the average standard deviation significantly decreases from 0.17405 (for $m_P = 1$) to 0.15719 (for $m_P = 5$). For the cases in a rather stable environment no significant differences can be observed. The significance at the 99%-level was confirmed using an F-test. Thus, increasing the principal's cognitive capacity in an unstable environment significantly reduces the variance of the effort induced by the incentive scheme (and exerted by the agent). In other words, if the principal manages to increase her memory in an turbulent environment, she not only increases the average normalized effort level but also significantly reduces the risk of extreme deviations from this value.

Finally, we take a look on the stability of the averaged normalized effort level. We regard a solution to be stable as soon as (i) the averaged normalized effort level at period t

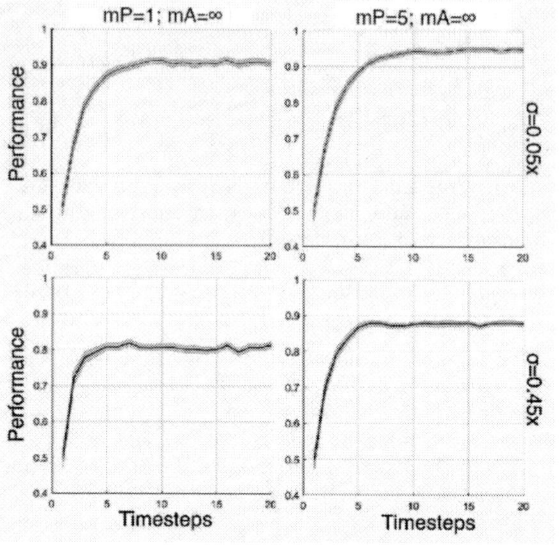

Figure 2. Situations with advantage regarding cognitive capacity for the agent (A) and the cognitive capacity of the principal (P) with either $m_P = 1$ or $m_P = 5$. Scenarios a plotted for two different environmental situations, stable ($\sigma = 0.05x$) and unstable $\sigma = 0.45x$..

is not significantly different from the same measure in period $t-1$, and given that (ii) this condition does not change after this point in time. For this analysis, we perform a T-test and set $\alpha = 0.01$. First, we focus on rather stable environments: For cases with a low (high) cognitive capacity for the principal of $m_P = 1$ and $m_P = 5$, we observe a stable solution for periods $t = 7$ and $t = 9$ onwards, respectively. For unstable environments, we can observe that a stable solution emerges earlier in both scenarios. For $m_P = 1$ ($m_P = 5$) the solution becomes stable in period $t = 4$ ($t = 6$). This is a counter-intuitive result as one would expect that turbulence in the environment leads to instability in the emergent solution.

B. Result 2: Advantage in information for the principal

This section analyses the cases in which the principal has an advantage in information. In stable environments ($\sigma = 0.05x$), we cannot observe significant differences: For the agent's memory of $m_A = 1$ and $m_A = 5$, the observed final averaged normalized effort levels are 0.9784 and 0.9786, respectively (see the two top subplots in Figure 3). The same result can be observed for unstable environments ($\sigma = 0.45x$). Here, the final performances are 0.9507 and 0.9512 for $m_A = 1$ and $m_A = 5$, respectively (see the two bottom subplots in Figure 3). Additionally, in line with intuition, we can observe that an increase in environmental turbulence leads to a decrease in the effort exerted by the agent.

Further, we analyze the effects of the agent's memory on the average variance of the results (i.e., the average variance of the effort exerted by the agent throughout the entire observation period). For unstable environments ($\sigma = 0.45x$), the observed results are similar to the ones presented in the previous section: The variances of the exerted effort levels are significantly different at the 99%-level for $m_A = 1$ and $m_A = 5$, for the former (latter) we observe a standard deviation of 0.1953 (0.15781). For stable environmnents, the results indicate that increasing the agent's memory significantly decreases the standard deviation of the exerted effort at the 95%-level:

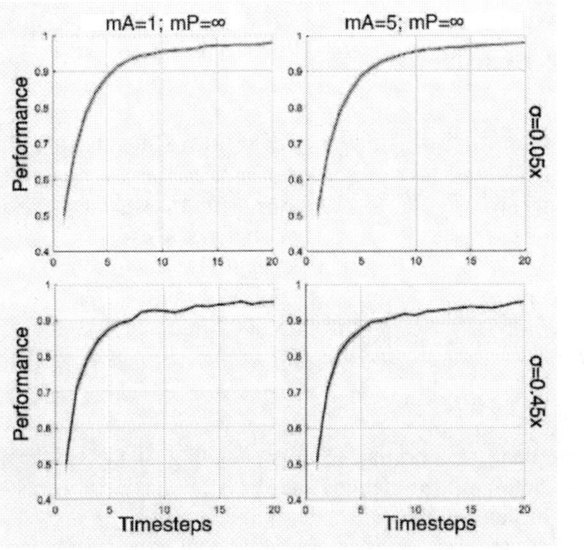

Figure 3. Scenarios with advantage regarding cognitive capacity for the principal (P) and the cognitive capacity of the agent (A) with either $m_A = 1$ or $m_A = 5$. Scenarios a plotted for two different environmental situations, stable ($\sigma = 0.05x$) and unstable $\sigma = 0.45x$.

We observe 0.14089 and 0.13821 for $m_A = 1$ and $m_A = 5$, respectively. Thus, increasing the agent's cognitive capacity significantly reduces the variance of the effort induced by the incentive scheme (and exerted by the him). In other words, if the agent manages to increase his memory, he significantly reduces the risk of extreme deviations from the performance value.

Finally, we investigate the stability of the averaged normalized effort level. First, we focus on the scenarios with rather stable environments: For the cognitive capacity of the agent of $m = 1$ and $m = 5$ we reach the stable point at period $t = 14$ and $t = 13$, respectively. For unstable environments we can observe in both scenarios that a stable solution emerges earlier. For $m = 1$ ($m = 5$) the performance reaches a stable point at period $t = 9$ ($t = 7$). This leads to the same counter-intuitive result as in the section before, as one would expect that turbulence in the environment leads to instability in the emergent solution.

IV. Conclusion and Future Work

The results presented in this paper deliver some insights about the effects of heterogeneous agents in a hidden-action setting:

- Our results suggest, that gathering information about the environment is a good strategy for the principal to increase his utility especially situations in which the environment is rather turbulent.
- In turbulent environments, increasing the memory of both the principal and the agent always has a positive effect on the variance of the results. This means that increasing the memory significantly reduces the risk of extreme deviations from the performance measures reported above.
- In stable environments, the results, on the contrary, suggest that only an increase of the agent's memory leads to an significant decrease in the exerted effort's variance.
- Surprisingly, the presented results indicate, that turbulence has a positive effect on stability, so that a stable solution emerges earlier in turbulent environments.

Future work might want to deeper investigate the effects of heterogeneous memory in the hidden-action setting (e.g, more memory length) and also include cognitive biases when characterizing the principal's and the agent's cognitive capabilities (such as the recency or the primacy effect [12]). Another potentially fruitful option avenue for future research might be to limit the principal's knowledge about the characteristics of the agent (such as the utility function).

Acknowledgment

This work was supported by funds of the Oesterreichische Nationalbank (Austrian Central Bank, Anniversary Fund, project number: 17930).

References

[1] B. Holmström, "Moral hazard and observability," The Bell Journal of Economics, vol. 10, no. 1, 1979, p. 74.

[2] R. L. Axtell, "What economic agents do: How cognition and interaction lead to emergence and complexity," The Review of Austrian Economics, vol. 20, no. 2-3, 2007, pp. 105–122.

[3] C. Schneeweiss, "On a formalisation of the process of quantitative model building," European Journal of Operational Research, vol. 29, no. 1, 1987, pp. 24–41.

[4] M. C. Jensen, "Organization Theory and Methodology," The Accounting Review, vol. 58, no. 2, 1983, pp. 319–339.

[5] K. M. Eisenhardt, "Agency theory: An assessment and review," The Academy of Management Review, vol. 14, no. 1, 1989, p. 57.

[6] S. P. Shapiro, "Agency Theory," Annual Review of Sociology, vol. 31, no. 1, 2005, pp. 263–284.

[7] S. Leitner and F. Wall, "Decision-facilitating information in hidden-action setups: an agent-based approach," Journal of Economic Interaction and Coordination, 2020, pp. 1–36.

[8] O. A. Guerrero and R. L. Axtell, "Using Agentization for Exploring Firm and Labor Dynamics," in Emergent Results of Artificial Economics, S. Osinga, G. J. Hofstede, and T. Verwaart, Eds. Berlin, Heidelberg: Springer Berlin Heidelberg, 2011, pp. 139–150.

[9] S. Leitner and D. A. Behrens, "On the efficiency of hurdle rate-based coordination mechanisms," Mathematical and Computer Modelling of Dynamical Systems, vol. 21, no. 5, 2015, pp. 413–431.

[10] R. A. Lambert, "Contracting theory and accounting," Journal of Accounting and Economics, vol. 32, no. 1-3, 2001, pp. 3–87.

[11] K. J. Arrow, "The Role of Securities in the Optimal Allocation of Risk-bearing," The Review of Economic Studies, vol. 31, no. 2, 1964, p. 91.

[12] A. Mantonakis, P. Rodero, I. Lesschaeve, and R. Hastie, "Order in choice: effects of serial position on preferences," Psychological science, vol. 20, no. 11, 2009, pp. 1309–1312.

On the Effectiveness of Minisum Approval Voting in an Open Strategy Setting: An Agent-Based Approach

Joop van de Heijning
Digital Age Research Center
University of Klagenfurt
Klagenfurt, Austria
johannes.vandeheijning@aau.at
ORCID 0000-0002-6246-9379

Stephan Leitner
Department of Management Control and Strategic Management
University of Klagenfurt
Klagenfurt, Austria
stephan.leitner@aau.at
ORCID 0000-0001-6790-4651

Alexandra Rausch
Department of Management Control and Strategic Management
University of Klagenfurt
Klagenfurt, Austria
alexandra.rausch@aau.at
ORCID 0000-0002-9275-252X

***Abstract*—This work researches the impact of including a wider range of participants in the strategy-making process on the performance of organizations, which operate in either moderately or highly complex environments. Agent-based simulation demonstrates that the increased number of ideas generated from larger and diverse crowds and subsequent preference aggregation lead to the rapid discovery of higher peaks in the organization's performance landscape. However, this is not the case when the expansion in the number of participants is small. The results confirm the most frequently mentioned benefit in the Open Strategy literature: the discovery of better-performing strategies.**

Keywords-Open Strategy; minisum approval voting; strategy as a practice; NK model; agent-based modeling.

I. INTRODUCTION

This paper shows that aggregating ideas from a diverse pool of participants using a specific aggregation mechanism leads to the rapid discovery of high-performing strategies. Including a wider range of participants in strategy-making is in line with a recent approach to strategy development, called Open Strategy (OS): OS is inclusive vs. restricted to the organizational elite, transparent vs. intransparent, and enabled by social information systems vs. merely supported by traditional IT [1]. Due to advances in (social) technology, changing societal norms, and several benefits, the interest in Open Strategy (OS) is on the rise [2][3].

Benefits of OS identified in empirical and conceptual research are the generation of better-performing strategies, increased buy-in and commitment, increased employee motivation, and improvements in an organization's reputation [4]. Tapping into the knowledge and intuition of nontraditional participants in the strategy process such as external stakeholders and access to a broader range of ideas are mentioned as reasons for the generation of better-performing strategies. The theory of the *Wisdom of the Crowd* poses similar reasoning [5].

In general, there is a lack of experimental evidence on when and how these claims might materialize, marked by calls for more longitudinal studies [3]. The goal of this work is to address this lack of evidence by evaluating with which number of participants and under which level of environmental complexity OS's most frequently mentioned benefit, the generation of better-performing strategies, eventuates. The results may contribute to a normative understanding of the OS approach and help guide academics and decision-makers towards better OS design.

This research turns to computational experimentation with an agent-based model for the following reasons [6]:

(a) Using empirical methods, it is impossible to disentangle the effects caused by the considered independent variables from the effects of other influences (the environment, competitors, the market, etc.) based on obtainable data such as from surveys and experiments, especially for strategic decision making. Additionally, on this topic, it is almost impossible to carry out longitudinal studies.
(b) Formal models frequently employed in economics would not be mathematically tractable due to their complexity.

Agent-based simulation, the form of the simulation method employed herein, fits the research's objective: The firm and its stakeholders that participate in strategy-making are the agents. They are heterogeneous, boundedly rational, and act autonomously in an explicit space of local interactions. As summarized in [7], these characteristics of the model define an agent-based model [8]. The individual search processes, individual decision-making, and individual learning result in the macrobehavior of the firm, incrementally finding better-performing strategies.

This work makes use of the strategy as a practice perspective. In contrast to the planning and process view on strategy-making, the focus of strategy as a practice is on how the participants in strategy development act and interact with each other and with the organization [9]. To make sure we model aspects relevant to a realistic OS setting, we turn to the strategy as a practice perspective adapted to OS [10].

The paper continues with a review of the literature in Section II and a description of the model in Section III, discusses the simulation setup and the results in Section IV, and ends with the conclusion and future work in Section V.

II. LITERATURE REVIEW

When implementing OS, organizations might opt for including both internal and external participants, or for limiting the inclusion scope to internal stakeholders only. Malhotra, Majchrzak, and Niemiec [11] employ an action research approach and describe OS as an online collaboration process in which mainly external stakeholders are involved. They identify the risks of contentious conflict and self-promotion. Careful risk-mitigating actions led to a successful conclusion of the process. The company Siemens opted for directing inclusion internally by opening up strategy-making to all employees [12]. The case study shows that different forms of participation, i.e., commenting, evaluating, or merely submitting ideas, generate divergent effects on employees' engagement with the company, with the first two making a positive contribution, but not the latter.

Other lines of research, e.g., [13], elaborate on the impact of the organization's characteristics on the implementation of OS. The double case study in [13] illustrates how a centralized organization tends to limit inclusion and transparency vs. a more decentralized organization.

Other research investigates OS across time, i.e, during different phases. Research suggests that during the exploration of new products or markets, OS is more attractive than during the later phases in a product cycle [14]. In addition, [15] and [16] highlight that also within the strategy process temporal effects exist: Organizations might do better by opening up strategy-making during the generation of ideas for new strategies than during the subsequent selection of new strategies.

There are social network connections among stakeholders and between the organization and its stakeholders. Four themes related to the intersection between network research and OS are identified in [17], leading to the following advantages of the network perspective when studying OS: First, it is possible to move toward a more relational understanding. Second, the availability of data in IT-based initiatives in OS provides opportunities to apply quantitative methods. Third, it could enable multilevel research. Finally, network analysis can be highly appropriate for studying the outcomes of increased openness.

While OS is associated with a wide range of beneficial outcomes, trade-offs exist [18]. E.g., the possibility of obtaining better-performing strategies is reported as a benefit in [11], while there is a risk of loss of commitment among participants when expectations about the impact of contributions remain unmet [19]. Long term studies on how better-performing strategies emerge are, however, still missing.

III. Model Description

The purpose of the model is to investigate how the number of participants and the level of complexity of the environment affects an organization's performance in an OS approach.

The strategy-making process is simulated in the *Open Strategy as a Practice* framework introduced in [10]. The three main components of the framework are a) the practitioners representing the people making strategy, b) the praxis component standing for what happens in an iterative process with the episodes taking place in a certain organizational context, and finally c) the set of practices representing the tools and mechanisms used to develop a strategy. When strategy-making is open, the set of practitioners includes stakeholders along with the firm's upper echelon, some types of voting mechanisms are typically part of the practices, and the praxis is transparent by including feedback to the stakeholders involved.

The model features a single firm that seeks and implements high-performing strategies in an iterative manner. The firm may or may not choose to include stakeholders in the strategy-making process. It operates in a static, complex environment.

The firm is represented by its upper management and it is always included in the simulation as P_1 in the set of practitioners $\{P_j : j \in \{1,..,S\}\}$ where S is the total number of practitioners. In an OS setting, strategy-making also includes $S-1 \geq 1$ stakeholders from inside or outside the firm such as employees and customers. While this work studies the performance of strategies for the firm that are being discovered and implemented, all practitioners are assumed to gain a personal utility from these strategies and want to maximize their utility.

The praxis is modeled as a cyclic process in the order of months, where each episode $t \in \{1,..,T\}$ consists of phases as in [10]. Hautz [16] and references therein propose that in a strategy-making process, first comes generating a range of strategy ideas, next comes selecting the most appropriate one, followed by implementation. Mack and Szulanski [13] present case illustrations showing that a similar framework can describe reality. As in [4], we distinguish the following four phases in an episode: 1) preparation phase, 2) generation phase, 3) selection phase, and 4) implementation phase. Strategies are modeled as bitstrings $\mathbf{s} \in \{0,1\}^N$ consisting of N binary decisions $s_i,\ i \in \{1,..,N\}$. Parameter K signifies the number of interactions between decisions and can be considered as a proxy for how tightly departments within an organization are interwoven, thereby also shaping the complexity of the task environment [20].

In condensed form, the sequence of events is as follows (see Figure 1): The simulation runs for T episodes with the number of stakeholders S and the number of decision interactions K as independent variables. In each episode, 1) the simulation's environment is set up in the preparation phase, 2) the practitioners come up with ideas for a new strategy, and a preference aggregation mechanism distills these ideas to a shortlist in the generation phase, 3) the practitioners vote for the new strategy in the selection phase, and 4) the performance for the firm of the new strategy is recorded as the dependent variable depending on independent variables S and K, and choices made in the OS process such as the type of the aggregation mechanism used, in the implementation phase. The subsections below describe the four phases and the model in more detail.

A. Preparation Phase

The firm starts with a random current strategy $\mathbf{s}_{cur}$. The simulator (the simulation software is written in Python 3.7) also generates the practitioners' utilities of the strategies the firm might implement. Strategies are mapped to performances for practitioners P_j in *performance landscapes* $F_j : \{0,1\}^N \rightarrow [0,1]$ defined by the NK model [21]. I.e.,

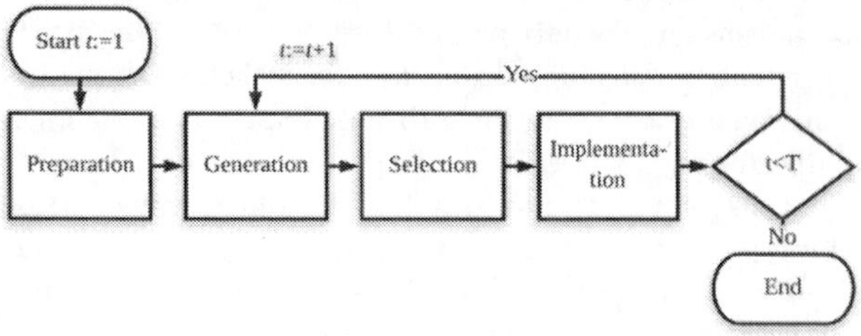

Fig. 1. Flow diagram of one simulation.

the strategies related to higher numerical values correspond to high-performing variants in the space of possibilities, and vice versa. A higher $K \in \{0, N-1\}$ leads to rugged, highly nonlinear performance landscapes with more local peaks, whereas a lower K gives rise to a smoother search space, see also [22].

As all practitioners including the firm are assumed to be correlated in their preferences toward strategies, the simulation generates random performance landscapes $F_j(\mathbf{s})$ with a pairwise correlation coefficient ρ in line with [23] (with a random interaction matrix). To account for the diversity in the pairwise correlations, the algorithm in [23] is extended to use a perturbed correlation matrix [24].

Evaluating strategies is not without error: Assuming limited cognitive capacity [25], practitioners' views of their landscapes are somewhat obfuscated. Hence, every time a practitioner P_j evaluates a strategy $\mathbf{s}$, the model adds a random error term ϵ from a Gaussian with mean 0 and standard deviation E_j:

$$\begin{aligned} F_j(\mathbf{s})' &= F_j(\mathbf{s}) + \epsilon, \\ \epsilon &\sim \mathcal{N}(0, E_j). \end{aligned} \tag{1}$$

We assume practitioners are diverse in their cognitive capacities. Consequently, at the start of a simulation, we draw random variables D_j, $j \in \{1, .., S\}$ from a Gaussian with mean 0 and standard deviation E and then take the absolute value of them to obtain the individualized E_j:

$$\begin{aligned} E_j &= |D_j|, \\ D_j &\sim \mathcal{N}(0, E). \end{aligned} \tag{2}$$

This phase takes place in episode $t = 1$ only, otherwise, the episode starts off with the generation phase directly.

B. Generation Phase

This phase generates a shortlist of L *candidates*; strategies that can be taken into consideration in the selection phase when practitioners vote for the firm's strategy in $t+1$. As the firm has a limited capacity for change in each episode, *appropriate* candidates $\mathbf{s}$ for $t+1$ do not differ in more than C decisions from $\mathbf{s}_{cur}$, i.e., they have a *Hamming distance* $d_H(\mathbf{s}, \mathbf{s}_{cur})$ of C decisions maximum, assuming $N > C$.

As the first step in this phase, each practitioner enters one idea from the set of appropriate candidates for the firm's new strategy in $t+1$ on a list of ideas. Entering ideas is modeled as follows: Practitioners observe the firm's current strategy $\mathbf{s}_{cur}$. Assuming limited cognitive capacity [25], each practitioner imagines a personal random subset of only Q strategies out of the set of appropriate candidates. They rank these Q strategies by evaluating them one by one in their performance landscapes. Every practitioner then enters their preferred strategy on the list of S ideas. Duplicates may occur.

As the second and last step in this phase, the preference aggregation mechanism *minisum approval voting* [26] distills these ideas into a shortlist of L candidates for the selection phase in this episode t. Let $\mathbf{s}$ be an appropriate candidate for the firm's strategy in $t+1$ and let $\mathbf{s}_j$ be P_j's idea. Then, the minisum score for $\mathbf{s}$ equals $\sum_{j=1}^{S} d_H(\mathbf{s}, \mathbf{s}_j)$, the sum of the Hamming distances between $\mathbf{s}$ and all $\mathbf{s}_j$. The candidates are ranked by score (candidates with the same score are ranked in random order) and the L lowest-ranked candidates win. As this algorithm takes the sum of distances, discontent from single practitioners with particular candidates may not influence the ranking. Therefore, minisum approval voting is a *utilitarian* preference aggregation mechanism.

C. Selection Phase

The shortlist of L candidates is extended by $\mathbf{s}_{cur}$. The practitioners evaluate the $L+1$ candidates and communicate their rankings to the *Borda count* voting rule from the set of practices [26]. Every time a practitioner ranks a candidate first, the candidate adds L scores to its total count. Every practitioner's second ranking rewards a candidate with $L-1$ scores, etc., with a last ranking giving zero scores. The winning candidate $\mathbf{s}_{new}$ is the candidate with the highest total count. If there are multiple candidates with the maximum total count, the simulation picks one at random.

D. Implementation Phase

The firm communicates $\mathbf{s}_{new}$ to its stakeholders and implements the strategy, thereby ending episode t. The model evaluates $\mathbf{s}_{new}$ in the firm's landscape and stores the result, relating time step t to performance $F_1(\mathbf{s}(t))$ as the dependent variable. If $t < T$, the simulation, skipping over the preparation phase, continues with the generation phase in $t+1$. The winning candidate $\mathbf{s}_{new}$ now has become $\mathbf{s}_{cur}$ in $t+1$.

IV. Results

The previous section presented features of the model that are relevant when considering the impact of multiple practitioners on strategy-making. The subsections below define the simulation setup and discuss the results.

A. Simulation Setup

Table I shows the variables used in the model. Starting with the control variables, we set $N = 10$ giving sufficient combinatorial richness while not putting too much demand on computational resources. The pairwise correlation coefficient ρ is set to the moderate positive value of 0.5. C, the maximum Hamming distance with the current strategy that makes a strategy a viable candidate, equals 2; while constraining the strategy updates in subsequent episodes to only 2 decisions, it still leaves plenty of choices for practitioners to imagine ideas as the set of appropriate candidates scales with the sum of Binomial coefficients $\binom{N}{k}$, with $k \in \{1, .., Q\}$. The number of ideas per practitioner Q is set to 2 due to the assumption of limited cognitive capacity [25]. The size L of the shortlist of candidates for selection is set to 3 as to not overburden voters in the selection phase. With $E = \frac{1}{16}$, the evaluation error E_j will average out to a small $\frac{E\sqrt{2}}{\sqrt{\pi}} \approx 0.05$ as the mean of the folded normal distribution with standard deviation E. The number of episodes T in a simulation is set to 100 as in all cases the results stabilize at this value.

The independent variables are K and S. The number of decision interactions K is varied to a moderate setting, i.e., 4 and a high setting, i.e., 7 for contrast. The number of practitioners S equals either 1, when strategy-making is exclusive for the firm as in a traditional Closed Strategy setting, and 10 or 100 when stakeholders are introduced in an OS setting.

The dependent variable $F_1(\mathbf{s}(t))$, the performance for the firm at time t, is recorded at the end of every episode from $t = 1$ to T with F_1 normalized to $[0, 1]$. To mitigate random effects, it was found sufficient to average the scenarios over 4000 simulation repetitions [27]. Confidence intervals over $F_1(\mathbf{s}(t))$ are calculated at 95%.

B. Simulation Results and Discussion

Figure 2 shows the performance of the firm $F_1(\mathbf{s}(t))$ over one hundred episodes at the moderate level of interactions $K = 4$. Included are results for $S = 1$, when strategy-making is restricted to the firm as the only practitioner involved in strategy development. When $S = 10$ or $S = 100$, strategy-making is opened up to include an additional nine, respectively, 99 practitioners, which are stakeholders of the firm. In $t = 1$, just one episode after starting with a random strategy, Figure 2 shows already a significant difference between performance at $S = 1$ or $S = 10$ on the one hand and $S = 100$ on the other. At $t = 5$, also the OS setting with ten practitioners starts outperforming the closed strategy-making. Over the entire range of episodes, $S = 100$ outperforms both $S = 10$ and $S = 1$.

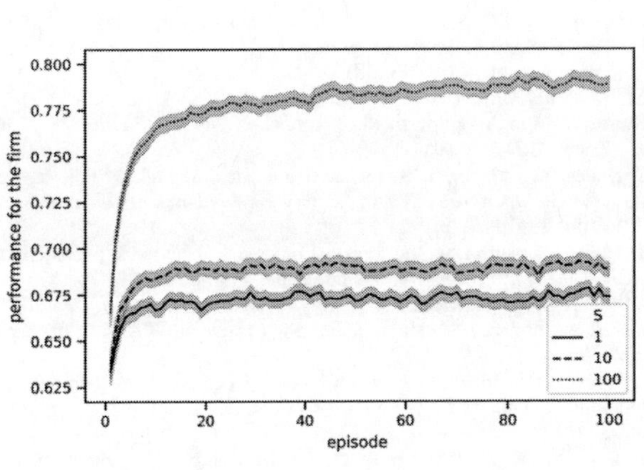

Fig. 2. Graph of performance for the firm over episodes at $K = 4$.

Figure 3 illustrates that when $K = 7$, the additional ruggedness of the landscapes produces lower performances for all values of S as it is more difficult to find peaks with high performing strategies for the firm. Still, $S = 100$ outperforms both $S = 1$ and $S = 10$. In contrast to $K = 4$, with $K = 7$, the OS setting with ten practitioners does not significantly outperform the Closed Strategy setting.

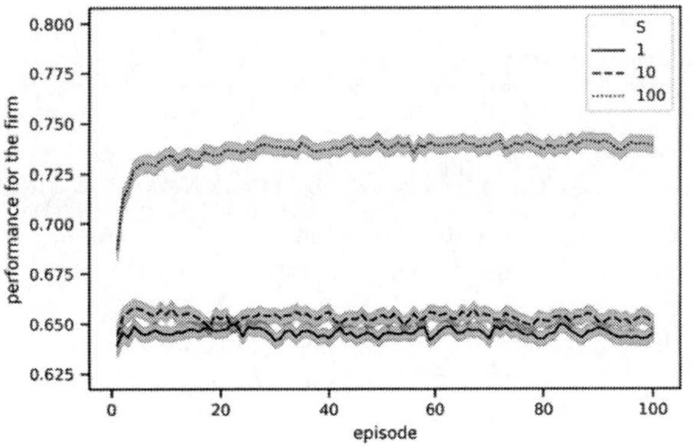

Fig. 3. Graph of performance for the firm over episodes at $K = 7$.

The results demonstrate that in our model the performance improves or is at least the same when opening up strategy-making for both $K = 4$ and $K = 7$, already in the initial episodes. This finding confirms the most frequently mentioned benefit of an OS approach: the discovery of better-performing strategies [4]. In a Closed Strategy setting, the firm has access to fewer ideas; access to a larger, diverse pool of ideas helps in exploring the landscape faster. In a sense, an OS approach gives a wider view, without needing to resort to uncertain big jumps in the searching process as in [20].

The result that with higher K the advantage of an OS approach for $S = 10$ seems to disappear can be explained as follows: The theory of the Wisdom of the Crowd states that in many discovery processes a group outperforms the individual, even if the single person is an expert [5]. Wisdom of the Crowd is especially effective when individual judgments cluster around the correct central value [28]. However, even when judgments among a wide group average to the central value, querying a small subset of the group can have a detrimental effect on the discovery of the correct value [29]. In our model, while the practitioners' performance landscapes are correlated, there is nothing that guarantees that the "central value" in the set of landscapes is the firm's landscape. Our findings suggest that when a landscape is very rugged, a small bias can have large effects, countering the advantage of the added number and diversity of ideas that an OS approach can bring. Sensitivity analysis with variations in ρ confirms the expectation that in ceteris paribus, a higher correlation among practitioners leads to higher performance.

TABLE I
VARIABLES

Classification	Symbol	Value/Range	Description
Control	N	10	The number of binary decisions in a strategy **s**.
	ρ	0.5	The average correlation coefficient between practitioners' performance landscapes.
	C	2	Maximum Hamming distance from the current strategy that makes a strategy an appropriate candidate.
	Q	2	The number of strategies practitioners can imagine in the generation phase.
	L	3	The size of the shortlist of candidates for the next episode's strategy.
	E_j	0.05	Standard deviation of practitioner's P_j evaluation error.
	E	0.0625	Standard deviation of each E_j.
	T	100	The number of episodes per simulation.
Independent	K	$\{4, 7\}$	The number of interactions between decisions.
	S	$\{1, 10, 100\}$	The number of practitioners.
Dependent	$F_1(\mathbf{s}(t))$	$[0, 1]$	Performance for the firm of strategy **s** at episode t.

V. Conclusion and Future Work

The results suggest that the often stated benefit of an OS approach, namely, the discovery of better-performing strategies [4], can indeed be obtained through preference aggregation of a diverse group of practitioners with minisum approval voting, even if voters' preferences are not 100% aligned with the firm's preference. Moreover, the results indicate that a larger group of practitioners ($S = 100$) outperforms a smaller group ($S = 10$) in organizations operating in both moderately ($K = 4$) and highly ($K = 7$) complex environments. With $K = 7$, when it is more difficult to navigate the firm's landscape, the advantage of OS, at least with a smaller number of participants, disappears due to the drawback of practitioners' preferences that are on average not necessarily 100% aligned with the firm's preference.

A limitation of our methodology is that external validation is hard, as data is difficult to obtain by empirical methods [30]. To focus on the core aspects of the research question, much complexity, such as communication between stakeholders, the effects of memory, and network effects, was eliminated that might capture critical aspects of reality. Additionally, this paper would benefit from sensitivity analysis over the control variables.

Future work can extend the model by including network effects among practitioners, strategic voting, and the consequences of voter dissatisfaction. Simulations could consider the effects of restricting the opening of strategy-making to specific phases in the strategy process or investigate the impact of temporal opening up depending on exploratory or exploitative demands in organizations' life cycles. Furthermore, egalitarian vs. utilitarian preference aggregation mechanisms [31] can be evaluated for their impact on the drawback of loss of commitment by dissatisfied practitioners [18]. Additional research can also investigate the apparent dilemma between the posed benefits of a broader range of ideas [32] (high diversity in preferences) and the requirement of low bias (low diversity) observed in this research.

References

[1] A. Tavakoli, D. Schlagwein, and D. Schoder, "Open strategy: Consolidated definition and processual conceptualization," in *2015 International Conference on Information Systems: Exploring the Information Frontier, ICIS 2015*. Association for Information Systems, 2015.

[2] R. Whittington, L. Cailluet, and B. Yakis-Douglas, "Opening strategy: Evolution of a precarious profession," *British Journal of Management*, vol. 22, no. 33, pp. 531–544, 2011.

[3] D. Seidl, G. Von Krogh, and R. Whittington, Eds., *Cambridge Handbook of Open Strategy*. Cambridge University Press, 7 2019.

[4] A. S. Sailer, D. Schlagwein, and D. Schoder, "Open Strategy: State of the Art Review and Research Agenda," *ICIS 2017: Transforming Society with Digital Innovation*, 2018.

[5] M. P. Silverman, "The Wisdom of Crowds." *American Journal of Physics*, vol. 75, no. 2, pp. 190–192, 2007.

[6] S. Leitner and F. Wall, "Simulation-based research in management accounting and control: an illustrative overview," *Journal of Management Control*, vol. 26, no. 2-3, pp. 105–129, 2015.

[7] S. Leitner and D. A. Behrens, "On the efficiency of hurdle rate-based coordination mechanisms," *Mathematical and Computer Modelling of Dynamical Systems*, vol. 21, no. 5, pp. 413–431, 2015. [Online]. Available: http://dx.doi.org/10.1080/13873954.2014.973885

[8] J. M. Epstein, "Agent-based computational models and generative social science," *Complexity*, vol. 4, no. 5, pp. 41–60, 1999.

[9] R. Whittington, "Strategy as Practice Mapping the Terrain," *Long Range Planning*, vol. 29, no. 5, pp. 731–735, 1996.

[10] A. Tavakoli, D. Schlagwein, and D. Schoder, "Open strategy: Literature review, re-analysis of cases and conceptualisation as a practice," *Journal of Strategic Information Systems*, vol. 26, no. 3, pp. 163–184, 2017.

[11] A. Malhotra, A. Majchrzak, and R. M. Niemiec, "Using Public Crowds for Open Strategy Formulation: Mitigating the Risks of Knowledge Gaps," *Long Range Planning*, vol. 50, no. 3, pp. 397–410, 2017.

[12] K. Hutter, B. A. Nketia, and J. Füller, "Falling Short with Participation — Different Effects of Ideation, Commenting, and Evaluating Behavior on Open Strategizing," *Long Range Planning*, vol. 50, no. 3, pp. 355–370, 2017.

[13] D. Z. Mack and G. Szulanski, "Opening Up: How Centralization Affects Participation and Inclusion in Strategy Making," *Long Range Planning*, vol. 50, no. 3, pp. 385–396, 2017.

[14] M. M. Appleyard and H. W. Chesbrough, "The Dynamics of Open Strategy: From Adoption to Reversion," *Long Range Planning*, vol. 50, no. 3, pp. 310–321, 2017.

[15] J. Hautz, K. Matzler, J. Sutter, K. Hutter, and J. Füller, "Practices of Inclusion in Open Strategy," in *Cambridge Handbook of Open Strategy*, 2019, pp. 87–105.

[16] J. Hautz, "Opening up the strategy process – a network perspective," *Management Decision*, vol. 55, no. 9, pp. 1956–1983, 2017.

[17] ——, "A Social Network Perspective on Open Strategy," in *Cambridge Handbook of Open Strategy*. Cambridge University Press, 7 2019, pp. 272–288.

[18] J. Hautz, D. Seidl, and R. Whittington, "Open Strategy: Dimensions, Dilemmas, Dynamics," *Long Range Planning*, vol. 50, no. 3, pp. 298–309, 2017.

[19] J. Baptista, A. D. Wilson, R. D. Galliers, and S. Bynghall, "Social Media and the Emergence of Reflexiveness as a New Capability for Open Strategy," *Long Range Planning*, 2017.

[20] D. A. Levinthal, "Adaptation on rugged landscapes," *Management Science*, vol. 43, no. 7, pp. 934–950, 1997.

[21] S. A. Kauffman and E. D. Weinberger, "The NK model of rugged fitness landscapes and its application to maturation of the immune response," *Journal of Theoretical Biology*, vol. 141, no. 2, pp. 211–245, 1989.

[22] F. A. Csaszar, "A note on how NK landscapes work," *Journal of Organization Design*, vol. 7, no. 1, p. 15, 2018.

[23] S. Verel, A. Liefooghe, L. Jourdan, and C. Dhaenens, "On the structure of multiobjective combinatorial search space: MNK-landscapes with correlated objectives," *European Journal of Operational Research*, vol. 227, no. 2, pp. 331–342, 2013.

[24] G. Marsaglia and I. Olkin, "Generating Correlation Matrices," *SIAM Journal on Scientific and Statistical Computing*, vol. 5, no. 2, pp. 470–475, 1984.

[25] H. A. Simon, "A Behavioral Model of Rational Choice Author (s): Herbert A . Simon Published by : Oxford University Press," *The Quarterly Journal of Economics*, vol. 69, no. 1, pp. 99–118, 1955.

[26] F. Brandt, V. Conitzer, U. Endriss, J. Lang, and A. D. Procaccia, Eds., *Handbook of computational social choice*. Cambridge University Press, 2016.

[27] I. Lorscheid, B. O. Heine, and M. Meyer, "Opening the 'Black Box' of Simulations: Increased Transparency and Effective Communication Through the Systematic Design of Experiments," *Computational and Mathematical Organization Theory*, vol. 18, no. 1, pp. 22–62, 2012.

[28] A. Lyon and E. Pacuit, "The Wisdom of Crowds: Methods of Human Judgement Aggregation." in *Handbook of Human Computation*, P. Michelucci, Ed. Springer, 2013, pp. 599–614.

[29] F. A. Csaszar, "Limits to the wisdom of the crowd in idea selection," *Advances in Strategic Management*, vol. 40, pp. 275–297, 2018.

[30] J. P. Davis, K. M. Eisenhardt, and C. B. Bingham, "Developing theory through simulation methods," *Academy of Management Review*, vol. 32, no. 2, pp. 480–499, 2007.

[31] D. Baumeister and S. Dennisen, "Voter dissatisfaction in committee elections," in *Proceedings of the International Joint Conference on Autonomous Agents and Multiagent Systems, AAMAS*, vol. 3, 2015, pp. 1707–1708.

[32] H. W. Chesbrough and M. M. Appleyard, "Open innovation and strategy," *California Management Review*, vol. 50, no. 1, pp. 57–76, 2007.

A Recurrent Neural Network for the Detection of Structure in Methylation Levels along Human Chromosomes

Wim De Mulder, Rafel Riudavets, Martin Kuiper

Norwegian University of Science and Technology
Trondheim, Norway
Emails: wim.demulder@kuleuven.be, rafelriudavets@gmail.com, kuiper@ntnu.no

***Abstract*—Recurrent Neural Networks (RNN) have been used in multiple tasks such as speech recognition, music composition and protein homology detection. In particular, they have shown superior performance in predicting structure in time series data. To our knowledge, RNN have not been used on DNA methylation data. Methylation patterns on chromosomal DNA represent an important form of epigenetic imprinting, a form of epigenetics that results in heritable gene expression and phenotype changes. DNA methylation is one of the mechanisms that a cell uses to fine-tune the expression levels of its individual genes, and it has been shown to affect very specific areas around specific genes. The methylation state of the human chromosomal DNA can be readily assessed with microarray technology, allowing the determination of the methylation status of thousands of positions along the individual chromosomes of the genome. With RNN analysis, we show that these methylation patterns have substantial structure, when relatively large stretches of chromosomes are tested. Furthermore, we show that each chromosome appears to have its own distinctive sequential methylation structure, but that this structure breaks down, to some extent, when normal cells develop into a tumour.**

Keywords*–*Recurrent neural networks; Nash-Sutcliffe efficiency; Epigenetics.

I. INTRODUCTION

A. Biological background to the research problem

Methylation of cytosine residues in DNA represents an important form of epigenetic modification [1]. Although an organism's form and function is based on its genome, characterized by a specific DNA sequence, the epigenetic state of the genome adds an important regulatory component to how specific genes in the genome are expressed and together define an organisms' phenotype, and it is a heritable trait [2]. Epigenetic modifications are not encoded by the nucleotide sequence of the genome [3], but by small modifications in the form of methyl groups or hydroxymethyl groups that are attached either to cytosine residues that are part of so-called CpG stretches ('CpG islands') within the DNA sequence, or to proteins that are bound to the DNA, together forming the biologically active form of DNA called chromatin [4]. The epigenetic state of the chromatin has a considerable plasticity, allowing a cell to adapt to new environmental challenges and demands. DNA methylation can for instance regulate gene expression by recruiting proteins involved in gene repression or by inhibiting the binding of one or more transcription factors to DNA [5]. The epigenetic state, however, is also prone to malfunctions that can result in diseases. Cancer cells represent an important cellular malfunction where among others the methylation state of the chromosomal DNA is affected [6].

A popular technique for determining the methylation status across the genome uses microarray-based Illumina Infinium methylation assays [7]. DNA is denatured (i.e., converted to single strands) and treated with sodium bisulfite, which deaminates the normal, unmethylated cytosine residues and effectively converts them to uracil, while methylated cytosine residues are resistant to this treatment [8]. To estimate the methylation status at a specific CpG site of a chromosome, the Illumina Infinium assay utilizes a pair of DNA probes that can distinguish between sequences with the native cytosine and the converted uracil. Illumina's primer-extension assay measures the intensities of methylated and unmethylated forms (alleles) of individual sites of the genome and the methylation level is calculated based on the signals of this pair of probes. It is convenient to express the methylation level as a value ranging from 0 to 1, referred to as the beta value, and which can be interpreted as the percentage of methylation [9]. Beta values are typically low, as illustrated by the histogram shown in Fig. 1. This histogram is taken from [9] and represents a typical sample measured by the Illumina Infinium HumanMethylation27 BeadChip, which interrogates 27,578 CpG sites where methylation primarily occurs [10].

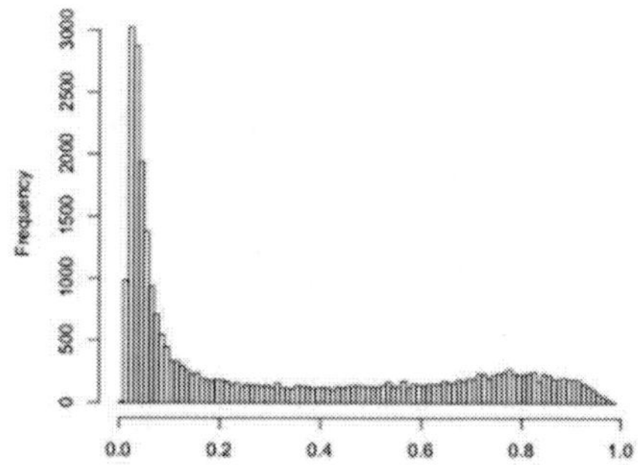

Figure 1. A histogram of beta values (from [9]).

B. Goal and organization of this paper

The methylation levels along a given chromosome have similarities to a time series, where the role of time is substituted by the location of the probes with respect to the DNA. However, whereas time series data are often equidistant, the measurement of methylation sites across a chromosome relies on assays using probes that are designed based on very specific local DNA sequence characteristics (is there a gene? is there a CpG island close to the gene?), resulting in a much more irregular distribution of measured points. The research question we consider here is whether there is still some structure in the sequence of beta values that correspond to probes of which the methylation level is consecutively measured along a given chromosome. Given the fact that the probes are not equidistantly located and that methylation levels arise as the result of complex biological processes, it is not clear whether one should expect some predictable structure to begin with. Fig. 2 shows the beta values of 500 consecutive probes that were collected from a randomly chosen chromosome of some patient that was arbitrarily selected from our data set. The apparently erratic pattern in the figure makes it clear that the human eye alone is not advanced enough to answer our research question. We will, therefore, rely on recurrent neural networks in investigating this research topic. More concretely, we set out to analyze whether recurrent neural networks detect structure among a stretch of consecutive methylation sites and use it to predict the next beta value adjacent to that stretch. If so, this would show that structure is present.

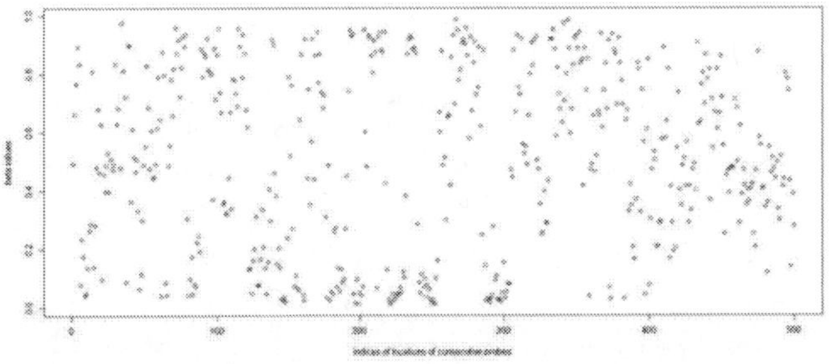

Figure 2. Sample of beta values corresponding to 500 consecutive probes from a randomly chosen chromosome and patient.

RNNs have previously been applied to DNA modification data with various objectives. In [11], the authors built a model combining DNA sequence together with DNA methylation in order to predict missing values in methylation data. The CpG module of the joint model uses a RNN in order to account for correlations between neighbouring CpG sites within and across different cells. Another study from [12] aimed at predicting DNA modifications such as DNA methylation based on training a RNN on raw electric data. In this work we considered DNA methylation events as a time series, where we tested whether methylation events of a position in the DNA are associated to methylation events in its neighbourhood.

The paper is organized as follows. In Section II we provide a brief introduction to recurrent neural networks, and we explain how examples, to be fed into the network, are typically constructed from a sequence of observations. Section III describes the experimental details, which include: 1. the description of the data set, 2. the set of recurrent neural network architectures that are tried on the data set, 3. the construction of training, validation and test sets from the data set, and 4. the performance measures that are used in evaluating the different recurrent neural network architectures. Results are described in Section IV. We first show how a suitable architecture is chosen from the set of considered architectures, and this architecture is then used when addressing the research question. In addition to an RNN performance analysis, we have conducted some additional analyses that are interesting from a biological perspective. Section V concludes the paper.

II. Methods

A. Background on recurrent neural networks

We employ artificial neural networks, more specifically RNNs, to detect structure, if any, in vectors of beta values representing consecutively measured probes. RNNs have shown to achieve state-of-the-art results in many applications with time series or sequential data [13], and enjoy several nice properties such as strong prediction performance as well as the ability to capture long-term temporal dependencies [14]. The distinctive feature of an RNN is that the output of the hidden layer is not only a function of the input at the current iteration, such as in feedforward neural networks, but also of the output of the previous iteration. In fact, since the hidden layer in RNNs takes the output of a previous iteration into account, it takes the output of *all* previous iterations into account, since the output at iteration n depends on the output at iteration $n-1$, which in turn depends on the output at iteration $n-2$, etc. The importance of this feedback loop is that it assigns RNNs a 'memory'. This makes RNNs ideally suited to be used in applications where all information contained in a sequence of values is of potential use to predict the value that comes next. For further details on recurrent neural networks, we refer to [15].

B. Construction of examples

The purpose of a recurrent neural network is often, as in our work here, to find structure in a data set D that consists of an ordered sequence of values $a_1, \ldots, a_n$. A recurrent neural network will learn this structure from given examples. A common procedure to extract examples from D is to consider a subsequence containing a predefined number of values as input, after which this subsequence is shifted by one position to be used as corresponding output. This algorithm is performed over all possible subsequences to obtain the complete set of examples. The predefined number of consecutive values that is used as input is referred to as the window size w. For example, if $w = 3$, then the first three examples $(\mathbf{x}_1, \mathbf{y}_1), (\mathbf{x}_2, \mathbf{y}_2), (\mathbf{x}_3, \mathbf{y}_3)$ extracted from D are given by

$$\begin{aligned} \mathbf{x}_1 &= (a_1, a_2, a_3) \\ \mathbf{y}_1 &= (a_2, a_3, a_4) \\ \mathbf{x}_2 &= (a_4, a_5, a_6) \\ \mathbf{y}_2 &= (a_5, a_6, a_7) \\ \mathbf{x}_3 &= (a_7, a_8, a_9) \\ \mathbf{y}_3 &= (a_8, a_9, a_{10}) \end{aligned}$$

Notice that the examples depend on the window size and that, by construction, the number of input neurons and the number of output neurons both equal the window size.

III. Experimental details

A. Data set

The data set we consider is collected from the Cancer Genome Atlas [16]. More specifically, the data set was produced in the project named TCGA-BRCA [17], which studies

Breast Invasive Carcinoma, and we downloaded it using the TCGAbiolinks R package [18] (version 2.8.4). We selected the samples mapped to the GRCh38 reference genome that had been assessed with the Illumina Human Methylation 450k platform.

For our purpose, it is especially relevant that this data set contains beta values for 24 chromosomes (22 non sex chromosomes plus X and Y chromosome) for 1095 patients in 2 conditions (normal and tumor). However, we do not consider the Y chromosome, since the data set contains only a very few beta values for this chromosome. Furthermore, due to missing data, it turns out that only for 96 patients data is available for normal tissue condition, whereas there is data for 782 patient tumors. To limit computation time, we consider the 96 patients in normal condition and the first 96 patients in tumor condition. Some additional experimental analysis has shown us that this number of patients is large enough to obtain stable results (see also Section IV-B). Thus the data set to be analyzed consists of beta values for 23 chromosomes in 96 patients in normal condition and 96 patients in tumor condition. On average, the data set contains about 17 000 measured beta values per chromosome.

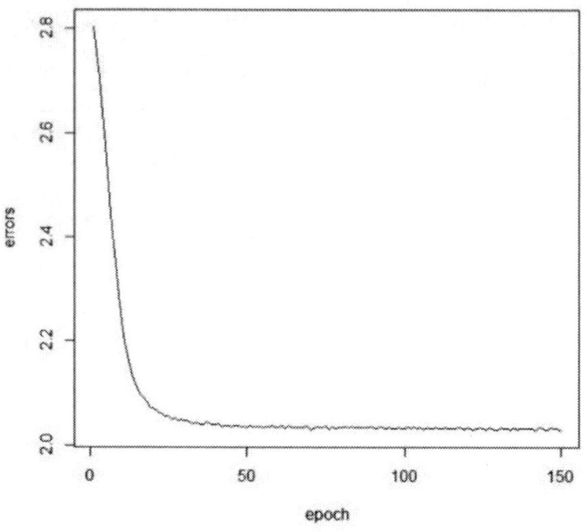

Figure 3. Evolution of the error of a RNN over 150 epochs on some set of examples

B. *Set of RNN architectures*

The parameters of a RNN that need to be given a value by the user are the number of iterations (also called epochs), the window size w and the number of hidden neurons n_h.

The number of epochs should be chosen low enough to limit computation time, but also large enough to ensure convergence of the weights of the RNN. We have performed a concise preliminary analysis on several sets of examples, running a RNN for 150 epochs and computing the error between real output values and values generated at the output neurons. The analysis showed that 40 epochs is sufficient to reach convergence, as all graphs are very similar to the one shown in Fig. 3, which represents the error over the 150 epochs corresponding to one of these experiments. Consequently, all RNNs are run for 40 epochs.

We consider RNNs with the following window sizes:

$$W = \{10, 30, 50, 70, 90\}$$

To determine suitable choices of numbers of hidden neurons, we can rely on some heuristics. One heuristic is to choose n_h as 2/3 of the sum of the number of input neurons and the number of output neurons [19]. Since the number of input neurons equals the number of output neurons, which in turn equals the window size, we try as number of hidden neurons at least

$$n_{h_1} = \text{round}(2/3 \times 2 \times w)$$

where *round* refers to rounding to the nearest integer. We also try several values that are close to the above value n_{h_1}, namely:

$$\begin{aligned} n_{h_2} &= \text{round}(0.9 \times n_{h_1}) \\ n_{h_3} &= \text{round}(0.8 \times n_{h_1}) \\ n_{h_4} &= \text{round}(1.1 \times n_{h_1}) \\ n_{h_5} &= \text{round}(1.2 \times n_{h_1}) \end{aligned}$$

Finally, we also try n_h as 2/3 of the number of input neurons, since some authors claim that the number of hidden neurons should be between the size of the input layer and the size of the output layer [20], and this heuristic restriction is not fulfilled by any of the number of hidden neurons already chosen (they are all larger than the size of the input layer, and thus also larger than the size of the output layer). We denote this value by n_{h_6}:

$$n_{h_6} = \text{round}(2/3 \times w)$$

This gives the following set of numbers of hidden neurons that we will consider:

$$N_h = \{n_{h_1}, n_{h_2}, n_{h_3}, n_{h_4}, n_{h_5}, n_{h_6}\}$$

Thus, in total we consider $|W| \times |N_h| = 5 \times 6 = 30$ different RNN architectures (the notation $|A|$ for a finite set A refers to the number of its elements).

C. *Training, validation and test sets*

For each combination of patient, condition and chromosome, we train a separate RNN. A first motivation for this is that the beta values on a specific chromosome of a particular patient in a given condition can have its own characteristics; that is, the distribution of these beta values can be significantly different from the other distributions. Secondly, obtaining different RNNs allows to compare results with respect to the patients, the chromosome and the condition. Finally, since the number of given beta values per chromosome is very large (as mentioned above, there are on average some 17 000 measured beta values for each individual chromosome), each RNN will still have enough examples to learn from.

The beta values for each triplet of the form (patient, chromosome, condition) are converted into examples according to the method described in Section II-B. Each set of examples is then split into a training set, a validation set and a test set, as follows: the first 60% of the examples are used as training examples, the next 20% as validation examples, and the last 20% as test examples. The training set is used to train the selected RNN architectures described in Section III-B for each (patient, chromosome, condition) triplet, the validation set is used to select the best RNN architecture, and the test set allows to evaluate the performance of the selected architecture on the task of detecting structure in the sequences of beta values.

D. *Performance measures to evaluate RNNs*

To evaluate the performance of an architecture on a given test set containing the examples $(\mathbf{x}_1, \mathbf{y}_1), \ldots, (\mathbf{x}_m, \mathbf{y}_m)$, where $\mathbf{x}_i$ and $\mathbf{y}_i$ refer to input vectors and output vectors, respectively, we will use several performance measures. These measures all evaluate performance in terms of the difference between the real outputs $\mathbf{y}_1, \ldots, \mathbf{y}_m$, and the outputs $\hat{\mathbf{y}}_1, \ldots, \hat{\mathbf{y}}_m$, generated by the considered RNN. We will use the notation $\mathbf{y}_k(i)$ to refer to the ith component of $\mathbf{y}_k$. By construction it holds that $\mathbf{y}_k(i) = \mathbf{x}_k(i+1)$ for $1 \leq i < w$ (see Section II-B). Therefore, all output components, except for the last one (given by $\mathbf{y}_k(w)$), are also components of the input vector. The consequence is that evaluation in terms of the difference between *all* true and estimated output values might result in a biased view on performance, so we also evaluate performance by restricting to the last output component. For each considered performance measure P we therefore have a first version that evaluates performance by comparing $\mathbf{y}_1(1), \ldots, \mathbf{y}_1(w), \ldots, \mathbf{y}_m(1), \ldots, \mathbf{y}_m(w)$ to $\hat{\mathbf{y}}_1(1), \ldots, \hat{\mathbf{y}}_1(w), \ldots, \hat{\mathbf{y}}_m(1), \ldots, \hat{\mathbf{y}}_m(w)$, and we denote this instance of the performance measure by P_a. But we also consider a second version P_b where the values $\mathbf{y}_1(w), \ldots, \mathbf{y}_m(w)$ are compared to the estimated values $\hat{\mathbf{y}}_1(w), \ldots, \hat{\mathbf{y}}_m(w)$.

We use the following performance measures: Root Mean Square Error (RMSE), Nash-Sutcliffe efficiency (NSE) and Index of Agreement (IA). All measures P are described below in their P_a version; the P_b counterpart is simply obtained by restricting the output values to the one corresponding to the last component.

The RMSE is given by

$$RMSE_a = \sqrt{\sum_{k=1}^{m}\sum_{i=1}^{w} \frac{(\mathbf{y}_k(i) - \hat{\mathbf{y}}_k(i))^2}{mw}}$$

It is clear that the lower the RMSE, the better the network.

The NSE, proposed in [21], is given by

$$NSE_a = 1 - \frac{\sum_{k=1}^{m}\sum_{i=1}^{w}\Big(\mathbf{y}_k(i) - \hat{\mathbf{y}}_k(i)\Big)^2}{\sum_{k=1}^{m}\sum_{i=1}^{w}\Big(\mathbf{y}_k(i) - \overline{\mathbf{y}}\Big)^2}$$

where $\overline{\mathbf{y}}$ refers to the average of all $\mathbf{y}_k(i)$ values. The NSE lies between -∞ and 1.0, where 1 denotes perfect fit. An NSE lower than zero indicates that the simple average $\overline{\mathbf{y}}$ is a better predictor than the obtained approximations $\hat{\mathbf{y}}_k(i)$.

The IA was proposed in [22], and is defined as:

$$IA_a = 1 - \frac{\sum_{k=1}^{m}\sum_{i=1}^{w}\Big(\mathbf{y}_k(i) - \hat{\mathbf{y}}_k(i)\Big)^2}{\sum_{k=1}^{m}\sum_{i=1}^{w}\Big(|\hat{\mathbf{y}}_k(i) - \overline{\mathbf{y}}| + |\mathbf{y}_k(i) - \overline{\mathbf{y}}|\Big)^2}$$

The range of the IA is $[0, 1]$. The higher the value, the better the model, with 1 denoting perfect fit.

IV. RESULTS

A. *Application to a small subset of patients*

Since each triplet (patient, chromosome, condition) is associated with a different data set, there are in total $96 \times 23 \times 2 = 4416$ individual data sets. Ideally, each of these data sets is modeled by the RNN architecture that is most suitable to this specific data structure. To find the best architecture among the selected set of 30 architectures (cf. Section III-B) would require the training of $4416 \times 30 = 132\,480$ RNNs, a prohibitive task in terms of computation time. Therefore, we select the first five patients in normal condition and the first five patients in tumor condition, and train each of the considered architectures only on these patients. In Section IV-B we analyze the performance of the trained networks on the validation sets related to this subsample of patients, and check if there exists one specific architecture that is suitable for the whole subsample. It is then hypothesized that this single architecture will also perform well for all 96 patients in both conditions. The application of this architecture to all patients is performed in Section IV-C. To compare architectures on the subsample of validation sets, in order to find a single suitable one, we only use $RMSE_a$, described in Section III-D. The complete set of performance measures will be used in Section IV-C, where we evaluate the architecture that is presumably suitable for all patients.

B. *Choice of a suitable recurrent neural network architecture*

As outlined in the previous section, we trained the 30 selected RNN architectures on each of the 23 chromosomes on a patient subsample consisting of five normal and five tumor conditions. This implies that each architecture is trained on $23 \times 5 \times 2 = 230$ individual data sets (23 chromosomes, five patients, two conditions). One possible way to compare the performance of the different architectures, is to plot the lowest, the highest and the average $RMSE_a$, over the selected ten different patient conditions and over the chromosomes, and this for each architecture. The result is shown in Fig. 4, where the X-axis denotes the architectures; for example, 50_5 refers to the architecture with $w = 50$ and $n_h = n_{h_5}$. The following observations can be drawn:

- Low window sizes, up to and including 50, perform better than higher window sizes, at least in terms of the average and the highest RMSE (the lowest RMSE is more or less the same for all architectures).
- For all window sizes that are 50 or smaller, the choice of the number of hidden neurons has no effect on the performance.

Another way to evaluate the different architectures is to record the number of times that a given architecture performs best, i.e. the number of times that it has lowest RMSE, and that a given architecture performs worst, i.e. that it has the highest RMSE, and this over all (patient, chromosome, condition) triplets from the subsample. Experiments in this respect show that the first architecture, with $w = 10$ and $n_h = n_{h_1} = 7$, performs best in most cases.

Based on these findings, we decide to use the architecture ($w = 10, n_h = 7$) as the overall best architecture. We will use this architecture in the next section to analyze the complete data set. Since the best architecture happens to be the one with smallest window size among the selected set of window sizes

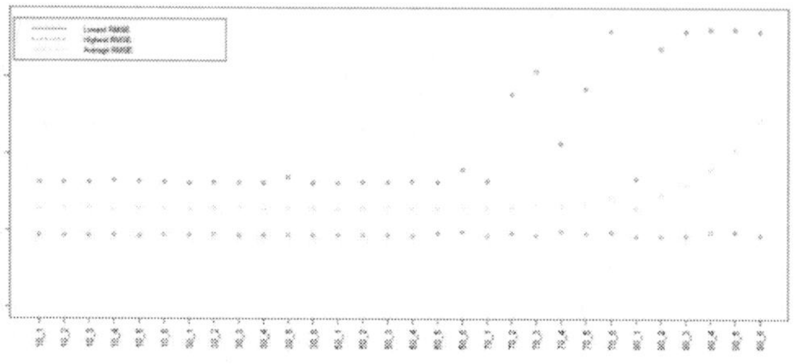

Figure 4. Lowest, highest and average RMSE over the selected patients and over the chromosomes, and this for each architecture

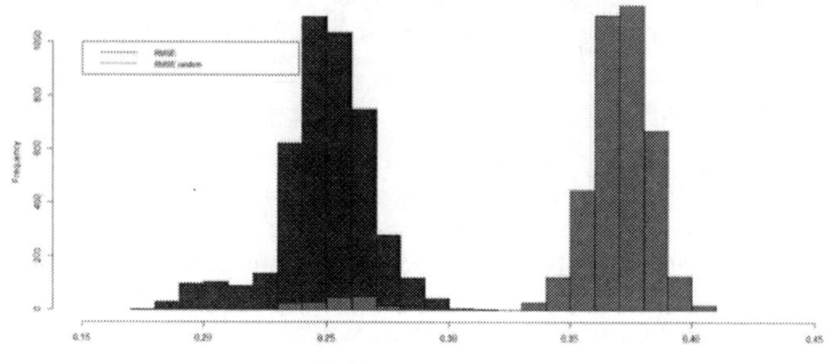

Figure 5. $RMSE_a$

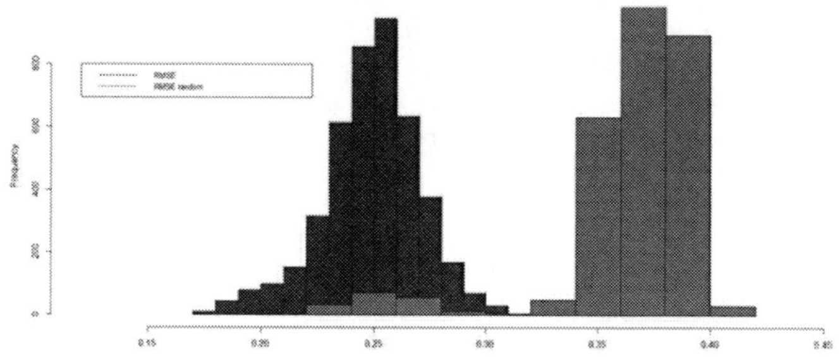

Figure 6. $RMSE_b$

W (which has as smallest element ten), one might wonder if even smaller window sizes perform better. Therefore, we also tried window size five, with varying numbers of hidden neurons, and performed several experiments. However, the obtained results were very similar to the results for window size ten. Therefore, we restrict attention to the $(w = 10, n_h = 7)$ architecture, the results of which are outlined in the next section.

Although our subsample of ten patients is small, we applied the $(w = 10, n_h = 7)$ architecture on the associated subsample of test sets to obtain some preliminary results. However, since this architecture was also applied to the much larger set of 96 patients, and since the results on the corresponding test sets turned out to be very similar to those obtained on the small subsample, we discuss the results only for the large set of 96 patients (cf. next section). The fact that the results for the small subsample and for the large set are similar indicate that the set of 96 patients is large enough to safely assume that the obtained outcomes are significant.

C. Application to all patients

We now evaluate the $(w = 10, n_h = 7)$ architecture on the set of 96 patients in tumor condition and in normal condition. Evaluation is done by training this architecture on each of the $96 \times 23 \times 2 = 4416$ corresponding training sets, and then measuring the performance on the associated test sets using the measures described in Section III-D. As a benchmark, performance is also evaluated with respect to a random permutation of the training sets.

The results are shown in Figs. 5-10. Each figure contains one of the two versions of each of the performance measures P (the version being P_a or P_b, cf. Section III-D). Furthermore, each figure contains two histograms of values of P: one that relates to performance on the test sets after training has been performed on the original training sets, and one where training has been done on a random permutation of the training sets. The figures indicate the following:

- There is a substantial difference between the results related to the permutated training sets and the non-permutated ones. The important implication is that the beta values along a chromosome are non randomly distributed. There is structure in a given sequence of consecutively measured beta values, and recurrent neural networks are able to detect this structure, at least to some extent.

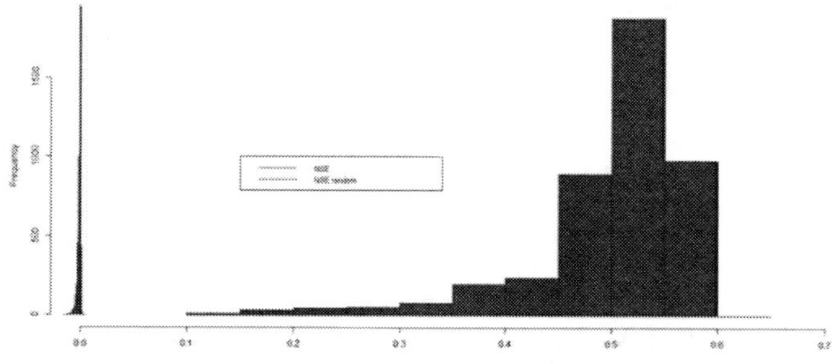

Figure 7. NSE_a

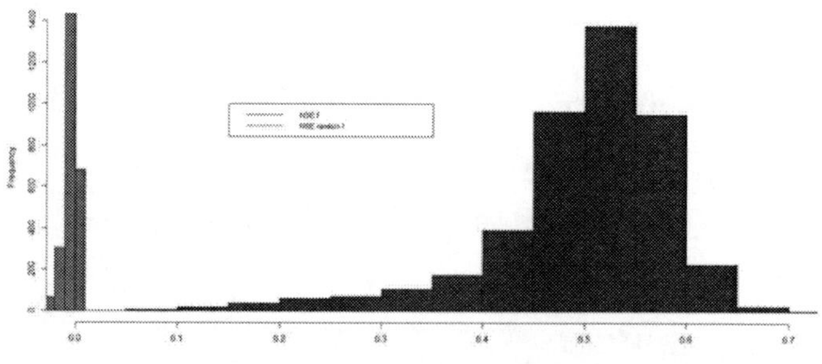

Figure 8. NSE_b

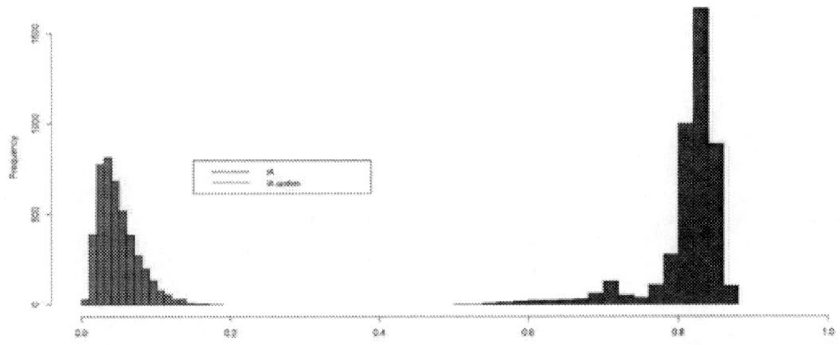

Figure 9. IA_a

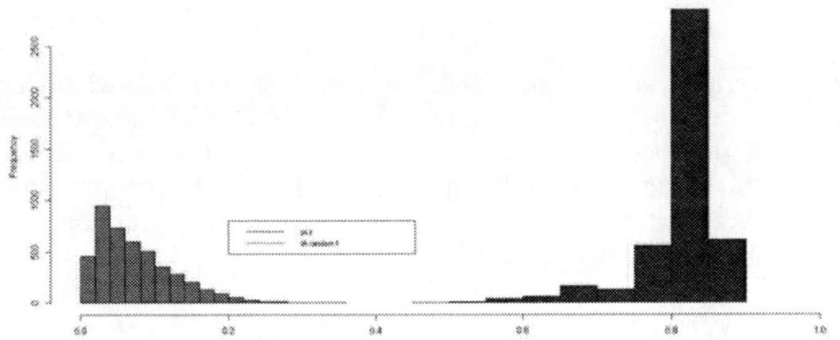

Figure 10. IA_b

- There do not exist theoretically derived thresholds on the values of each of the performance measures to demarcate good and bad models. However, it seems justified to conclude that the values of the performance measures related to the non permutated training sets are acceptable or even very good. Especially the IA attains very high values, with most values higher than 0.8.
- As expected, the P_b version of the performance measures (which takes only the last output component into account) has worse values than its P_a counterpart (taking all output components into account). However, the histograms of both versions are not substantially different (roughly speaking, the histograms of P_b appear to be shifted to the right over only a small distance), implying that the recurrent neural network performs still reasonably well when evaluation is limited to the last output component, i.e. the only component that is truly predicted.

V. Conclusion

In this paper, we have shown the applicability of recurrent neural network analysis for the detection of structure in sequences of measured methylation levels along human chromosomes. The considered task is inherently challenging, due to the fact that a specific methylation value is the result of complex biological processes and because probes where measurements are collected are not equidistantly located. Nevertheless, our work demonstrates that structure is present in sequences of methylation levels, and that recurrent neural networks are able to detect this structure. The obtained results are relevant to both the machine learning and the biological community.

References

[1] P. Jones and D. Takai, "The Role of DNA Methylation in Mammalian Epigenetics," Science, vol. 293, 2001, pp. 1068–1070.

[2] T. Atkinson and M. Halfon, "Regulation of Gene Expression in the Genomic Context," Computational and Structural Biotechnology Journal, vol. 9, 2014, p. e201401001.

[3] B. Jin, Y. Li, and K. Robertson, "DNA Methylation: Superior or Subordinate in the Epigenetic Hierarchy?" Genes Cancer, vol. 2, 2011, pp. 607–617.

[4] E. Greer and Y. Shi, "Histone Methylation: a Dynamic Mark in Health, Disease and Inheritance," Nature Reviews Genetics, vol. 13, 2012, pp. 343–357.

[5] L. Moore, T. Le, and G. Fan, "DNA Methylation and its Basic Function," Neuropsychopharmacology, vol. 1, 2013, pp. 23–38.

[6] M. Eirlich, "DNA Methylation in Cancer: Too Much, but also Too Little," Oncogene, vol. 21, 2002, pp. 5400–5413.

[7] C. Thirlwell et al., "Genome-wide DNA Methylation Analysis of Archival Formalin-fixed Paraffin-embedded Tissue Using the Illumina Infinium HumanMethylation27 BeadChip," BMC Bioinformatics, vol. 52, 2010, pp. 248–254.

[8] M. Frommer et al., "A Genomic Sequencing Protocol that Yields a Positive Display of 5-methylcytosine Residues in Individual DNA Strands," BMC Bioinformatics, vol. 89, 1992, pp. 1827–1831.

[9] P. Du et al., "Comparison of Beta-value and M-value Methods for Quantifying Methylation Levels by Microarray Analysis," BMC Bioinformatics, vol. 11, 2010.

[10] Y. Xin et al., "Role of CpG Context and Content in Evolutionary Signatures of Brain DNA Methylation," Epigenetics, vol. 6, 2011, pp. 1308–1318.

[11] Q. Liu et al., "Detection of DNA base modifications by deep recurrent neural network on Oxford Nanopore sequencing data," Nature Communications, vol. 10, 2017, p. 2449.

[12] ——, "Detection of DNA base modifications by deep recurrent neural network on Oxford Nanopore sequencing data," Nature Communications, vol. 10, 2019, p. 2449.

[13] J. Connor, R. Martin, and L. Atlas, " Recurrent Neural Networks and Robust Time Series Prediction," IEEE Transactions on Neural Networks, vol. 5, 1994, pp. 240–254.

[14] Z. Che, S. Purushotham, K. Cho, D. Sontag, and Y. Liu, "Recurrent Neural Networks for Multivariate Time Series with Missing Values," Scientific Reports, vol. 8, 2018.

[15] W. De Mulder, S. Bethard, and M.-F. Moens, "A Survey on the Application of Recurrent Neural Networks to Statistical Language Modeling," Computer Speech & Language, vol. 30, 2015, pp. 61–98.

[16] C. G. Atlas, https://cancergenome.nih.gov/, last access: August 20, 2020.

[17] TCGA-BRCA, https://portal.gdc.cancer.gov/projects/TCGA-BRCA, last access: August 20, 2020.

[18] TCGAbiolinks, https://bioconductor.org/packages/release/bioc/html/TCGAbiolinks.html, year = last access: August 20, 2020, language = english,.

[19] F. Panchal and M. Panchal, " Review on Methods of Selecting Number of Hidden Neurons in Artificial Neural Network," IJCSMC, vol. 3, 2014, pp. 455–464.

[20] A. Blum, Ed., Neural networks in C++. Wiley, 1992.

[21] J. Nash and J. Sutcliffe, "River flow forecasting through conceptual models, Part I - A discussion of principles," Journal of Hydrology, vol. 10, 1970, pp. 282–290.

[22] C. Willmot, "On the validation of models," Physical Geography, vol. 2, 1981, pp. 184–194.

RUL Prediction for Cold Forming Production Tooling

Wim De Mulder and Alessandro Di Bucchianico

Department of Mathematics and Computer Science
Eindhoven University of Technology
Eindhoven, The Netherlands
Email: wim.demulder@ugent.be
a.d.bucchianico@tue.nl

Haije Zijlstra

Philips
Drachten, The Netherlands
Email: haije.zijlstra@philips.com

***Abstract*—This paper presents a work-in-progress contribution that involves a collaboration with Philips, where the goal is to predict the remaining useful lifetime for cold forming production tooling. As the data set is complex, with many outliers and missing data points, we plan to integrate multiple techniques to reliably predict the time until maintenance is required, at least including machine learning methods, bootstrapping and change point detection techniques. The latter two methods are seldomly employed in the domain of remaining useful lifetime prediction, although they deliver very useful additional information compared to mainstream prediction techniques. Despite the fact that times of failure are currently lacking, we were able to perform a useful preliminary data analysis, which resulted in the extraction of several features to be used later as input variables for RUL prediction, and we obtained an interesting unsupervised clustering of a set of selected production runs.**

***Keywords*–Remaining useful lifetime; Bootstrapping; Change points; Cold forming production tooling.**

I. INTRODUCTION

This paper presents a work-in-progress contribution that is part of the ambitious Prophesy project on predictive maintenance [1]. Predictive Maintenance (PdM) refers to the data-driven process of predicting when operational equipment may fail and deploying preventive maintenance to avoid any down-time [2]. The idea is that maintenance should be performed as far in the future as possible, in order to minimize costs, ideally just before serious failure occurs. The predicted output variable by a PdM algorithm is the Remaining Useful Lifetime (RUL) [3], which indicates how long the machine is expected to continue to run without failure. This variable is expressed in units that depend on the application at hand, e.g., the number of cycles that a turbofan engine is expected to run before it breaks down [4].

The goal of the project entails a collaboration with two major industrial companies, namely Jaguar Land Rover and Philips, whose maintenance costs consume a considerable amount of all expenses. In this paper, we describe the Philips use case, involving a very complex data set containing many variables, measured continuously over time, with a lot of missing data points and outliers. Currently, we are focusing on measured force-signals at different angles during the forming process of the involved metal part [5]. The main purpose is to predict the remaining number of die hits (which are accompanied by the generation of a force-signal) that the considered tool is able to produce before breakdown.

Unfortunately, for the considered tool no times of failure are currently available. Nevertheless, the unlabelled large amount of data that has already been collected is suitable for an unsupervised cluster analysis. Furthermore, collaboration with engineers from Philips allowed a useful feature extraction, where the features can later be used as input variables in a supervised RUL prediction method.

The paper is organized as follows. Section II gives some background on the use case, while Section III describes how the (currently unlabelled) data set has been collected. Section IV explains how feature extraction has been performed, despite the fact that times of failure are currently unavailable. Unsupervised cluster analysis of 13 selected production runs has been applied for each of the features, as outlined in Section V. Finally, Sections VI and VII describe two interesting future research lines for this particular use case, but also for RUL prediction in general.

II. DESCRIPTION OF THE USE CASE

Philips Consumer Lifestyle in Drachten develops a wide range of innovative products like rotary shavers, beard trimmers, hairdryers, epilators, vacuum cleaners, SENSEO coffeemakers and Wake-up Lights. Philips Drachten employs 2000 people, amongst which 600 developers with 35 different nationalities. Philips Drachten is also world leader in mass production of rotary shaving devices, occupying over 50% market-share of a €1 billion market.

Multiple production lines take care of cold forming metal parts. Each production line creates a product mix. On these production lines over 50 individual metal products are created. In total, there are over 300 individual dies. The project goal is dedicated to a single production line and a single die set. When this goal will be accomplished, the developed model will be expanded to cover more production lines and more dies.

Tooling maintenance is performed in the tool workshop. A production run for the tool maintenance is triggered by production for the following reasons:

- Production run finished.
- Pre-defined lifetime threshold reached.
- Product quality issue or tool malfunction.

About 600 production runs are triggered yearly. The accuracy and the diversity of the wear parts, together with the interactions between these parts during processing, is a big challenge for maintenance. Therefore, the quality of work is strongly dependent on the skills and craftsmanship of the maintenance engineers. In many cases, highly skilled,

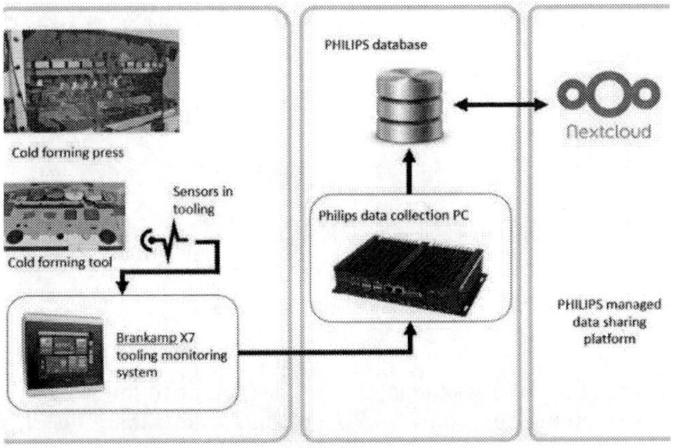

Figure 1. Global overview of the use case.

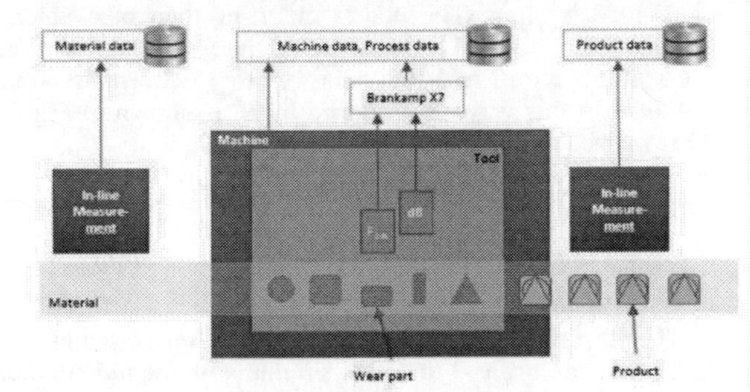

Figure 2. Some technical details of the use case.

second-line support is needed in case of non-standard problem solving. Breakdowns come with high maintenance costs, which explains the need to investigate modern technologies that enable the shift from breakdown maintenance to predictive maintenance.

The Philips predictive maintenance use case is defined around the cold forming tooling for high precision metal parts. Although the cold forming tool consists of a high number of parts, for the sake of clarity in this use case, two wear parts are considered: one cutting punch and one die-plate. Figure 1 gives a global overview of the use case, while Figure 2 displays some more technical details.

III. Data collection

The data set includes the force-signal as registered during the cold-forming operation, and is collected from several sources. To enable data extraction from existing machines, modifications to the machine control systems have been made and additional measurements have been programmed in the in-line measuring machines and a Brankamp X7 process monitoring system [6].

Figure 3 shows such a Brankamp X7 system, as well as some possible process curves. The X7 system allows up to 24 channels for an extended process monitoring. The HMI part of the system runs on a Windows Operation System, so that an easy connection to other Prophesy parts is possible. Furthermore, the X7 Cockpit provides a switchable mask design with flexible arrangement of the monitoring channels (according to the machine configuration). Binary input signals can be monitored with up to three monitoring windows to ensure the

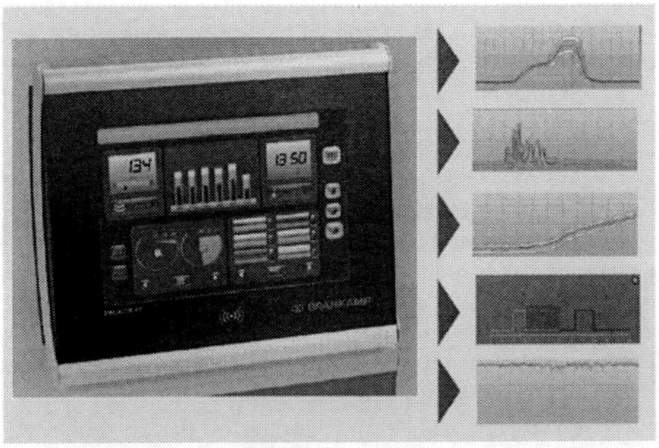

Figure 3. Brankamp X7 process monitoring system.

earliest possible fault detection. The failure distribution shows machine downtimes and the frequency of process failures for a quick and easy failure analysis.

During one stroke of the cold forming press, the cutting force, as measured by a sensor manufactured by United Electric Controls, is stored at 500 measurement points. These 500 measurement points correspond to force-signals at angles ranging from 50 degrees to 110 degrees in steps of 0.12 degrees. At a normal production rate, 1 stroke is stored every 60 seconds, in CSV format, and then pushed to the Philips Manufacturing Execution System, from where it can be downloaded by the Prophesy partners in order to perform data analysis.

IV. Feature extraction

A careful analysis that was performed together with engineers from Philips showed that only 13 production runs that were obtained during the Prophesy project, are eligible to be used as training data. As there are 500 input variables (cf. Section III), it is necessary to perform a dimensionality reduction [7]. Five features were extracted:

1) Variable 1: the 90% percentile force at angle 71.72 degrees. The 90% percentile is taken over windows consisting of 251 time points, as follows: for a given time point, consider the set of forces at 71.72 degrees together with those at the 125 time points to the left and together with those at the 125 time points to the right. From this set the 90% percentile is taken. The reason to consider the 90% percentile is that the maximum force is more interesting than, e.g., the average force, from a mechanical point of view, but because of the presence of outliers the 90% percentile force was taken as a more robust alternative to the maximum force. For time points at the beginning or at the end of a production run, for which less than 125 time points are available to either the left or the right, additional time points from the other side are taken in computing the 90% percentile force.
2) Variable 2: the Area Under the Curve (AUC) [8] of the forces between 70 and 75 degrees.
3) Variable 3: the 90% percentile force at 79 degrees, where the 90% percentile is computed as for variable 1.
4) Variable 4: the AUC of the forces between 78 and 80 degrees.

The features were extracted by analyzing the time series of the forces for the considered production runs, and discussing with engineers from Philips the mechanical meaning and relevance of the observed patterns.

V. Cluster analysis of the production runs

An important disadvantage of the current data set is that no production runs end in failure, implying that RULs are missing. Consequently, supervised machine learning cannot be applied, and the best we can currently do is performing an unsupervised analysis [9]. Cluster analysis [10], and in particular k-means [11], is a typical unsupervised tool to gain some insight into the structure of an unlabelled data set.

The k-means algorithm is applied to the 13 time series that correspond to the production runs, using the Euclidean distance measure. Clustering is repeated for each of the four feature variables. However, because the production runs do not all have the same number of time points, we truncate all production runs at 1640 time points, which is the number of time points of the shortest production run. Unfortunately, the optimal number of clusters is unknown. Therefore, we applied three validation measures that try to detect the optimal number of clusters, using the clValid package from the statistical software R: connectivity, the Dunn index and the Silhouette index [12]. The result is shown in Table I.

Table I. Optimal number of clusters according to three selected cluster validation measures.

	Connectivity	Dunn	Silhouette
Variable 1	2	9	2
Variable 2	2	10	2
Variable 3	2	2	2
Variable 4	2	2	2

Although the measures do not agree on the optimal number of clusters for all variables, it is clear that two clusters is overall the best choice. Table II shows the cluster index for each production run for each of the variables, where clustering is performed with two clusters.

Table II. Clustering of the production runs for each of the feature variables.

	Variable 1	Variable 2	Variable 3	Variable 4
Production run 1	1	1	1	1
Production run 2	1	1	1	1
Production run 3	1	1	1	1
Production run 4	1	1	1	1
Production run 5	1	1	2	2
Production run 6	1	1	2	2
Production run 7	1	1	2	2
Production run 8	1	1	2	2
Production run 9	2	2	2	2
Production run 10	2	1	2	2
Production run 11	2	1	2	2
Production run 12	2	1	2	2
Production run 13	2	1	2	2

It is seen that the clustering is not the same for each of the variables. However, for variables 3 and 4 the clustering *is* exactly the same; these variables group the first four production runs together, while the other production runs belong to the other cluster. Variable 1, on the other hand, considers the first eight production runs as similar, while the other production runs are clustered in another group. Finally, variable 2 seems not to result in a meaningful clustering: all production runs are clustered together, except production run 9.

We can integrate the different clusterings into one summary clustering as follows. Each clustering can be represented as a matrix M with elements $M[i,j]$ defined as follows: $M[i,j] = 0$ if production run i and j belong to the same cluster, and $M[i,j] = 1$ otherwise. The four resulting matrices can then be averaged over the number of variables, i.e., each $M[i,j]$ is divided by four. The matrix elements then take values in $\{0, 0.2, 0.4, 0.6, 0.8, 1\}$. For ease of interpretation we round the value 0.2 to 0 and the value 0.8 to 1. The matrix that is obtained in this way, as produced by R, is shown in Figure 4. This matrix provides the following information:

```
      [,1] [,2] [,3] [,4] [,5] [,6] [,7] [,8] [,9] [,10] [,11] [,12] [,13]
 [1,]  0.0  0.0  0.0  0.0  0.4  0.6  0.6  0.6  1.0   1.0   1.0   0.6   1.0
 [2,]  0.0  0.0  0.0  0.0  0.4  0.6  0.6  0.6  1.0   1.0   1.0   0.6   1.0
 [3,]  0.0  0.0  0.0  0.0  0.6  0.4  0.4  0.4  1.0   0.6   0.6   1.0   0.6
 [4,]  0.0  0.0  0.0  0.0  0.4  0.6  0.6  0.6  1.0   1.0   1.0   0.6   1.0
 [5,]  0.4  0.4  0.6  0.4  0.0  0.0  0.0  0.0  0.6   0.4   0.4   0.0   0.4
 [6,]  0.6  0.6  0.4  0.6  0.0  0.0  0.0  0.0  0.4   0.0   0.0   0.4   0.0
 [7,]  0.6  0.6  0.4  0.6  0.0  0.0  0.0  0.0  0.4   0.0   0.0   0.4   0.0
 [8,]  0.6  0.6  0.4  0.6  0.0  0.0  0.0  0.0  0.4   0.0   0.0   0.4   0.0
 [9,]  1.0  1.0  1.0  1.0  0.6  0.4  0.4  0.4  0.0   0.0   0.0   0.4   0.0
[10,]  1.0  1.0  0.6  1.0  0.4  0.0  0.0  0.0  0.0   0.0   0.0   0.0   0.0
[11,]  1.0  1.0  0.6  1.0  0.4  0.0  0.0  0.0  0.0   0.0   0.0   0.0   0.0
[12,]  0.6  0.6  1.0  0.6  0.0  0.4  0.4  0.4  0.4   0.0   0.0   0.0   0.0
[13,]  1.0  1.0  0.6  1.0  0.4  0.0  0.0  0.0  0.0   0.0   0.0   0.0   0.0
```

Figure 4. Average clustering matrix, with values 0.2 rounded to 0, and values 0.8 rounded to 1.

- Production runs 1 to 4 are similar.
- Production runs 5 to 8 are similar.
- Production runs 9, 10, 11 and 13 are similar.
- Production runs 10 to 13 are similar.

The last two observations could also be rephrased as saying that production runs 9 to 13 are similar, with the note that there is some dissimilarity between production runs 9 and 12.

Currently we started discussing if the results of this cluster analysis may be used in future RUL prediction. This requires to analyze whether production runs 1 to 4, production runs 5 to 8, and production runs 9 to 13 share certain properties that might be related to the 'health' of the involved mechanical parts. If so, this knowledge can be used in a later stage, together with times of failure when they become available, to predict the RUL.

VI. Future work: bootstrapping and prediction interval

Applications on RUL prediction often restrict to returning a single RUL value. However, it is very useful to have an indication of the reliability of this prediction, for example in terms of a prediction interval. Although many machine learning techniques, e.g., artificial neural networks, only return a predicted value, it is easy to obtain a prediction interval by means of bootstrapping [13]. By randomly sampling from the training set and training a model on each sample, one obtains a set of models, each having a slightly different view on the data set. Consequently, averaging the predictions of all these models results in a robust prediction, and the set of predictions itself can be considered as a range of possible RUL values that vary with certain peculiarities in the data set. From the set of predictions, which represent a histogram of values, it is very simple to obtain a 95% prediction interval. Noteworthy advantages of bootstrapping are its simplicity in terms of implementation, and the observation that it is asymptotically more accurate than the standard intervals obtained using sample variance and assumptions of normality [14]. Prediction intervals offer more decision-making power to industrial partners. For example, very conservative engineers will be inclined not to rely on the predicted value, but on the left endpoint of the prediction interval when scheduling maintenance.

Even if prediction intervals are taken into account, it is often neglected to evaluate them. That is, evaluation of a prediction model is often restricted to the predicted values. However, validation measures have been developed to evaluate prediction intervals. For example, the interval score [15] rewards narrow intervals, while at the same time penalizing lack of coverage. It is defined as

$$\Big(u(\mathbf{x}) - l(\mathbf{x})\Big) + \frac{2}{\alpha}\Big(l(\mathbf{x}) - \nu(\mathbf{x})\Big)\mathbf{1}_{\{\nu(\mathbf{x})<l(\mathbf{x})\}} + \frac{2}{\alpha}\Big(\nu(\mathbf{x}) - u(\mathbf{x})\Big)\mathbf{1}_{\{\nu(\mathbf{x})>u(\mathbf{x})\}}$$

for a $(1-\alpha)\%$ prediction interval $[l(\mathbf{x}), u(\mathbf{x})]$, where $\mathbf{1}_{\{expr\}}$ refers to the indicator function, being 1 if expression *expr* holds and 0 otherwise. In our view, implementations related to RUL prediction should always produce a prediction interval, and these prediction intervals should be taken into account when performance is evaluated by comparing to the results of other models. We will do so in our future research on the Philips use case.

VII. Future work: Change point detection

Change point detection refers to identifying when certain properties of a probability distribution, in particular the mean and the variance, of a time series change [16]. As far as we know, change point detection methods are rarely used in RUL prediction. This is unjustified, as such methods are complementary to traditional RUL prediction methods: whereas most RUL methods, e.g., artificial neural networks, implicitly assume continuity in the time series, change point detection is able to handle sudden discontinuities or trends. In this way, it might prove useful to combine traditional machine learning techniques with change point detection methods in RUL prediction. For example, as long as no change point is detected, engineers might rely on the midpoint value of the prediction interval for maintenance. However, whenever a change point is notified, indicating a change in regime (possibly due to the failure of a non critical part of the involved tool), engineers might react properly by relying on the left endpoint of the prediction interval instead, thereby discounting the danger of a premature failure.

We experimented with the package 'changepoint' in R [17]. For example, Figure 5 shows the forces during a selected production run at angle 71 degrees, together with the jumps in an otherwise constant mean trend. One changepoint (jump) was detected, as seen from the figure.

Change points deliver additional information compared to mainstream RUL predictors. For our case study, we envisage developing a measure that takes into account the number of angles at which a change point arises: if a change point occurs at a high number of angles at the same time, this indicates a more serious warning compared to a change point occurring at only one or a small number of angles at the same time. In the first case, a more conservative RUL should be predicted than in the second case.

VIII. Conclusion

In this work-in-progress contribution we have described a use case from a cold forming production tooling process that involves collaboration with Philips in the context of a major EU project named Prophesy. The purpose is to predict the remaining useful lifetime of certain tools that come with high maintenance costs. Our plan is to combine several techniques in order to fulfill this goal:

- Machine learning techniques, in particular artificial neural networks, to produce the RUL.
- Bootstrapping, to obtain a prediction interval for the predicted RUL.
- Change point detection, to ensure that not only gradual changes in performance of the tool are detected, but that also more abrupt changes are identified.

An important challenge will be to integrate all these methods into a reliable and efficient RUL prediction mechanism.

Bootstrapping and change point detection are often neglected in RUL prediction, although these techniques create additional relevant information on the predicted RUL. Perhaps these methods just need to find their way in the domain of RUL prediction. Our work might be an incentive for other researchers in RUL prediction to consider the use of these techniques.

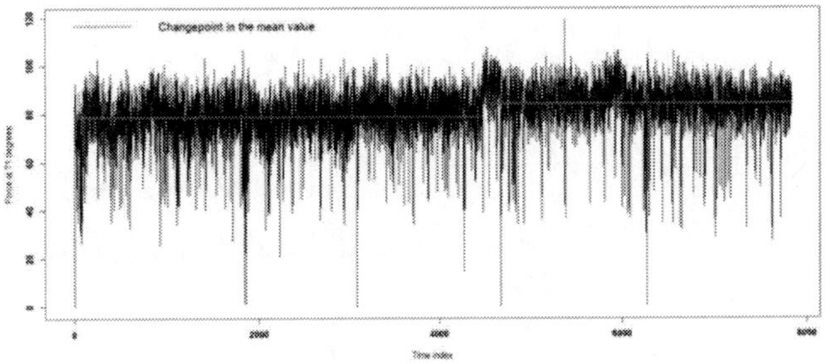

Figure 5. Change point detection for the mean during a certain production run for forces measured at angle 71 degrees.

Acknowledgment

This work was supported by European Union's Horizon 2020 grant no.766994 (PROPHESY).

References

[1] Prophesy, https://prophesy.eu/, last access: August 20, 2020.

[2] J. Levitt, Ed., Complete Guide to Preventive and Predictive Maintenance. Industrial Press, 2011.

[3] X. Si, W. Wang, C. Hu, and D. Zhou, "Remaining Useful Life Estimation – A Review on the Statistical Data Driven Approaches," European Journal of Operational Research, vol. 213, 2011, pp. 1–14.

[4] V. Mathew, T. Toby, V. Singh, M. Rao, and M. Kumar, "Prediction of Remaining Useful Lifetime (RUL) of Turbofan Engine Using Machine Learning," in Proceedings of the IEEE International Conference on Circuits and Systems (ICCS), 2007, pp. 306–311.

[5] I. Suchy, Ed., Handbook of Die Design. McGraw-Hill Education, Jan. 2005.

[6] Brankamp, http://www.brankamp.com/en/index.php?page=brankamp_x7_artificial_intelligence_is_the_key, last access: August 20, 2020.

[7] H. Lu, K. Plataniotis, and A. Venetsanopoulos, Eds., Multilinear Subspace Learning: Dimensionality Reduction of Multidimensional Data. Chapman and Hall/CRC, Jan. 2013.

[8] A. Bradley, "The Use of the Area Under the ROC Curve in the Evaluation of Machine Learning Algorithms," Pattern Recognition Letters, vol. 30, 1997, pp. 1145–1159.

[9] M. Kyan, P. Muneesawang, K. Jarrah, and L. Guan, Eds., Unsupervised Learning: A Dynamic Approach. Wiley-IEEE Press, Jan. 2014.

[10] D. Xu and Y. Tian, "A Comprehensive Survey of Clustering Algorithms," Annals of Data Science, vol. 2, 2015, pp. 165–193.

[11] A. Jain, "Data Clustering: 50 Years Beyond K-means," Pattern Recognition Letters, vol. 31, 2010, pp. 651–666.

[12] G. Brock, V. Pihur, S. Datta, and S. Datta, "clValid: An R Package for Cluster Validation," Journal of Statistical Software, vol. 25, 2008, p. i04.

[13] J. Shao and D. Tu, Eds., The Jackknife and Bootstrap. Springer, Jan. 1996.

[14] T. DiCiccio and B. Efron, "Bootstrap Confidence Intervals," Statistical Science, vol. 11, 1996, pp. 189–228.

[15] T. Gneiting and A. Raftery, "Strictly proper scoring rules, prediction, and estimation," Journal of the American Statistical Association, vol. 102, 2007, pp. 359–378.

[16] S. Aminikhanghahi and D. Cook, "A Survey of Methods for Time Series Change Point Detection," Knowledge and Information Systems, vol. 51, 2017, pp. 339–367.

[17] R. Killick and I. Eckley, "changepoint: An R Package for Changepoint Analysis," Journal of Statistical Software, vol. 58, 2014, pp. 1–19.

Mixed Reality Autonomous Vehicle Simulation: Implementation of a Hardware-In-the-Loop Architecture at a Miniature Scale

Robin Baruffa
Univ. de Technologie de Belfort-Montbéliard
Belfort, France
email: robin.baruffa@utbm.fr

Jacques Pereira
Univ. de Technologie de Belfort-Montbéliard
Belfort, France
email: jacques.pereira@utbm.fr

Pierre Romet
CIAD (UMR 7533)
Univ. Bourgogne Franche-Comte, UTBM
Belfort, France
email: pierre.romet@utbm.fr

Franck Gechter
CIAD (UMR 7533)
Univ. Bourgogne Franche-Comte, UTBM
Belfort, France
email: franck.gechter@utbm.fr
Mosel Loria (UMR CNRS 7503)
Université de Lorraine
Vandoeuvre-lès-Nancy-54506, France

Tobias Weiss
CIAD (UMR 7533)
Univ. Bourgogne Franche-Comte, UTBM
Belfort, France
Institute of Energy Efficient Mobility
Univ. of Applied Science
Hochschule, Karlsruhe, Germany
email: tobias.weiss@hs-karlsruhe.de

***Abstract*—Validation of autonomous vehicles is a resource intensive and time-consuming endeavour because of their *safety critical* nature. *X-In-the-Loop* proposes a development method that uses a simulated environment to overcome real-world constraints to test and improve autonomous vehicle capabilities. Development time can be reduced as each iteration on the control software does not necessarily require real-world testing. This paper focuses on studying the influence of switching from simulated to real-world camera data on control algorithms execution time in the context of a preliminary work consisting in implementing a *Hardware-In-the-Loop* architecture on a *miniature car*.**

Keywords*—*Hardware-In-the-Loop; autonomous vehicles; miniature car.

I. Introduction

The project detailed in this paper is part of a new alternative freight transportation system in cities and in the countryside called SURATRAM (Système Urbain et Rural Autonome de TRansport de Marchandises). It aims to revitalize small businesses struggling to meet the level of flexibility and competitiveness that e-commerce companies can offer. The proposed solution is to deploy an autonomous fleet of cargo vans in various areas to facilitate the transportation of goods, lowering transportation fees by optimizing the path of each package and lessening the need for maintaining extensive stocks; and improving logistic chains' flexibility and speed. The increase in traffic caused by the additional number of vehicles among cities would be mitigated by restricting these autonomous vans to follow existing human-operated public transport vehicles such as tramway or buses in a *platoon* formation. Thus, the next logical step in the development of this transportation system is using a real vehicle as a testbed in order to assess the state of the art platoon algorithms [1]. This *System-under-Test* (SuT) must demonstrate its reliability in various extreme scenarios such as an imminent collision with a pedestrian or an emergency stop performed by any vehicle from the convoy. Extensive testing of hardware in real driving conditions can be very costly as it requires having access to special facilities, and in our case, renting a bus with a driver during the whole test campaign. A solution to this problem is to develop a simulated replica of the real-world system dynamic and its sensors, allowing for thorough validation of the SuT by breaking free from physical and time constraints. With this method, known in the literature as *Hardware-In-the-Loop* (HIL) [2], the real hardware is used to process the simulated sensor data and outputs actions that are fed back in the simulation.

Figure 1. Image of the miniature car.

In order to pave the way for the future design of a complete HIL implementation of a full-sized car, a *miniature car* has been designed to verify the relevance and performance of the chosen HIL architecture (Figure 1).

This preliminary work aims at highlighting the difference in the control algorithm execution time when fed with real-world or with simulated camera data. It is an important metric to check as if the gap is too wide, the control algorithm will not behave as expected when tested in real conditions.

In Section II, we first present the current state of the art in the autonomous vehicle development field. Section III then describes our implementation of the HIL framework on a miniature car. Section IV provides a description of the experimental protocol and the preliminary results regarding the gap between car and its cyber-twin. Finally, in Section V, we close this paper with a summary and an outlook on the future improvements needed to validate the simulation.

II. State of the Art

In the literature, the general framework *X-In-the-Loop* is the subject of numerous works [3][4], especially in the robotics and autonomous vehicle field where the SuT can be a *safety-critical system* [5].

The classical approach is to use *Model-In-the-Loop* [6] as a first step to create a mathematical representation of the system's dynamics.

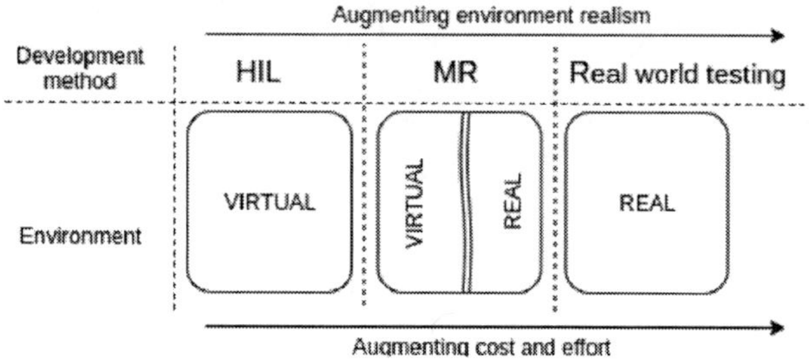

Figure 2. Environment in HIL architecture to MR [7].

In some cases, limitations can occur both in simulation (e.g., in terms of fidelity) and in the real world (e.g., in terms of price and safety), therefore a hybrid framework like *Mixed Reality* (MR) [8] can be used to mitigate this. Its purpose is to create hybrid observations by mixing simulated and real observations in order to add entities such as pedestrians, cars or obstacles [9][10]. It can provide an intermediary step between the relatively easy and inexpensive HIL, and costly real-world testing [7]. Figure 2 shows how much time and financial investment is required for each development method.

As it is critical to make sure that the SuT will perform similarly in real world testing and in its virtual world, numerous works [11][12] focus on quantifying the difference in dynamics between the real world model and the simulated model. We think software execution time differences deserve to be studied in more detail as they can influence the overall behaviour of the SuT.

III. Proposition

The short-term goal of this project is to implement HIL on a miniature car and its cyber-twin to have it *follow a simulated bus,* both in the simulation and in the real world. Our architecture allows for testing the control algorithm with sensor data coming from the simulation or from the real car interchangeably, which is a key component of HIL methods. Additionally, when using only simulated observations, it is possible to execute the actions in an *open-loop configuration* on the real-world car, with the purpose of verifying the fidelity between the simulated vehicle dynamics and its real counterpart.

Related work focuses first on developing the control algorithm in simulation, then implementing it in a test platform. A key advantage of our miniaturisation method is its simplicity and low cost. After a description of the global architecture, this section will go into details about the subsystems architecture.

A. Global architecture

On the one hand, a computer runs the simulation, which updates the car's position and velocity when receiving an action, then sends the simulated sensors readings over the network. On the other hand, the raw data is fed to a decision making unit running on the real car's hardware, which outputs an action composed of throttle level and steering angle. This action will be transmitted to both the simulator and the *Electronic Control Unit* (ECU), controlling the real vehicle.

Figure 3 shows the overall architecture. The top simulation part is executed on a computer because of its computationally intensive nature, while the bottom part is executed on the *miniature car*'s embedded hardware.

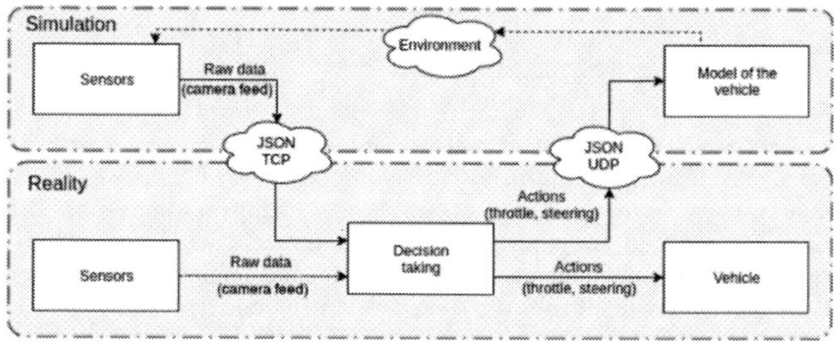

Figure 3. Global architecture of our HIL implementation.

B. Simulator architecture

Simulators have different goals and capabilities. The requirements are that they must offer both a realistic and customizable graphical environment, along with realistic physics. In literature, the use of a robotic simulator like *Gazebo* [7][9][10][13] or game-based engines such as *Unity* [8][14] or *Unreal-Engine* [15] are standard.

For this work, it was decided to choose Unity3D (which uses the *PhysX 4.1* physical engine), as it comes free of charge for non-commercial use and has good rendering capabilities which are needed for realistic camera sensors.

A generic 3D model of a car and a bus are used (Figure 5). Their dynamical parameters are set arbitrarily, as having an accurate physics model is currently beyond the scope of this project, but it will be investigated in future works. The bus can either be user-controlled or driven by a predefined spline. A virtual camera and a tachometer measuring the rotation speed of the wheels are used as sensors.

C. Software architecture

The simulation layer is managed by Unity3D. A script parses the JSON (JavaScript Object Notation) output from the simulator (camera feed and odometry), then forwards it through the local network to the real car. The latter sends the received observation information to be processed over the *Robotic Operation System* (ROS) network. An output action

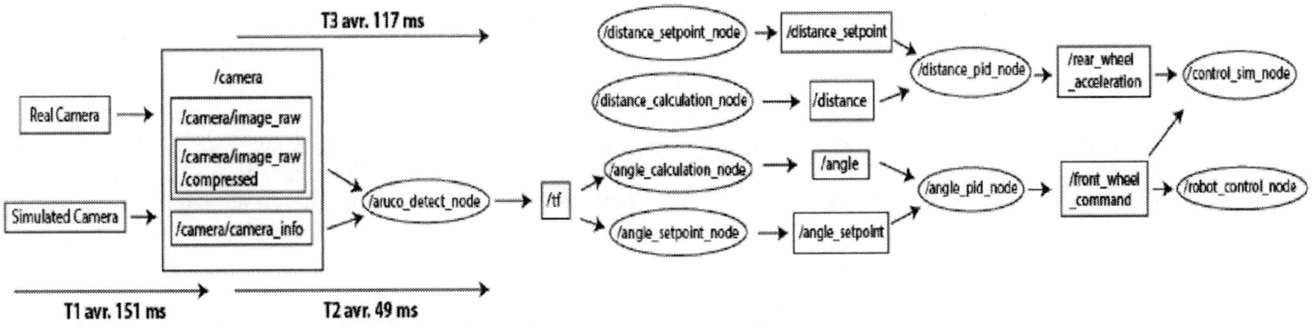

Figure 4. ROS computation graph along with measured computation time.

is then forwarded simultaneously to the ECU and back to the simulation. The ROS middleware is very convenient and often used in the literature [7][9] as it integrates many sensors drivers, natively supports multi-machine communication, integrates various visualization packages and offers the possibility to record and replay every incoming observation and outgoing actions in a deterministic manner.

Since the scope of this project is not about the sensor processing nor about the control algorithm, both have been simplified in the following way :

1) Camera processing: An *ArUco marker* (Figure 5) is used on the back of the bus. These markers are widely used for robotic and autonomous vehicles applications [16], as their detection and position estimation is made easier thanks to their simple binary shape. A ROS node called /aruco_detect_node receives the camera stream (from the simulation or the real sensor) and outputs the marker's coordinate system concerning the camera (shown as /tf in Figure 4). A copy of the video feed with the detected axis system overlaid is used for debugging purposes.

2) Control algorithm: The relative distance between the car and the bus is calculated and fed into a PID (Proportional Integral Derivative) controller that outputs a throttle command based on this distance and a user-defined distance setpoint parameter. The car's heading error is defined as the angle between the centre of the camera and the lateral position of the ArUco marker. This heading error is fed to a PID controller along with the desired heading angle (null in this case) and outputs a steering command.

D. Hardware architecture

The model car is a $25cm$ long and $14cm$ wide four-wheel drive with front steering wheels and rear propulsion. Its onboard computer is a *Raspberry PI 4* running the ROS server which communicates with the simulation computer via a Wi-Fi connection. The steering angle and throttle commands are transmitted to an external ECU that controls the motors in an open-loop configuration through GPIO (General Purpose Input Output) pins. The front-mounted camera is set to have a resolution of $640 \times 480px$ at $10Hz$.

IV. Experiments

This section will present two different experiments. The first one consists in controlling the bus manually in the simulation while the car will follow it from a safe distance. Then it is visually confirmed if the miniature car movements are both synchronized and coherent with the simulation.

The second experiment will aim to demonstrate that our HIL infrastructure can operate in real testing conditions: a manually controlled three-wheeled robot will represent the bus in the real world. The model car will run the same software and its performance will be visually assessed. In the two experiments, measurements are performed to quantify both delays in sensor data transmission from the simulation to the car's local network and the camera processing time resulting in usable information for the control algorithm. Comparing response time in HIL and real-world configuration permits to assess the coherence between both systems, which is critical since any delay discrepancy in the control loop can lead to different behaviours.

In Figure 4, T_1 represents the delay between the rendering of the virtual camera and its reception on the ROS network, and T_2 and T_3 are the times taken by the ArUco detection node to compute the marker coordinate from simulated and real camera data respectively. Delays measurements of the robot using simulated observations were performed on 308 samples and 343 samples when using real-world observations. The camera framerate was set to $5\ Hz$, which is the maximum frequency the ArUco detection package would handle on our hardware before starting to drop measurements.

Figure 4 shows a significant difference in delay between the two experiments, even though it is performed by the same code running on the same hardware. The only difference is the content of the video stream, as it has been setup to use the same compression format, encoding, framerate and resolution.

A. Real car guided by the simulated one

The leading virtual bus is placed at a distance from the virtual car, which will have to accelerate then slow down to get to its distance setpoint from the bus and maintain it while the simulated bus follows a predefined spline trajectory. The real miniature car will perform the same actions as its virtual twin.

The laptop running the simulation and the embedded computer were synchronized beforehand to avoid timing issues.

In the current absence of additional sensors allowing for precise location, we visually confirm that the miniature car follows the same trajectory as its cyber-twin.

B. Real hardware in real world condition

The purpose of this specific experiment is to demonstrate that the same software can be used in real conditions with real sensor data. Since the physical car is at a smaller scale, a robotic platform will act as the leading bus and will be user-controlled. This robot also uses ROS, which facilitated its implementation. The distance setpoint and the ArUco marker width were edited to take into account the scale difference.

Figure 5. Miniature car in real-world test condition.

An overview of the experimental apparatus can be seen in Figure 5. Visual observation confirms that the car follows the robot from a safe distance, without significant change in behaviour compared to Subsection IV-A.

The latency increase in real-world conditions is likely to be caused by the increased complexity of the video stream. The execution time of image processing algorithms with an adaptive number of iterations, such as the one used for detecting ArUco markers, can be shorter if the input image is sharp and contains little noise. Thus, adding noise to simulated observations is not only needed for ensuring that the sensor processing algorithm will be robust in non-ideal condition, but it can also be a source of discrepancy in the behaviour of the same algorithm given different sensor data.

V. Conclusion and Future Work

This paper has presented a use case of HIL for autonomous vehicle implementation at a smaller scale. It has proven the effectiveness of the chosen combination of simulation, software and hardware. The global architecture proved to yield similar dynamics behaviour when sensory information comes from a simulated or a real-world environment, but a difference in computation time has been observed. The specific scope of use will dictate whether this delay discrepancy is acceptable.

Throughout the development of our preliminary platform, we learned the importance of choosing algorithms that take a fixed amount of time to execute, regardless of the input complexity. One of the most challenging tasks was to measure delays at every step of the computation graph without interfering significantly with the normal execution of the code.

Future work will focus on quantifying the dynamical differences between the simulated car and its real counterpart by adding additional sensors, either on the car or in the test environment, to get "ground truth" measurements. We will also investigate how ROS2, the new version of the ROS middleware, performs to further lower latency. A simple yet effective implementation would be to use additional fixed ArUco markers to estimate the car's position with good accuracy [16]. The next step towards a practical solution could be to use more advanced computer vision algorithms that do not require modification on the vehicle that needs to be followed.

These incremental improvements will ultimately lead to using a real autonomous vehicle platform that will be used as a testbed for developing novel MR architectures. It would be possible to overlay virtual obstacles on top of the real-world camera feed to improve the control algorithm's performance and lower development time.

Acknowledgment

This work is carried out as part of our studies at the Université de technologie de Belfort-Montbéliard, in the context of the SURATRAM Project. The SURATRAM project is made possible thank to the support of Région Bourgogne-Franche-Comté.

References

[1] F. Gechter, J.-M. Contet, S. Galland, O. Lamotte, and A. Koukam, "Virtual intelligent vehicle urban simulator: Application to vehicle platoon evaluation," *Simul. Model. Pract. Theory*, vol. 24, pp. 103–114, 2012.

[2] J. A. Ledin, "Hardware-in-the-loop simulation," in *Embedded Systems Programming*, vol. 12, 1999, pp. 42–60.

[3] W. Huang, K. Wang, Y. Lv, and F. Zhu, "Autonomous vehicles testing methods review," in *2016 IEEE 19th International Conference on Intelligent Transportation Systems (ITSC)*, 2016, pp. 163–168.

[4] J. E. Stellet, M. R. Zofka, J. Schumacher, T. Schamm, F. Niewels, and J. M. Zöllner, "Testing of advanced driver assistance towards automated driving: A survey and taxonomy on existing approaches and open questions," in *2015 IEEE 18th International Conference on Intelligent Transportation Systems*, 2015, pp. 1455–1462.

[5] O. Gietelink, "Design and validation of advanced driver assistance systems," in *TRAIL Research School*, 2007.

[6] A. R. Plummer, "Model-in-the-loop testing," *Proceedings of the Institution of Mechanical Engineers, Part I: Journal of Systems and Control Engineering*, vol. 220, no. 3, pp. 183–199, 2006.

[7] M. R. Zofka, M. Essinger, T. Fleck, R. Kohlhaas, and J. M. Zöllner, "The sleepwalker framework: Verification and validation of autonomous vehicles by mixed reality lidar stimulation," in *2018 IEEE International Conference on Simulation, Modeling, and Programming for Autonomous Robots (SIMPAR)*, 2018, pp. 151–157.

[8] F. Gechter, B. Dafflon, P. Gruer, and A. Koukam, "Towards a hybrid real/virtual simulation of autonomous vehicles for critical scenarios," in *In The Sixth International Conference on Advances in System Simulation (SIMUL 2014)*, 10 2014, pp. 14–17.

[9] M. R. Zofka et al., "Traffic participants in the loop: A mixed reality-based interaction testbed for the verification and validation of autonomous vehicles," in *2018 21st International Conference on Intelligent Transportation Systems (ITSC)*, 2018, pp. 3583–3590.
[10] I. Y. Chen, B. MacDonald, and B. Wunsche, "Mixed reality simulation for mobile robots," in *2009 IEEE International Conference on Robotics and Automation*, 2009, pp. 232–237.
[11] C. Koehler, A. Mayer, and A. Herkersdorf, "Determining the fidelity of hardware-in-the-loop simulation coupling systems," in *2008 IEEE International Behavioral Modeling and Simulation Workshop*, 2008, pp. 13–18.
[12] N. Seegmiller, F. Rogers-Marcovitz, G. Miller, and A. Kelly, "Vehicle model identification by integrated prediction error minimization," in *The International Journal of Robotics Research*, vol. 32, 07 2013, pp. 912–931.
[13] I. Chen, B. A. MacDonald, and B. Wünsche, "A flexible mixed reality simulation framework for software development in robotics," in *Journal Of Software Engineering In Robotics*, vol. 2, 2011, pp. 40–54.
[14] M. Wu, S.-L. Dai, and C. Yang, "Mixed reality enhanced user interactive path planning for omnidirectional mobile robot," *Applied Sciences*, vol. 10, p. 1135, 2020.
[15] M. Broy, "Challenges in automotive software engineering," in *Proceedings of the 28th International Conference on Software Engineering*, ser. ICSE '06. New York, NY, USA: Association for Computing Machinery, 2006, pp. 33–42.
[16] J. Bacik, F. Durovsky, P. Fedor, and D. Perdukova, "Autonomous flying with quadrocopter using fuzzy control and aruco markers," in *Intelligent Service Robotics*, vol. 10, 2017, pp. 185–194.

The Digital Twin as a Design Tool in Industry 4.0: A Case Study

Ivan Arturo Renteria-Marquez
Tzu-Liang (Bill) Tseng
Department of Industrial, Manufacturing and Systems Engineering
University of Texas at El Paso
El Paso, USA
E-mails:{iarenteria | btseng }@utep.edu

Anabel Renteria
Department of Mechanical Engineering
University of Texas at El Paso
El Paso, USA
E-mail: arenteriamarquez@miners.utep.edu

Abstract— **This manuscript reports the findings of a study conducted in a manufacturing assembly plant that is in the journey of incorporating Industry 4.0 technologies on its production floor. In this manufacturing company, some manual operations will be replaced with painting robots, because of that, a digital twin was created to quantify the influence of them. Specifically, during this investigation, the influence of the buffer size over the proposed manufacturing system with painting robots on it was quantified. This study demonstrates the relevance of the digital twin as a design tool that one can employ to plan a gradual transition from a classical manufacturing production floor to a modern production floor with Industry 4.0 technologies.**

Keywords- digital twin; discrete-event simulation; industry 4.0; manufacturing.

I. INTRODUCTION

The new industrial revolution, most of the times referred to as Industry 4.0 or Smart Manufacturing has the potential to transform and reactivate the manufacturing industry in the USA [1].

Industry 4.0 is a term used to describe the vision of manufacturing systems integrated by processes with a high degree of automation, which are fully connected between them. The technologies that integrate this vision for manufacturing systems are: internet of things, robotics, automation, cloud computing, cybersecurity, data analytics, additive manufacturing (i.e., 3D printing), and simulation [2].

In recent years, the government of the USA was leading different initiatives to develop and implement smart manufacturing technologies. The goal of these initiatives is to generate new manufacturing opportunities within the USA and support the competitiveness of local manufacturers. For instance, the creation of the Clean Energy Smart Manufacturing Innovation Institute (CESMII) is one of these initiatives of the government focused on boosting Industry 4.0 technologies.

Inspired by public and private initiatives, a considerable number of manufacturing companies across the USA are trying to move from a traditional production floor to a smart production floor. Nevertheless, the introduction of Industry 4.0 technologies on the production floor is a challenging task since it is difficult to visualize how the production system will perform after the introduction of them.

Hence, the development of strategies to introduce Industry 4.0 technologies on the production floor is required. Consequently, the focus of this manuscript is to report the methodology followed and the findings of a project deployed in an assembly manufacturing company located in the USA that focused on the implementation of a manufacturing digital twin to predict the effects of introducing robotic systems in their production process. The rest of the paper is organized as follows. Section II includes a literature review of important concepts related to the developed project. In section III the manufacturing system is described. One can find in section IV the solution approach and the results obtained. Finally, in section V the conclusion of this manuscript is presented.

II. LITERATURE REVIEW

We will start by defining the concept of a digital twin. The concept was originally established by a NASA team [3][4], in this context, they defined the digital twin as a simulation model of a vehicle that integrates multi-physics, multi-scale, and probabilistic models. This digital twin uses physical models, sensor updates, and fleet history. Reference [5] describes a digital twin as a coupled model of a real machine that is available in the cloud and is used to simulate the health condition of that machine. Reference [6] defines the digital twin as a simulation model with the ability to describe events in time and space. These digital twins can be used during the design phases of the system and during the operational phases of the system.

A digital twin of a manufacturing system can be defined as a virtual representation of a manufacturing system that allows one to see how the system will perform in the real world; where the digital twin can be used to design, optimize and operate the system. In a manufacturing facility with Industry 4.0 technologies, the digital twin can be connected online through the Industrial Internet of Things (IIoT) and access in-real time the Enterprise Resource Planning (ERP) and the Manufacturing Execution System (MES) System updating the model according to the current status of the physical system.

One can find in the literature a limited number of case studies of digital twin's applications in manufacturing systems. Reference [7] reports the implementation of a digital twin to support manufacturing and maintenance planning in a roll shop. One can find in [8] the description of a plan to implement a digital twin in a drive shaft manufacturing plant.

Now that the concept for digital twin of manufacturing systems was established, we will define the concept of capacity analysis. One can define capacity analysis as the process used to measure the capacity of one operation in a manufacturing plant. More specifically, production capacity analysis refers to the maximum number of production orders that can be manufactured under specific conditions.

One can study problems related to production capacity analysis and optimization from different angles. For instance, reference [9] describes a case study of a production capacity analysis of a shock absorber assembly line where the configuration of the layout was modified to improve production rates. In this study, the production capacity was increased by 32%.

Reference [10] remarks on the lack of studies in the literature focused on the investigation of the influence and effects of limited buffer size in the production capacity of reentrant hybrid flow shops. The goal of this study was to develop scheduling strategies that will optimize production capacity. This type of problem demands a non-trivial solution since this problem is NP-hard. In this work, a hybrid harmony search and genetic algorithm were proposed.

III. OVERVIEW OF THE MANUFACTURING SYSTEM AND PROBLEM DEFINITION

As previously mentioned, the manufacturing plant presented in this manuscript is an assembly plant. The value stream of this manufacturing plant is composed of a complex internal structure where the workers currently perform all the processes with manual operations. The four main groups forming the processes of this facility are assembly, pre-painting, painting, and testing, where these groups have the flexibility to produce five different product types. One can find a schematic of this facility in Fig. 1.

The production processes of the assembly lines are configured as a hybrid flow shop. This is formed by a series of workstations, where some operations are performed in workstations with a parallel connection; the flow of this process runs in one direction.

The production processes of the painting area are arranged as a job shop with reentrances. The different products run through the painting shop in small batches of the same product type. Each product type requires a specific sequence with a specific set up. Not all the product types require to pass through all the processes, and most of the time a product needs to pass by a specific process several times. The workstations that perform the same function are grouped together. After the product types pass through all the required painting processes, they pass by a functional test.

As previously mentioned, one can classify the manufacturing operations of this system as manual operations. However, this manufacturing plant is on the journey of incorporating Industry 4.0 technologies into their processes. This manuscript reports the initial steps of this long-term initiative.

In this manufacturing system, some manual operations of the painting shop will be replaced with automatic operations performed by painting robots. The presented manuscript focuses on a capacity analysis with a limited buffer size prior to the implementation of these robots. The motivation for predicting the proper buffer size capacity prior to the implementation of these robots is based on the fact that these robots will affect the dynamics of the entire system and a proper buffer size needs to be determined. The buffers are located before and after the painting area.

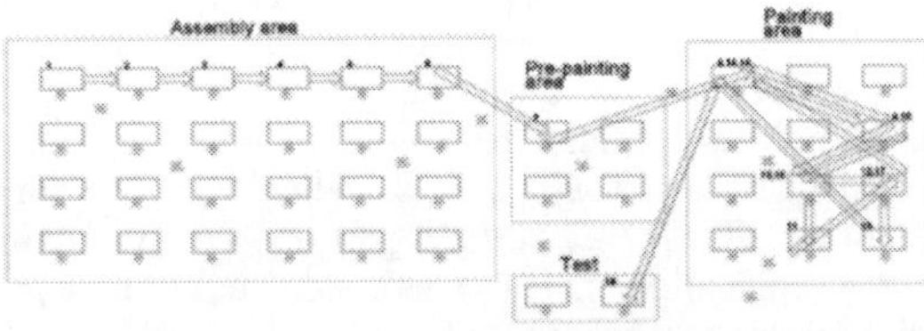

Figure 1. Assembly manufacturing plant.

IV. SOLUTION APPROACH AND RESULTS OBTAINED

The presented project was accomplished by systematically developing four key tasks. These four tasks are: definition of the logical model of the system, data collection, programming of the digital twin, and perform the analysis.

Task 1: Definition of the logical model of the system. The starting point to develop a digital twin of a manufacturing system is to define a logical model of it. Hence, the entire process of this manufacturing plant was mapped. In order to document the current state of the entire process, Value Stream Map (VSM) techniques were used [11]. VSMs were used because they offer an industrial engineering language that is well known around the world. After that, a spaghetti diagram was defined for each product type. One can see in Fig. 1 an example of a spaghetti diagram created for a product type. Different meetings were organized with the engineering group of this company to define the logical model generated for this facility for each product type. This process is typically interactive, especially for projects where it is required to develop a digital twin for an entire facility.

Task 2: Data collection. After the logical model was approved for each product type, the second task consists of working on the data collection and calculation of probabilistic distributions. This is a time-consuming process that requires a big effort [12].

It was found that the majority of the processes involving this production system can be modeled using triangular distributions. These are continuous probability distributions defined by the minimum value, most likely value, and maximum value.

Also, in order to accurately model the behavior of the painting robots, experiments with these robots were run to collect enough data to feed later the digital twin.

Task 3: Programming of the digital twin. Firstly, one needs to choose the proper software to program the digital twin. Simio simulation software was chosen for this project because this software offers the four discrete-event modeling paradigms developed for simulation of queuing systems; these paradigms are events, processes, objects, and agent-based modeling. Also, the Simio software is prepared to be connected online and driven by data received from the MES and ERP systems [2]. For this project, the digital twin was connected online to the

MES system, allowing starting the simulation as a non-empty and idle system.

The logical model previously defined in Task 1 was programmed using the Simio software. The paradigms that were used to develop the digital twin are objects, events, and processes. The programing task was divided into two phases. During the first phase, a digital twin that mimics the current state of the system was created to have a point of departure, which subsequently was used to develop a digital twin of the future state of the system. This digital twin was broken down into small parts and those were systematically programmed one at a time. Every time a small part of the digital twin was created, a verification analysis was conducted to prove that the model is behaving as expected.

Subsequently, the output of the digital twin of the system's current state was compared versus the output of the real system. The digital twin's programming, verification, and validation steps were done iteratively until the group of modelers and the engineering team of the manufacturing plant agreed that the digital twin was an accurate representation of the current system.

Also, a sensitivity study was conducted using linear regression. The input parameters that were chosen for the analysis are one station of the assembly and pre-painting areas, and the painting station. Fig. 2 shows a Tornado chart with the results obtained in the Simio software. The sensitivity coefficients of the previously mentioned workstations are 0.044, 0.039, and 0.018 hours, respectively.

Afterward, the programming of the digital twin of the current system was modified to mimic the previously defined logical model of the proposed system with painting robots.

Task 4: Perform the analysis. After the digital twin of the proposed process with painting robots was completed during the third task, the analysis task started. As mentioned before, this analysis focuses on quantifying the influence of limited buffer size in the production capacity of the proposed system with painting robots.

The presented study is focused on the calculation of the total number of products produced over the pre-defined buffer size of the painting area. In order to determine the influence of the buffer size, a what-if analysis was run.

The simulation runs for 365 days (i.e., 8,760 hours). An infinite demand was considered for this analysis, which means that it was considered that the system is able to ship all the units that are produced. For this analysis, the manufacturing orders of the product types were pushed through the value stream.

During the analysis, the average total number of parts was calculated for buffer sizes of 7, 8, 9, 10, 20, 30, 40, 50, 100, 200 and infinity.

Table I shows the average results obtained from fifty replications of the total number of parts produced. Also, one can see in Fig. 3 a graph that shows the total number of parts produced versus the different buffer sizes. It was observed that the system converges at a buffer size of 200, where the total number of parts produced with this buffer size is 5200 parts.

In terms of theory of constrains [13], one can say that the painting area is the governing constraint that determines the throughput, because this area has the processes with longest processing times and the manufacturing sequences involves re-entrance of the WIP of the different products. The system converges at a buffer size of 200 units because the buffer placed before this area ensures a starving time of zero for this area. At the same time, the buffer placed after this area allows a starving time of zero for the Testing area.

Furthermore, one can see in Fig. 4 the inventory of the cluster with painting robots. It is observed that for the case of an infinity buffer capacity the inventory in the robotic cluster grows without control, because of that, a limited buffer serves also as a production strategy to maintain the inventory levels.

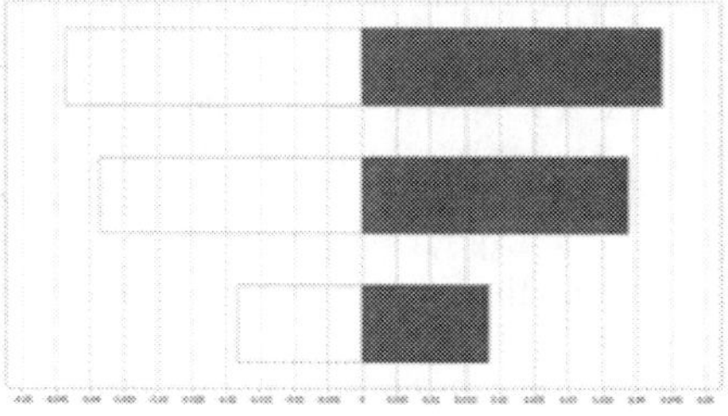

Figure 2. Sensitivity analysis of the selected processes.

TABLE I. NUMBER OF PARTS PRODUCED AS A FUNCTION OF THE BUFFER SIZE

Buffer size	Number of parts produced
7	4963
8	5006
9	5027
10	5065
20	5097
30	5129
40	5170
50	5185
100	5190
200	5200
Infinity	5205

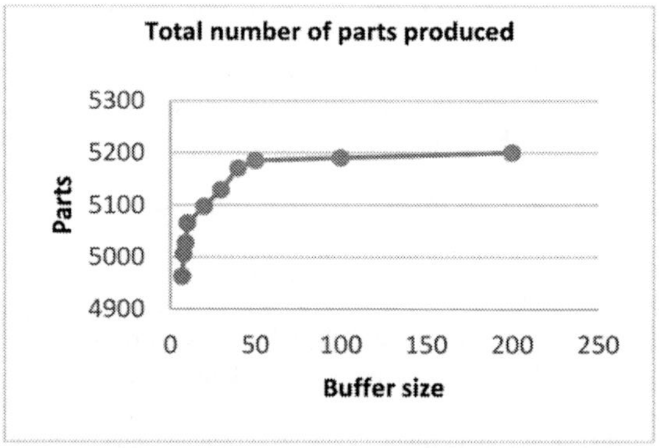

Figure 3. Total number of parts produced versus different buffer sizes.

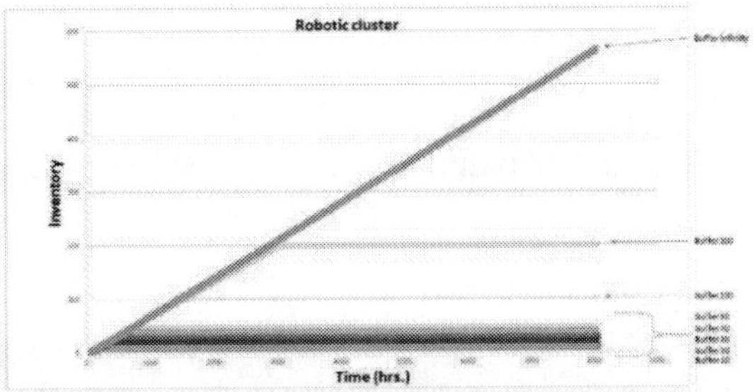

Figure 4. Inventory of the robotic cluster as a function of time.

V. CONCLUSION

In this manuscript, the initial efforts and findings of a company that is in the journey of incorporating Industry 4.0 technologies are presented. This research project reports an implementation of a digital twin of an entire manufacturing assembly plant that is used for design purposes. To be more specific, the digital twin was used to investigate the influence of the buffer size of the painting shop over the total production capacity for the future state of the manufacturing plant. The future state of the company consists on replacing some manual operations of the painting shop with painting robots.

The implementation of a digital twin enables us to quantify the influence of the painting robots before the insertion of them into the manufacturing system. The results of the analysis show that the system converges at a buffer size of 200, obtaining approximately a total number of 5200 parts produced. Also, it was observed that a limited buffer size helps to control the inventory on the production floor.

Furthermore, this manufacturing company will employ in the near future this digital twin as a foundation to quantify the different implications of adding additional technologies encompassed by Industry 4.0 on their production floor.

REFERENCES

[1] Industry 4.0: The Future of Competitiveness in U.S. Manufacturing, Innovative Manufactures Centers, retrieved: Aug., 2020, Available: http://imcpa.com/industry-4-0-future-competitiveness-u-s-manufacturing/.

[2] J. Smith, D. Sturrock, and W. Kelton, "Simio and Simulation: Modeling, Analysis, Applications", 5th ed., Pittsburgh, PA: Simio, 2018.

[3] M. Shafto et al., "DRAFT Modeling, Simulation, Information Technology & Processing Roadmap", NASA, DC, D.C., USA, Nov 2010.

[4] M. Shafto et al., " Modeling, Simulation, Information Technology & Processing Roadmap", NASA, DC, D.C., USA, April 2012.

[5] J. Lee, E. Lapira, B. Bagheri, and Hung-an Kao, "Recent Advances and Trends in Predictive Manufacturing Systems in Big Data Environment," Manufacturing Letters, vol. 1, pp. 38-41, Oct. 2013, doi.org/10.1016/j.mfglet.2013.09.005.

[6] T. Gabor, L. Belzner, M. Kiermeier, M. Beck, and A. Neitz, "A Simulation-Based Architecture for Smart Cyber-Physical Systems," 2016 IEEE International Conference on Autonomic Computing (ICAC), IEEE Press, July 2016, pp. 374 379, doi:10.1109/ICAC.2016.29.

[7] W. Terkaj, T. Tolio, and M. Urgo, "A virtual factory approach for in situ simulation to support production and maintenance planning," CIRP Annals, vol. 64, pp. 451-454, 2015, doi.org/10.1016/j.cirp.2015.04.121.

[8] F. Tao et al., "Digital Twin-driven Product Design, Manufacturing and Service with Big Data," The International Journal of Advanced Manufacturing Technology, vol. 94, pp. 3563-3576, March 2017, doi:10.1007/s00170-017-0233-1.

[9] N.S. Gujarathi, R.M. Ogale, and T. Gupta, "Production Capacity Analysis of a Shock Absorber Assembly Line Using Simulation," Proc. of the 2004 Winter Simulation Conference, IEEE Press, pp. 1-5, Dec. 2004, doi: 10.1109/WSC.2004.1371451.

[10] C.-C. Lin, W.-Y. Liu, and Y.-H. Chena, "Considering Stockers in Reentrant Hybrid Flow Shop Scheduling with Limited Buffer Capacity," Computers and Industrial Engineering, vol. 139, pp. 1-14, Jan. 2020, doi.org/10.1016/j.cie.2019.106154.

[11] Y.-H. Lian and H. Van Landeghem, "Analyzing the effects of Lean manufacturing using a value stream mapping-based simulation generator," The International Journal of Production Research, vol. 45, pp. 3037-3058, July 2007, doi.org/10.1080/00207540600791590.

[12] K. Vasudevan, E. Lammers, E. Williams, and O. Ülgen, "Application of Simulation to Design and Operation of Steel Mill Devoted to Manufacture of Line Pipes," Proc. 2010 Second International Conference on Advances in System Simulation, IEEE Press, Aug. 2010, pp. 1-6, doi: 10.1109/SIMUL.2010.11.

[13] E. M. Goldratt, "What is this thing called theory of constraints and how should it be implemented?," 1st ed., Great Barrington, MA, USA, The North River Press, pp. 117-118, 1990.

Event Triggered Simulation of Push and Pull Processes

Stefan Haag, Lara Zakfeld, Carlo Simon and Christian Reuter

Hochschule Worms
Erenburgerstr. 19, 67549 Worms, Germany
Email: {haag, lara.zakfeld, simon, reuter}@hs-worms.de

Abstract—**The development of conceptual models relies on a proper modeling language, the existence of a beneficial tool, and knowledge about modeling techniques. We use Petri nets as our preferred modeling language for decades, because Petri net models are illustrative and can be executed or simulated, respectively. However, since most of the Petri net tools that have been developed in the past are no longer executable, we developed a novel, Web-based Petri net modeling and simulation environment called Process-Simulation.Center (P-S.C). It facilitates the definition of individual data objects as tokens such that data-driven process simulations can be conducted within the tool. In the process, we realized the absence of a general modeling technique for the definition of such models. Generally, two different approaches exist: a clock-pulse simulation where the state of the modeled system is simulated for each point in time and an event triggered simulation that calculates new states only for those moments the system state changes. Using teaching in a logistics laboratory as an example, this paper demonstrates how event triggered simulation models can be developed and how they have to be interpreted. Concretely, the consequences of switching logistics processes from push to pull principles are considered concerning the storage costs.**

Keywords–Conceptual models of timed dynamic systems; Simulation; Petri nets; Logistics; Teaching.

I. INTRODUCTION

Reducing costs while at the same time increasing the production's flexibility is a combined goal for manufacturers. Beside an investment in better and faster machines, rethinking production strategies and processes is also feasible and potentially cheaper. Changing the production from push to pull is one option and its advantages have been demonstrated in many production lines. Nonetheless, push strategies are still widely in practical use. What is the reason for this? We assume that producers are uncertain about the consequences of such changes. In this case, conceptual and simulatable models of the current and the intended production lines could objectify decisions on the reorganization of the production.

This paper shows the effect of turning a push into a pull production using the example of a logistics training laboratory at the University of Applied Sciences Worms. For this, two different models of Petri nets with individual tokens have been developed and simulated: a clock-pulse simulation that – like a movie – demonstrates the behavior in every second, and an event triggered simulation that is the objective of this paper. Such a simulation, however, needs a powerful Petri net modeling and simulation tool that can handle individual tokens and that can also be used in a distributed environment. We chose to use the novel, Web-based Process-Simulation.Center (P-S.C) developed on our own, which is free to use for academic users.

Part of the research design for this tool is its use in various environments like production, logistics, trade and teaching in order to develop and understand different Petri net modeling techniques. For the concrete example, the P-S.C helps learners to predict the behavior of the processes to be reorganized.

Following this introduction, in Section II, a short explanation of the design science research method is given. Then, the logistics training laboratory for processes is explained as a sample application in Section III. Section IV provides an overview of push, pull, and kanban as well as possibilities for the modeling and simulation of timed dynamic systems with Petri nets and other modeling approaches. Also, some information about the P-S.C is given. Afterwards, in Section V, the utilized modeling approach and its push and pull based implementations are introduced. Lastly, in Section VI a conclusion both on the simulation results and the modeling approach is presented. The paper closes with an overview of planned and possible future work.

II. RESEARCH METHOD

Research on new and comparison of different modeling techniques for Petri nets with individual tokens relies on the existence of proper modeling and simulation tools. For this, we work on the P-S.C for several years following the guidelines for design science research as per [1]. Application to a simulative learning environment is one more step in this process. A brief overview of conducted research is as follows:

Design as an Artifact: The P-S.C is a Web-based specification and simulation software for processes encompassing both user defined and primitive data types (including date and time types), organizational structures and process maps. Process execution can be controlled by business relevant data that is linked by a data interface. Also, an interface can be used to control sensors and actors connected to a Raspberry Pi if installed on such a device.

Problem Relevance: A simulation permits the extension of real-world experiences in a learning environment. It helps to overcome typical limitations concerning time, resources, space, and people. The simulation environment, though, must be generic enough to assure the intended learning success. From a conceptual modeling perspective, it must be determined if all these aspects can be expressed and simulated due to a formal, semantic base.

Design Evaluation: The P-S.C has already been used by companies in logistics and trade. Students of an integrated logistics degree program developed a simulation model for the reorganization of a returns process [2]. The tool is also used for problem-based and research-oriented learning in bachelor and master degree programs [3].

Research Contribution: The P-S.C is a practical application on the theoretical basis of high-level Petri nets combined with views on organizational structures, process maps and data types. The tool offers a novel user experience and provides new insights in Petri net based modeling techniques. This is important since as an abstract concept Petri nets do not force specific modeling approaches such as flow diagrams, value stream diagrams or other pictorial modeling approaches.

Research Rigor: The benefits of a simulation approach in opposite to pure visual methods is evaluated in mentioned bachelor and master courses as well as in cooperation with partner companies of integrated degree programs.

Design as a Search Process: The presented prototype is the latest in a series that starts from the initial implementation of the underlying principles and ends in a productive system. Each implementation step has been evaluated and published (for instance, [4]-[6]).

Communication of Research: The results achieved so far are relevant for both research and practice. They are presented on pertinent conferences but also, more eidetic, for practitioners in advanced training programs.

III. A Simulation Laboratory for Processes in Logistics

The so-called *box game* has been developed at the University of Applied Sciences Worms to teach students in logistics. Despite its obvious simplicity, it effectively demonstrates different kinds of problems and processes that have a high impact for practical applications. We chose it as the modeling and simulation objective in order to enrich the learning experience of the students.

The concrete example is a simple construction process: students assemble big and small boxes, put the smaller into the bigger ones, and eventually check the quality. This production is conducted following varying strategies (push and pull) in order to observe influences on organizational issues, production time, and storage costs of these strategies as well as consequences when they are changed. Learners taking part in the game gain first-hand experience of different work situations and can recognize several types of waste (called *muda*) such as overproduction, waiting, and motion, but also the transformation of waste types. Discussing the shared experiences is a major part of the learning success. A complete simulation run of the box game lasts about two to three hours.

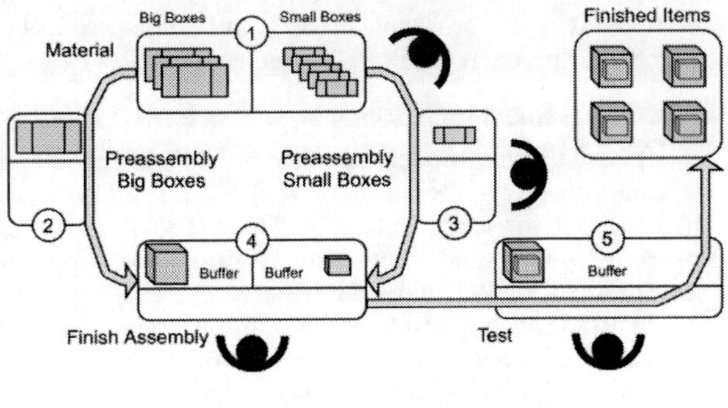

Figure 1. Layout Design of the *Box Game*

Despite the simplicity of the used material and the low level of technical requirements, the *box game* is easily transferable to assembly workstations in general and has a high practical impact. It focuses on the strategic principles and leaves out problems of a mechanical production such as shift patterns, changeover times and multiple machine set-ups.

Figure 1 shows the spatial organization of the *box game* in the learning laboratory: five worktables are arranged in a suitable location and standard positions like interim storages are marked with adhesive tape. As can be seen, the setting can also be built up in locations such as conference rooms, training rooms, or even canteens.

The following activities have to be conducted:

Storage (S): Deliver the boxes' building sets.

Preassembly big boxes (PBB): Fold the box, close the lid, and pass the box to the next processing step.

Preassembly small boxes (PSB): Fold the box, close the lid, and pass the box to the next processing step.

Finish assembly (FA): Open big box, insert small one, label small box with a package note (a simple post-it), close and seal big box lid (with adhesive tape), cut of tape with scissors if necessary, and pass the box to the test step.

Test (QA): Shake the sealed box for an acoustic quality check, apply a red dot to the upper left corner of the box to indicate a pass, and place the box in the storage.

The following players can partake in the game:

5 employees who will occupy the work stations.
3 timekeepers who record the processing times.
1 observer who records the inventory in the system.
1 observer who records productivity levels.
2 substitues who disassemble the boxes.

The initial stock of the *box game* is 75 big and small boxes each. However, the aim is not to produce the entire demand in the shortest time possible with all employees but to respect the customer's demand - one part every 15 seconds - without inventory and with as few employees as possible.

Typically, the simulation is played in four rounds with defined duration, for example 5 or 8 minutes. During the game two types of principles with two batch sizes are played.

Batch size 3 - push principle: The products are passed on in batches of size 3. Each process step works functionally independent from the other and the participants are rewarded based on the number of pieces they work on. Hence, it is the goal at each station to produce as much output as possible.

Batch size 3 - pull principle: Stations produce and pass on products in size 3 batches. Upstream stations have to hold their pieces and stop production until it is demanded internally or externally. Capacity of a station is limited to 3 items and items can only be replaced accordingly.

Batch size 1 - pull principle: The third round is played like the second one, but the batch size is reduced to 1.

Improvement - pull principle: The last round is used to find tweaks autonomously and to implement them as a team.

The advantage of this approach is that the participants gather personal experiences. This can hardly be replaced by a computer simulation. However, augmenting this hands-on experience by such a simulation helps to scale up both complexity and range of the considered process.

IV. RELATED WORK

Since this paper combines conceptual modeling with Petri nets and the simulation of laboratory processes in logistics, for both fields related work is considered.

A. Push, Pull and Kanban

In a push production, every workstation produces when supplied sufficiently regardless of a given demand. The advantages of this are steady production and a high utilization rate. In a pull production, the workstations only produce for a given actual demand, leading to lower stocks and a more flexible production. Which of these paradigms is better than the other depends on the circumstances. Sometimes, mixed solutions are best [7].

Kanban is a method to realize pull principles in logistics and hence to lower stocks by controlling the replenishment of material. If a threshold is recognized, a kanban signal initiates a pull request that includes information on the batch size, leading to stable production sizes. Dependent on the used variant, the replenishment can be controlled by cards, empty containers, via e-kanban or by use of a supermarket system [8] [9].

As the pull requests establish a chain starting at the dispatch warehouse, in kanban systems information flows upstream, while material flows downstream. Different types of kanban may be used to account for the type of material, set up times for production or internal factors [10].

B. Push and Pull Simulation with Petri Nets

Petri nets can be used to study the performance of push and pull approaches. Constraints like manufacturing and setup times, vehicle routing or concurrent processing become operational and, thus, flexible manufacturing systems can be examined [7]. Large and interlocked systems can be modeled by expanding on local components; applying different Petri net specifications suited for respective tasks is beneficiary [11].

Almost all of these approaches lack the handling of real time values and rely on some kind of generic times. We assume that this is because of the absence of proper modeling tools for timed Petri nets [12].

C. Time Concepts in Petri Nets

Since time is an important dimension for the modeling of processes and dynamic systems in general, there exist numerous approaches for handling time aspects in Petri nets. They differ concerning their expressiveness (discrete or continuous time) and which Petri net elements are used to express time constraints (place, transition, arc, or token).

One possible implementation puts one or two time values on transitions, the lower being a delay up to which the transition is not enabled while the higher presents the latest possible moment of firing. This may lead either to a forced firing, the reset of a clock - where the lower value describes a kind of preparation time and the higher one an expiration time from when a new preparation needs to be conducted - or even to a dead net. Variations include time consuming firing [13] as well as firing without time consumption [14].

Another obvious possibility is to assign time values to the places, again representing lower and upper bounds. These bounds represent the availability of tokens, either as delay until a token becomes available [15] or as time windows in which they are available [16] [17].

Yet, another possible implementation is to define the permeability of arcs relative to the moment an adjacent place was marked or an adjacent transition was enabled. The so far cited concepts are equivalent [18]. However, they have the disadvantage that the state of such nets does not only rely on the respective markings, but also on some kind of timer clocks.

D. Higher Petri Nets and Time

Originally, Petri nets have been defined as Place/Transition nets (P/T) with anonymous tokens indicating a system's state [19]. Diverse concepts for representing high level information in Petri nets exist, with the most widely known being Predicate/Transition nets (Pr/T) and Colored Petri Nets (CPN).

Pr/T and CPN omit anonymous tokens for ones carrying information that can be processed and altered by functions encoded on transitions and arcs. They are used to select tokens from the preset and to calculate new values for tokens on the postset of transitions. Places serve as predicates according to which transitions may fire. Thus, it is possible to model data-driven processes or dynamic systems in general. In CPN, elements are additionally provided with a color, hereby inducing a parallelization in representation: when determining the status of a transition, places and tokens are examined by color separately [20]-[22].

Timestamps are means to encode time information in the marking. In Timestamp Nets, tokens designate the moment the corresponding token was placed. Transitions may fire in time windows as given on the transitions' incoming arcs [23] [24]. Extended Timestamp Nets integrate the concepts of Pr/T and Timestamp nets such that tokens carry timestamps and any further information [25].

Some of the approaches may be transformed into each other effortlessly [26] [27]. All of the presented Petri net formalisms use artificial, abstract time units. To model and simulate real-world applications, real time values however should be used instead. To this end, date and time data types seem beneficial to be included as possible information on tokens.

E. Further Modeling Approaches

For reference, there are other modeling methods that were developed to combine time and process structures. One of these methods are Value Stream Diagrams, which are suitable for high-level overviews of processes as they consider whole value streams from customer to supplier [28] [29].

Also, Business Process Model and Notation (BPMN) is extensively used for modeling business processes due to the relative ease of both creating and understanding models. Using BPMN, it is possible to create both high-level models of companies and low-level models of single processes in a graphical approach similar to flowcharts [30].

F. Process-Simulation.Center

If conceptual models are to be developed for process simulation or even execution, tools are needed in addition to a formal mathematical base. The P-S.C is a novel, Web-based modeling and simulation environment supporting the development of P/T and Pr/T nets.

In P-S.C, it is possible to assign data types to places and use these places in analogy to tables in databases. Special types for date and time are important substructures for the simulation of processes in production and logistics and enhance the mentioned approaches to timed Petri nets.

In opposite to relational algebra and, hence, SQL, where operations like select or projection are applied to all affected tuples at once and the result of a relational operation is always a set, in P-S.C the processing of tuples on places is serialized. The reason for this design choice is that, in business and production processes, work items are also treated one after another. The concrete sequence is decided upon locally by the transitions of the net and its marking.

Moreover, the P-S.C can be used to connect the process view on a system with other views. For instance, usage of process maps may combine different processes with each other and express the strategic value of a specific process as a primary process, a support process or a process on the management level. Also, the organizational structure of an institution can be combined with the Petri net view on the processes by assigning its nodes to the swim lanes of the corresponding responsible organizational units. Organizational charts themselves complete the functions of the P-S.C.

It is worth mentioning that the P-S.C draws nodes in such a way that their labels can be presented within, which facilitates reading and understanding. To further strengthen visual clues of their functionality, nodes can be provided with symbols.

Contrary to most other conceptual modeling tools, especially those developed for Petri nets, a specification language rather than a graphical editor has been designed for the P-S.C with which all types of models are scripted. Due to strong algorithms for automatic layout, modelers can concentrate on structural aspects of the domain to be expressed.

The dearth of current Petri net tools, the quaint user experience of most of the still working ones and the unique approach of using textual programming instead of drag-and-drop modeling in combination with the added functionality are the main reasons for the implementation of the P-S.C.

Further information about the tool has already been referred to in Section II.

V. Event Triggered Simulation Models

One target of this paper is to develop an event triggered simulation model to determine the total costs of all involved stocks and to explain the applied modeling technique. Hence, the presented Petri net models mainly consist of places for these stocks, connected by transitions and arcs that represent the functionality. Since an ideal production flow is one with minimal stocks and short throughput times, the individual boxes are passed from one production step directly to the following, establishing a batch size of 1. Other batch sizes are implemented accordingly [9].

Transitions carry selection criteria about which tokens are to be processed next if there are several available (normally the one with the lowest id according to the FIFO principle is chosen). These criteria may be displayed on the transitions by clicking the plus symbol.

Further computation instructions are deposited on the arcs; they are required for the simulation's output as they provide information about how much time is needed for each production step in the complete process. Again, arc inscriptions can be shown or hidden as required.

A. The Push Model

Figure 2 shows the push version of the *box game*. Single boxes get delivered from the main storage *inStore* to the upstream buffers *inBB* and *inSB* of the assembly stations.

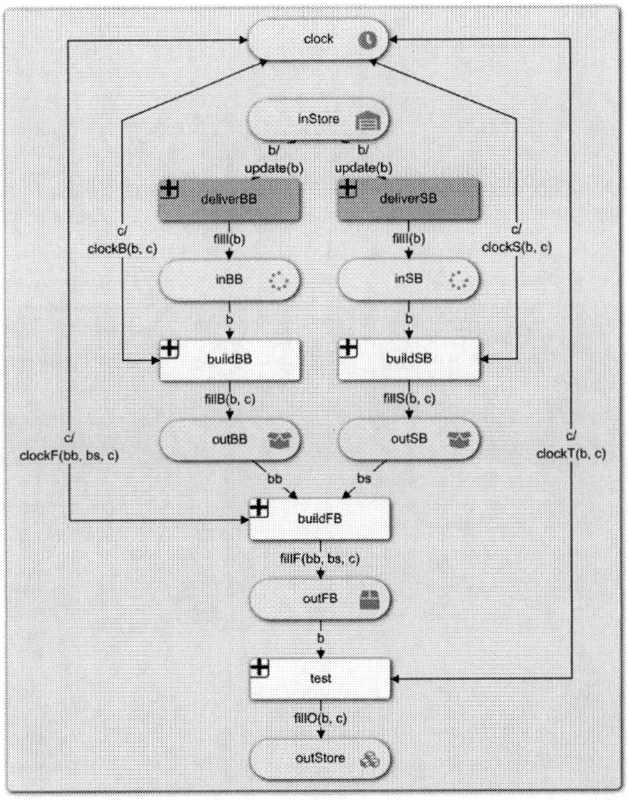

Figure 2. Event Triggered Push Model

Modeling and simulation of the workplaces themselves is abridged by use of the build transitions *buildBB*, *buildSB*, *buildFB* and later on the transition *test*. Successively, the boxes are stored in the outgoing buffers of the workplaces *outBB* and *outSB*, final assembly *outFB*, and the exit storage *outStore*.

The place *clock* establishes a possibility to track elapsed times. As the simulations runs, the time data on when items enter or leave a storage position - a part of the respective marking of the Petri net as provided by the *clock* - is logged and the whole data set is supplied in form of comma-separated values. The data set embraces the entire reachability set of all times and amounts which allows for a deep analysis of the net's behavior, especially of waiting times and storage costs.

B. The Pull Model

The pull version of the *box game* as depicted in Figure 3 is partly more complicated, as supplementary elements are needed to implement pull requests. On the other side, as time logging can be implemented by tracing tokens forward and backward, the *clock* and some arcs may be dropped.

In Section IV-A, it has been mentioned that information flows from the dispatch warehouse upstream. Thus, the kanban chain should start at *outStore* instead of where it is modeled. However, in the presented model theoretically necessary arcs between the storage places establishing single pulls may partly be omitted. Skipping these connections is feasible as all pulls beside the modeled one arise from working steps that require less time than *buildFB*, so their storage places are empty by specification at the relevant times. Modeling the full kanban chain becomes necessary when considering larger batch sizes.

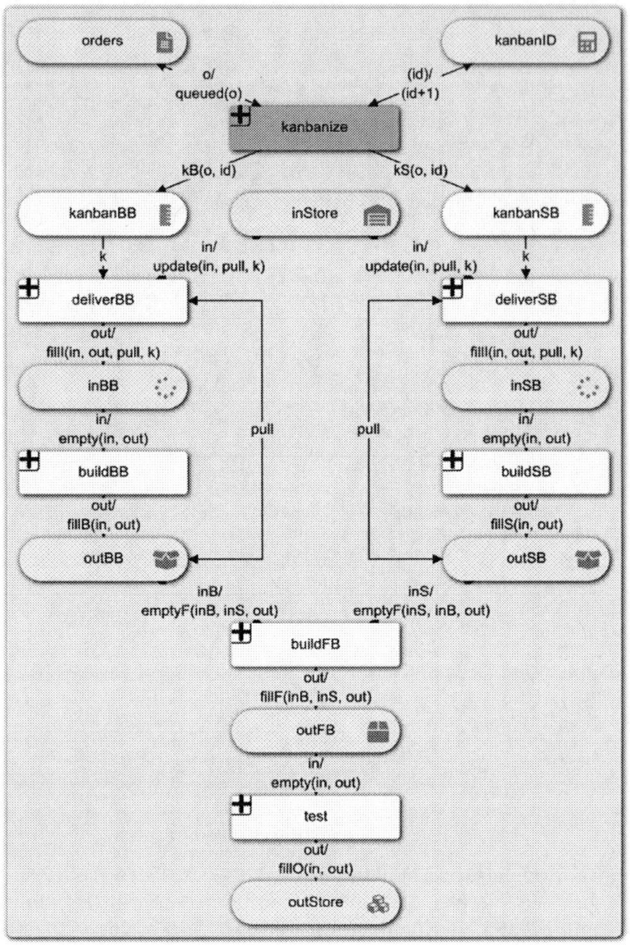

Figure 3. Event Triggered Pull Model

As a first step, tokens on *orders* are transposed into kanban tokens that adhere to the given batch size. These tokens are put on *kanbanBB* and *kanbanSB* in order to control the deliveries from the main storage *inStore*.

In connection with information flowing through additional *pull* arcs, the kanban principle is implemented. When there are no boxes on the preassembly's outgoing storage places *outBB* and *outSB* (which also serve as input buffer for *buildFB*), a pull request for raw material and, thus, production of the specified batch is initiated. The model accounts for both necessary delivery times from main storage to buffers and the longer processing time of the big boxes, leading to later dispatch times of the small boxes. This is done to minimize the waiting time of intermediates in the buffers.

The remainder of the model works like the push version.

VI. Conclusion and Future Work

As expected, the simulation of the two models show no difference in total processing or idle times for single workplaces. Differences on storage places become evident, though.

As the distribution of waiting times behind *buildFB* is the same for both models, only the first six storage places need to be analyzed. The upper part of Figure 4 shows the allocation of the boxes' waiting times to single stocks in the push model while the lower part shows the same for the pull model.

Stocks on *inStore* are split by type. The boxes themselves are aggregated into Five-Box-Clusters for clarity. The trend to successively longer waiting times is clearly visible.

The push model's *inStore* gets cleared as fast as possible. This, however, leads to large buffers just before the first concurrent production steps. As the preassembly requires less time than the final assembly, the two incoming buffers for *buildFB* are also highly occupied.

Although the accumulated waiting times are equivalent, the pull model unites them on the main storage *inStore* only.

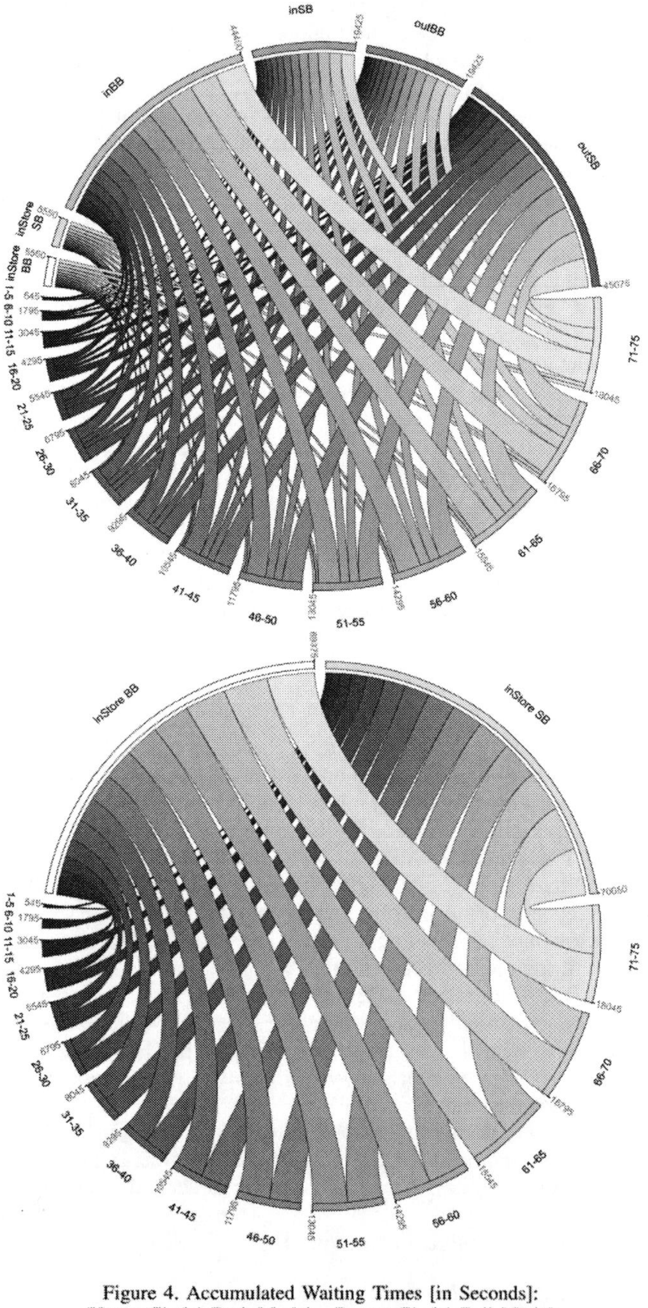

Figure 4. Accumulated Waiting Times [in Seconds]:
(Upper Circle) Push Model · (Lower Circle) Pull Model:
(Upper Half Circles) Named Storage Places · (Lower Half Circles) Clusters of Five Successive Boxes · (Circular Area) Distribution of Accumulated Waiting Times of Five-Box-Clusters to Individual Storage Places

As anticipated, the pull principle leads to zero interim buffer inventory throughout the stocks under consideration. For manufacturing companies, this opens up the possibility to externalize costs. One such alternative is to use consignment stores: suppliers maintain warehouses inside the customer's facility and, thus, must keep the material in their balance sheet. Another common possibility is just-in-time delivery. With high process stability and fast response times, even the use of a kanban cycle with the supplier is conceivable [10]. These options may lead to partial or total eradication of stocks.

An example for what is not accounted for in these models is the cost of transportation, as smaller batch sizes usually correspondent to higher transportation costs, leading to familiar knowledge: decreasing one muda typically increases others. Hence, batch size 1, which is optimal for interim storage costs, may not necessarily be the globally optimal solution.

Event triggered simulations show performance advantages over clock pulse simulations. In this example, the push model needs 79 calculation steps while the pull model requires 228, due to the additional kanban flows. However, both models outperform their respective clock pulse counterpart that both run for 1902 computation steps each - one step for every second elapsed. Hence, the presented approach scales better, which will be beneficial for an industrial application.

During development of the shown models, the following modeling techniques turned out to be helpful:

1. Define data types for the different stocks and other data objects, and initialize the corresponding places in accordance with the starting condition.
2. Augment the model by transitions for beginning and ending specific tasks like delivering raw materials, building or testing a box.
3. Identify the next item to be taken and the moment this will occur. This also allows for implementation of different prioritization strategies.
4. Start with modeling the simpler push principle and augment this model by pull principles.
5. Look for a proper visualization of the simulation results.

Event triggered and clock pulse simulation both react to discrete, clearly distinguishable events and calculate predictable new states. The world, however, is continuous and decisions are often fuzzy. Future work will, therefore, focus on further, different techniques for developing conceptual models for dynamic systems, taking this aspect into account. This work will also rely on the existence of a modeling and simulation environment and hence work on the P-S.C will be continued.

REFERENCES

[1] A. R. Hevner, S. T. March, J. Park, and S. Ram, "Design science in information systems research," MIS Quarterly, vol. 28, no. 1, 2004, pp. 75–106.

[2] C. Simon and S. Haag, "Simulatable Reference Models To Transform Enterprises For The Digital Age – A Case Study," in ECMS 2020: 34rd International Conference on Modelling and Simulation, M. Steglich, C. Müller, G. Neumann, and M. Walther, Eds., 2020, pp. 294–300.

[3] ——, "Digitale Zwillinge modellieren und verstehen: Eine Fallstudie zum problembasierten und forschenden Lernen," in MoHoL 2020 (Workshop): Modellierung in der Hochschullehre, J.-R. Rehse, M. Striewe, and M. Ullrich, Eds., Wien, Austria, 2020, pp. 101–112.

[4] S. Haag and C. Simon, "Simulation of Horizontal and Vertical Integration in Digital Twins," in ECMS 2019: 33rd International Conference on Modelling and Simulation, M. Iacono, F. Palmieri, M. Gribaudo, and M. Ficco, Eds., 2019, pp. 284–289.

[5] C. Simon and S. Haag, "Simulation vertikaler Integration: Vom Top-Floor zum Shop-Floor und zurück," in Tagungsband AKWI, T. Barton, F. Herrmann, V. G. Meister, C. Müller, C. Seel, and U. Steffens, Eds., 2018, pp. 104–113.

[6] C. Simon, "Eine Petri-Netz-Programmiersprache und Anwendungen in der Produktion," in Tagungsband AKWI, T. Barton, F. Herrmann, V. G. Meister, C. Müller, and C. Seel, Eds., 2017, pp. 61–70.

[7] M. Zhou and K. Venkatesh, Modeling, Simulation, and Control of Flexible Manufacturing Systems - A Petri net Approach, ser. Intelligent Control and Intelligent Automation. Singapore, New Jersey: World Scientific, 1999, vol. 6.

[8] U. Dombrowski and T. Mielke, Ganzheitliche Produktionssysteme: Aktueller Stand und zukünftige Entwicklungen. München: Springer Vieweg, 2014.

[9] J. Gottmann, Produktionscontrolling: Werströme und Kosten optimieren, 2nd ed. Wiesbaden: Springer Gabler, 2019.

[10] H. Wildemann, Kanban-Produktionssteuerung, 28th ed. München: TCW, 2020.

[11] L. Recalde, M. Silva, J. Ezpeleta, and E. Teruel, Lectures on Concurrency and Petri Nets: Advances in Petri Nets. Berlin: Springer, 2004, ch. Petri nets and manufacturing systems: An examples-driven tour, pp. 742–788.

[12] "Petri Nets Tools Database Quick Overview," https://www.informatik.uni-hamburg.de/TGI/PetriNets/tools/quick.html (last accessed 2020.09.01).

[13] C. Ramchandani, "Analysis of Asynchronous Concurrent Systems by Timed Petri Nets," MIT, Project MAC, Technical Report 120, 1974.

[14] P. Merlin, "The Time-Petri-Net and the Recoverability of Processes," University California, Irvine, Tech. Rep., 1974.

[15] J. Sifakis, "Use of petri nets for performance evalutation," in Measuring, modelling and evalutating computer systems, ser. IFIP, H. Beilner and E. Gelenbe, Eds., North Holland Publ. Co., 1977, pp. 75–93.

[16] H.-M. Hanisch, Petri-Netze in der Verfahrenstechnik. München: Oldenbourg, 1992.

[17] ——, "Dynamik von Koordinierungssteuerungen in diskontinuierlichen verfahrenstechnischen Systemen," in Petrinetze in der Automatisierungstechnik, E. Schnieder, Ed. München, Wien: Oldenbourg Verlag, 1992.

[18] R. König and L. Quäck, Petri-Netze in der Steuerungs- und Digitaltechnik. München, Wien: Oldenbourg Verlag, 1988.

[19] C. A. Petri, "Kommunikation mit Automaten," Schriften des Institutes für instrumentelle Mathematik, Bonn, Tech. Rep., 1962.

[20] H. J. Genrich and K. Lautenbach, "System Modelling with High-Level Petri Nets," Theoretical Computer Science, vol. 13, 1981.

[21] H. J. Genrich, "Predicate/Transition Nets," in High-level Petri Nets: Theory and Applications, K. Jensen and G. Rosenberg, Eds. Springer, 1991, pp. 3–43.

[22] K. Jensen, Coloured Petri-Nets, 1st ed. Berlin: Springer, 1992.

[23] C. Ghezzi, D. Mandrioli, S. Morasca, and M. Pezzè, "A unified high-level petri net formalism for time-critical systems," IEEE Transactions On Software Engineering, vol. 17, no. 2, 1991, pp. 160–172.

[24] H.-M. Hanisch, K. Lautenbach, C. Simon, and J. Thieme, "Timestamp Nets in Technical Applications," in IEEE International Workshop on Discrete Event Systems, San Diego, CA, 1998.

[25] K. Lautenbach and C. Simon, "Erweiterte Zeitstempelnetze," Universität Koblenz-Landau, Universität Koblenz-Landau, Fachberichte Informatik 03–99, 1999.

[26] K. Jensen, "High-Level Petri Nets," Informatik-Fachberichte, vol. 66, 1983, pp. 166–180.

[27] L. Popova-Zeugmann, Time and Petri Nets. Berlin: Springer, 2013.

[28] C. E. Knoeppel, Installing Efficiency Methods. The Engineering Magazine, 1915.

[29] T. Ohno, Toyota Production System. Milton Park, UK: Taylor & Francis, 1988.

[30] OMG, "BPMN 2.0 - Business Process Model and Notation," http://www.bpmn.org/ (last accessed 2020.09.01), 2011.

Designing a Model for Flu Propagation in Emergency Departments

[1]Morteza Ansari Dogaheh,
[1]Emilio Luque, [2]Manel Taboada
[1]Computer Architecture and Operating Systems Department
University Autonoma of Barcelona
Bellaterra, Barcelona, Spain
e-mail: morteza.ansaridogaheh@e-campus.uab.cat,
emilio.luque@uab.es
[2]Escuelas Universitarias Gimbernat: Computer Science School
Universitat Autonoma de Barcelona (UAB)
Barcelona, Spain
e-mail: manel.taboada@eug.es

Francisco Epelde
Medical Department
Hospital Universitari Parc Tauli
Sabadell, Barcelona, Spain
e-mail: fepelde@tauli.cat

Abstract—**Influenza is an acute viral infection that primarily attacks the upper respiratory tract. The disease occurs worldwide and spreads very quickly in populations, especially in crowded circumstances like Emergency Departments (ED). Influenza can be spread in three main ways, all of which are very feasible in ED environments: by the airborne route, by contaminated surfaces or from direct personal contact such as a handshake. Our research uses Agent Based Modeling and Simulation techniques to build the model and the simulation of the transmission of flu virus contact in ED. The simulator allows us to build virtual scenarios with the aim of understanding the phenomenon of flu transmission and the potential impact of the implementation of different policies in propagation rates. This work is an expansion of the previous one carried on by other members of our research group, with the aim of developing a more flexible and reasonable healthcare system simulation and modeling.**

Keywords- Emergency department Simulator; Agent based modeling and simulation; Influenza propagation.

I. INTRODUCTION

Influenza, known as the flu, is a respiratory infection caused by a virus. According to the Centers for Disease Control (CDC), the burden of Influenza during the 2017–2018 season was the highest since the 2009 pandemic, resulting in more than 22.7 million medical visits, 959,000 hospitalizations, and 79,400 deaths in the United States [1]. The flu virus usually spreads from person to person through coughing or sneezing. The flu can be contacted by touching a surface that includes the flu virus on it and then touching the nose or eyes [2]. Infection with the influenza virus can cause significant morbidity and mortality. This is specifically true in vulnerable populations with an underlying disease in an indoor situation like Emergency Department areas.

Emergency Departments are one of the most complex and dynamic healthcare systems, receiving an increasing demand, and usually being overcrowded. ED has a continuous activity, operating 24 hours a day every day of the year. The existence of a communicable disease within the emergency services, especially a seasonal contagious disease [3], can have a negative influence on the service offered, and increases the risk of both, the infection of health personnel and of worsening of the underlying disease of the patients attended in the ED. The resource planning of ED is complex because its activity is not linear, and it varies depending on time, day of the week, and season. Simulation becomes an important tool for modeling complex systems that include many elements, a large number of interdependencies among such elements, and/or considerable variability [4]. Discrete Event Simulation (DES), System Dynamics (SD), and Agent-Based Modeling and Simulation (ABMS) are the main three approaches used in the simulation of healthcare systems. However, the ability of ABMS to represent both human intention and interaction, makes it a better-suited approach than DES and SD for modeling systems like healthcare one, that are based on human behavior and interaction [5][6].

A solid example of an Agent-Based Model for Hospital Emergency Departments is presented in [7], which has been designed following a system analysis performed at different hospitals, under the advice of healthcare professionals with many years of experience. Agents are modeled using Moore state machines that interact inside a specified environment, enabling the study of the dynamics of complex systems without having challenges in getting exhaustive system definitions that are required by other modeling approaches. The validity of the model and the simulator for representing the real system have been checked applying the verification and validation process recommended by [8]. High Performance Computing (HPC) has been used due to the specific features of the model (a great number and variety of agents), the amount of data to be computed and finally the number of executions of the Simulator needed in the experiment.

In [9], the authors use such Emergency Department ABMS as the core component of a decision support system that aids healthcare managers to make the best-informed decisions possible, and causing better use of resources, achieving a more efficient and improved patient care system. A Length of Stay (LoS) index is used to evaluate the efficiency of ED. Among others, the experiment let to conclude that the estimated patient LoS can be reduced using a larger number of ED Staff, and/or more experienced ED staff, and/or the modularity in the ED different sections.

The aim of our work is to develop a model and a simulator that, used as Decision Support System, aids the administrators and heads of the ED to get additional knowledge about how the flu virus propagates, how it can influence over the patients ongoing treatment and the effects over sanitary staff, with the purpose of identifying strategies of improvement.

The remainder of this article is organized as follows. Section 2 presents the Emergency Department Simulation. The Flu Propagation Model is detailed in Section 3. Finally, Section 4 closes this paper with conclusions and future work.

II. Emergency Department Simulation

The Emergency Department is a healthcare unit that offers immediate care to patients, also called the emergency room, emergency ward, accident & emergency department, or casualty department [10]. ED is one of the most complex and dynamic areas in a hospital. Its activity is not linear and depends on several factors, including human behavior.

Simulation becomes an important tool for modeling complex systems that include many elements, a large number of interdependencies among such elements, and/or considerable variability [4]. It is impossible to model all the functionalities of such a complex system because there are lots of factors that can influence the different components and worth noting. Actually, it is useful to make a very abstract perception in mind from the considered real world. Moreover, we have to choose a proper methodology to find a better answer to our problems.

Discrete Event Simulation, System Dynamics, and Agent-Based Modeling and Simulation are the main three approaches used in the simulation of healthcare systems. DES simulates just the significant events of a system. It frequently is characterized by a series of tokens that hold up in turn for a service provider that forms them some time they proceed on to another portion of the system [7]. SD, which is used to simulate large systems, began to be used as a simulation method in healthcare operational supervision later than DES. An SD simulation is based on continuous space and does not model individuals, it simulates the whole system along time.

Healthcare systems are based on human interactions, and the ability of ABMS to represent both, human intention and interaction, makes it an appealing approach, while DES and SD are not well-suited approaches to model them [5][6]. A clear illustration of the potential use of ABMS in ED modeling is shown in [11].

Agent-Based Modeling and Simulation is considered as a systemic approach with a bottom-up architecture that can be used as a productive method to get the macro-level point of view from the micro-level evolution of agent interactions [12], [13]. The main components of an agent-based model are environment, agents, and interactions [14].

We based our model on a previous Emergency Department model (ED-Simulator) that has been developed as part of previous research work [7][9][13] by our research group, High Performance Computing for Efficient Applications and Simulation (HPC4EAS), of the Universitat Autònoma de Barcelona (UAB). Such model has been designed with the participation of ED staff from the Hospital of Mataro (Hospital of medium size that gives care service to an influence area of 250,000 people attending 110,000 patients/year in the ED), and the Hospital of Sabadell (one of large size that gives care service to an influence area of 500,000 people attending 160,000 patients/year in the ED). It is a pure Agent-Based Model, formed entirely of the rules governing the behavior of the individual agents which populate an ED.

Two kinds of agents have been identified, active, and passive. Active agents represent people, who act upon their own initiative: 1) patients; 2) admission staff (who receive patients just when they arrive at the ED); 3) sanitarian technicians (who help certain patients to move from one place to another of the ED); 4) triage and emergency nurses (the former receive patients after their admission for establishing their priority level and the latter are involved in the diagnosis and treatment phase); 5) and doctors. Passive agents represent systems that are solely reactive, such as the loudspeaker system (that is used by ED staff to communicate with patients that are in the waiting rooms), patient information system, pneumatic pipes (that are used to send the trials from the diagnostic zone to labs), and central diagnostic services (radiology service and laboratories).

As it is shown in Figure 1, ED is divided into different zones in which different types of agents may act, maintaining interactions that also may be different. Such interactions are carried out through communication. For this reason, the model includes both an environment and a communication model.

The input of our model are the patients who arrive to get emergency services. According to the Spanish Triage System [15], very similar to the Canadian Triage System, after the patient arrival, and the registration by the admission staff has been completed, based on the severity of their situation in triage, patients are categorized taking into account their priority level. There are 5 different values, level 1 is for the most critical situation and it is named resuscitation, and level 5 is for the least critical one (non-urgent).

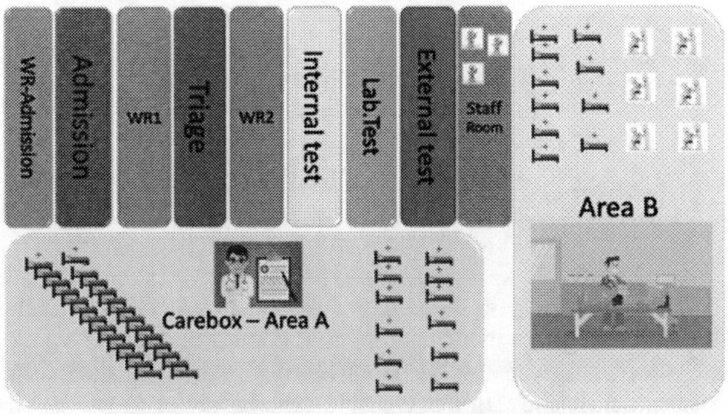

Figure 1. Different areas in Emergency Department.

There are different areas in EDs Spanish standard (Figure 1): Admissions Area, Triage Area, Diagnosis-Treatment Zone, Waiting Rooms, and etc. After triage, patients with diagnosed acuity level 1, 2, and 3 are treated separately and allocated in Area A, and patients 4 and 5 are treated in a separate area identified as Area B. The admissions and triage sections apply the same healthcare staff, but doctors and nurses are different for Area A and B [13].

III. FLU PROPAGATION MODEL

In order to create a contact propagation model of flu by ABMS method, we will define all actors involved in the ED process and their specific function and behavior such as: doctors, nurses, admission staff, laboratory technicians, auxiliary personnel, cleaning staff, patients and companions. Also, the following terms and items will be defined: "Transmission vector" as any agent capable of transmitting the flu virus, "Susceptible" as any agent that has a risk to acquire the influenza infection, and "Prevention policies" as behaviors performed by members of the sanitary staff in order to attempt to control the rate of propagation of flu and other contagion infections.

We propose four types of contact transmission in which a transmission vector is required:

a) Direct transmission: flu virus is transmitted from a transmission vector to another susceptible agent.
b) Semi-direct transmission: a transmission vector spreads the virus to an immune person and then s/he spreads that to a susceptible person.
c) Semi-indirect transmission: once a passive agent is infected by flu virus, then another passive agent touches it, and after a chain of contagion, an active agent is in contact with that.
d) Indirect transmission: when a transmission vector touches medical equipment or objects in the ED environment, and flu virus is transmitted to the object, later, a susceptible agent (patient or healthcare staff) has contact with the same object and acquires the microorganism.

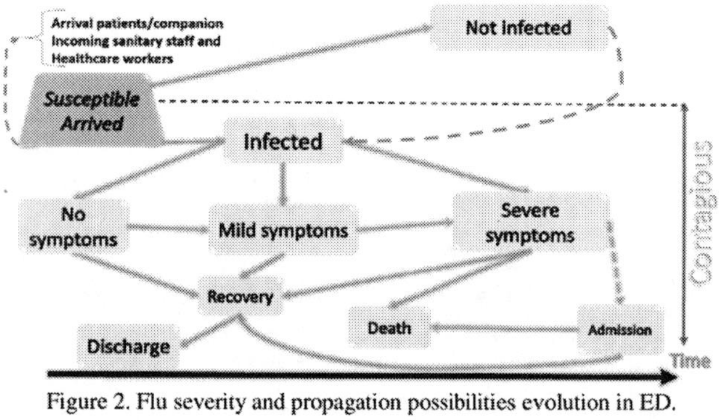

Figure 2. Flu severity and propagation possibilities evolution in ED.

As stated before, the aim of this research is to understand how the influenza is influencing and changing the acuity level of the patient, how it is affecting sanitary staff, and consequently, how this is changing the behavior of the ED. If we apply for a screening at the entry point of incoming individuals, we may find different types of individuals. People with a negative test result will be categorized as 'not infected'. Obviously, they are susceptible to get infected. Then, based on the results, we can categorize positive people with 'no symptom', 'mild symptom', and 'severe symptom' [16]. Figure 2 shows the different states of flu virus infection, in its lifecycle in a host patient.

In [17] the authors show the probability of MRSA infection in ED, and how many people are involved with MRSA contamination. However, in our research, the idea is not only how the propagation of the flu virus in ED is, but also how this propagation is affecting people. Affecting people or patients means that the acuity level of them could improve gradually if there was not any flu infection. If patients are exposed to a flu virus contamination, they will require more attention and more use of ED resources like health care staff, facilities, care boxes, etc. As a result, the LoS will be higher and ED will become closer to saturation. In some cases, this leads to overcrowd, and overcrowd means more risk of epidemic and propagation in the area. In this situation, the relative position of the body influences human thermal plume (e.g., a seated inclination of the body), which is considered to affect the air velocity of convective flows around a human being, and hence the ability to carry small droplets [18]. As an indoor area, every section of ED has a strong potential of getting infected by flu, and being beneath high risk of flu propagation. Places, where patients type 1, 2 and 3 have been held, have almost no risk, because they have no contact with others, and in addition they have not been waiting in any queue before admission. Contrary to that, patients with acuity level 4 or 5 spend long time in the waiting rooms and ED wards. So, probably they have a highest possibility to get infected. Figure 3 shows the different probabilities of risk infection for each section of the treatment process in ED.

The risk of propagation of the different areas in the ED also depends on the number of individuals that stay in. It is high in zones like waiting rooms, ED wards and admission zone, and low in triages room, examination room or care boxes. Flu propagation is being facilitated in limited (indoor) areas, so, quantifying the probabilities of the virus transmission in some specific areas like waiting rooms, wards, etc, is expected in this research, and this can also be considered as a framework because of its independent behavior [19]. Consequently, calculation leads to be more complicated. The key point that arises here is to find the relationship between the size of an indoor area and the propagation of infection there, and how many people should be there in max to minimize or reduce the rate of contagious. Therefore, some new variables like fragility and the ratio of area size per capita have to be added to our previous model. Fragility is an index that indicates how fragile anybody is: as more fragile anybody is, the more severe will be the flu infection. There are some indicators for each individual to show the amount of being at risk for getting an infection in a contagious situation.

A combination of patient age (ag), acuity level (al), underlying diseases (ud), etc. play a role to generate the fragility index of each person: $Fr(p)=f(ag,al,ud)$

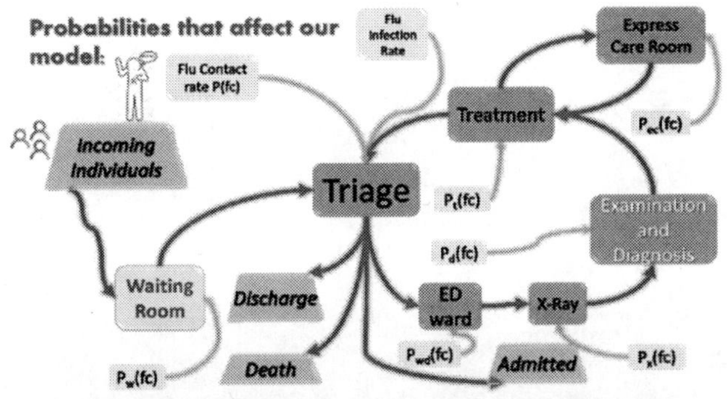

Figure 3. Flu severity and propagation possibilities evolution in ED.

As Figure 3 shows, there are different possibilities of getting the flu virus based on the flu contact rate of each area inside the ED:

$$P(getFlu): \{ P_t(fc), P_{ec}(fc), P_d(fc), P_{wd}(fc), P_w(fc), P_x(fc)\}$$

Moreover, Flu Contact rate *P(fc)*, Flu Infection rate is also calculated. *P(fc)* holds the probability of flu transmission in triage. We use $P_t(fc)$ to represent the probability of flu contact rate in the process of treatment. Pec(fc) shows the possibility of transmission in express care room, Pd(fc) represents the probability of propagation in the examination room, Pwd(fc) is the propagation probability in wards, Pw(fc) shows the probability in the waiting room and Px(fc) is for x-ray and labs. There is another variable named 'status' for each agent (active/passive) with the following possible values: Susceptible or non-carrier, Carrier, Infected, and Recovered. We can categorize patients into two parts. The first part includes patients who do not have a clear possibility of being carriers or infected with the flu virus. In this case, the healthcare staff assumes that this patient is non-carrier; and the second part is those patients who are known or can be assumed to be carriers or infected with the flu.

The authors in [17] conclude that some preventive facilities like isolation of patients can avoid the transmission of MRSA bacteria between patients. However, in flu not only physical contact between patients should be banned, but also they have to use some facial masks or facial shields because the flu virus is also airborne. Actually, as a result, we aim to limit the probability for propagation of flu in the ED, and, by taking some preventive actions in EDs, the number of patients who contact the flu can be reduced. On the other hand, the single best way to prevent seasonal flu is to be vaccinated each year, but good health habits, like covering one's cough and washing hands, often can help stop the spread of germs and prevent respiratory illnesses like the flu.

$$P(AgainstFlu)=f(Vaccinate, Handwashing, SanitizeHand, IsolatedMaterial, MedicalMask, MedicalShield, SocialDistancing, AreaSizeCapita)$$

There are passive indicators that are assumed to affect the propagation rate in an indoor area. We hypothesize that the flu transmission rate in Emergency Departments may be influenced by area temperature (T), humidity (H), air pressure (P), air condition speed (AS), air condition direction (AD), air pollution in ED (AP), UV radiation (UV), airborne particles in ED (AbP), etc. So, we can assume a strong correlation among these indicators:

$$C\,(FluTransmissionRate)= f\,(T, H, P, AS, AD, AP, UV, AbP)$$

IV. Conclusion and Future Works

In this paper, we opened a new idea on our group's previous work in the area of modeling and simulating the emergency department. Although we have experience in simulating MRSA in our ED-simulator, in this research we are initiating, to model and simulate how influenza propagates in different areas of an ED, how it influences patients underlying diseases, and furthermore, what are its effects on healthcare staff.

Our journey started with initiation and investigation on the topic area, and it continues with data gathering and problem articulation. Then, we initiate a conceptual model for our idea, and it will continue with model design and implementation, the model calibration, validation and verification. Finally, we will be able to analyze the results. The resemblance of this virus's lifecycle and its effects on ED with some other diseases like Covid19, Chickenpox, Mycoplasma pneumonia is also hypothesized.

Acknowledgment

This research has been supported by the Agencia Estatal de Investigacion (AEI), Spain and the Fondo Europeo de Desarrollo Regional (FEDER) UE, under contract TIN2017-84875-P and partially funded by a research collaboration agreement with the Fundacion Escuelas Universitarias Gimbernat (EUG).

References

[1] Center for Disease Control and Prevention: *Archived Estimated Influenza Illnesses, Medical visits, Hospitalizations, and Deaths in the United States- 2017-2018 influenza season.* Available from: https://www.cdc.gov/flu/about/burden/2017-2018/archive.htm

[2] D. Chumachenko, V. Dobriak, M. Mazorchuk, I. Meniailov, and K. Bazilevych, "On agent-based approach to influenza and acute respiratory virus infection simulation" in 14th International Conference on Advanced Trends in Radioelecrtronics, Telecommunications and Computer Engineering (TCSET), Feb. 2018, pp. 192-195.

[3] E. Davoli and World Health Organization, "A practical tool for the preparation of a hospital crisis preparedness plan, with special focus on pandemic influenza" (No. EUR/06/5064207). Copenhagen: WHO Regional Office for Europe, 2006.

[4] P. Babin and A. Greenwood, "Discretely Evaluating Complex Systems" in Industrial Engineer Magazine 43(2): pp. 34-38, 2011.

[5] E. Bonabeau, "Agent-based modeling: Methods and techniques forsimulating human systems" in Proceedings of the National Academy of Sciences of the United States of America, vol. 99, no. Suppl 3, pp.7280–7287, 2002.

[6] P. Escudero-Marin and M. Pidd, "Using ABMS to simulate emergency departments" in Proceedings of the 2011 Winter Simulation Conference, IEEE. pp. 1,239-1,250.

[7] M. Taboada, E. Cabrera, M. L. Iglesias, F. Epelde, and E. Luque, "An agent-based decision support system for hospitals emergency departments" in Procedia Computer Science, 4, pp. 1870-1879, 2011.

[8] R.G. Sargent, "Verification and validation of simulation models" in Proceedings of the 2010 Winter Simulation Conference, Ed. B. Johansson, S. Jain, J. Montoya-Torres, J. Hugan, and E. Yücesan, pp. 166-183.

[9] E. Cabrera, E. Luque, M. Taboada, F. Epelde, and M. L. Iglesias, "ABMS optimization for emergency departments" in Proceedings of the 2012 Winter Simulation Conference, IEEE. pp. 1-12.

[10] World Health Organization: *Emergency medical services systems in the European Union: report of an assessment project* co-ordinated by the World Health Organization-Data book (No. EUR/08/5086087). Copenhagen: WHO Regional Office for Europe, 2008).

[11] A. K. Kanagarajah, P.A. Lindsay, A.M. Miller, and D.W. Parker, "An exploration into the uses of agent-based modeling to improve quality of health care" in Proceedings of the 6th International Conference on Complex Systems, edited by A. Minai, D. Braha and Y. BarYam, pp. 471-478, 2010.

[12] D. M. Nguyen, "A Risk Analysis Framework for Nosocomial Influenza Infection Using Agent-Based Simulation", Doctoral Thesis, Tokyo Tech Research Repository. 2014, July 28th, Available from:

http://t2r2.star.titech.ac.jp/rrws/file/CTT100693389/ATD1000 00413/thesis_11D35078.pdf

[13] Z. Liu, D. Rexachs, E. Luque, F. Epelde, and E. Cabrera, "Simulating the micro-level behavior of emergency department for macro-level features prediction" in Proceedings of the 2015 Winter Simulation Conference, IEEE. pp. 171-182.

[14] L. Perez and S. Dragicevic, "An agent-based approach for modeling dynamics of contagious disease spread" Int J Health Geogr. 2009; 8:50. Published 2009 Aug 5. doi:10.1186/1476-072X-8-50.

[15] R. Sánchez et al., "El triaje en urgencias en los hospitales espanyoles", Emergencias: Revista de la Sociedad Española de Medicina de Urgencias y Emergencias, Vol. 25, Nº. 1, 2013, pp. 66-70, ISSN 1137-6821.

[16] S. Moghadas and M. Laskowski, "Review of Terms Used in Modelling Influenza Infection", National Collaborating Centre for Infectious Diseases, September 2014, ISBN 978-1-927-988-18-3.

[17] C. Jaramillo, M. Taboada, F. Epelde, D. Rexachs, and E. Luque, "Agent Based Model and Simulation of MRSA Transmission in Emergency Departments" in Proceedings of the 2015 International Conference of Computational Systems, pp. 443-452.

[18] N. Zhang et al., "Close contact behavior in indoor environment and transmission of respiratory infection" *Indoor Air*, 2020 30: pp. 645-661, Available from:

https://doi.org/10.1111/ina.12673

[19] M. A. Dogaheh, "Introducing a framework for security measurements", in 2010 IEEE International Conference on Information Theory and Information Security, IEEE. pp. 638-641.